मातृकाभेदतन्त्रम्
Matrkabheda-Tantram

CALCUTTA SANSKRIT SERIES

under the direction of

PANDIT AMARESWAR THAKUR, M.A. Ph.D.

No. VII

मातृकाभेदतन्त्रम्

Matrkabheda-Tantram

Edited by

CHINTAMANI BHATTACHARYA

GYAN

Published by

Gyan Publishing House
5, Ansari Road
Daryaganj, New Delhi-110002
Phone: 011-47034999, 9811692060
E-mail: books@gyanbooks.com

Distribution Network
gyanbooks.com
India, USA, Canada, UK, Australia, France

ISBN : 978-81-212-2796-4 (HB)
First Published, 1933

2nd Impression 2021

Printed at: Gyan Press, Delhi.

Matrkabheda-Tantram
Edited by: Chintamani Bhattacharya

CALCUTTA SANSKRIT SERIES

under the direction of

PANDIT AMARESWAR THAKUR, M. A., Ph. D.

No. VII

मातृकाभेदतन्त्रम्

MĀTṚKĀBHEDA-TANTRAM

Edited by

CHINTAMANI BHATTACHARYA

Published by

METROPOLITAN PRINTING & PUBLISHING HOUSE, LIMITED.

CALCUTTA

1933

भूमिका

अथेदमुपक्रम्यते मातृकाभेदतन्त्रं मुद्रापयित्वा प्रकाशयितुम्। तत्र तन्त्रशब्दस्यार्थस्तु बहुव्यापकः, केचित्तु शास्त्रमात्रमेव तन्त्रमित्याचचक्षिरे। ज्यौतिषशास्त्राभिज्ञास्तु ज्यौतिषस्यांशविशेषं तन्त्रत्वेन निर्णीतवन्तः। तथा हि—

"स्कन्धेऽस्मिन् गणितेन या ग्रहगतिस्तन्त्राभिधाना त्वसौ" (वराहमिहिरः)

इति। वेदशास्त्रस्यापि तन्त्रत्वेन व्यपदेशः, यथा "दर्शपौर्णमासौ तु पूर्वं व्याख्यास्यामस्तन्त्रस्य तत्राऽऽम्नातत्वात्" इत्याश्वलायनश्रौतसूत्रम्। एवमन्येऽप्यर्था कोषादिषु वर्त्तन्ते। तथा च मेदिनी—

'तन्त्रं कुटुम्बकृत्ये स्यात् सिद्धान्ते चौषधोत्तमे।
प्रधाने तन्तुवाये च शास्त्रभेदे परिच्छदे'॥ इति।

एषु च शिववक्त्रविनिर्गतं मन्त्रशास्त्ररूपं तन्त्रमेवास्माकं विषयः। केचिच्च षट्कर्मप्रधानं शास्त्रं तन्त्रत्वेन व्यपदिशन्तो महोदारास्तन्त्रशास्त्रं प्रधानतस्त्रिधा विभजन्ते हिन्दुतन्त्र-बौद्धतन्त्र-जैनतन्त्रभेदत इत्यन्यदेतत्। अपरे पुनरद्यत्वे प्रतीच्यप्रभावभाविता गवेषणागवाक्षविक्षिप्तदृष्टयः प्राचीनत्व एव तन्त्रशास्त्रस्य बहु विवदन्ते। तत्रैके तु हिन्दूनां तन्त्रशास्त्रमेव नासीत, बौद्धमतानुयायिनां तन्त्राणामुत्पत्तेरनन्तरं सनातनमतानुयायिनां तन्त्रे श्रद्धा जातेति ते बौद्धतन्त्राण्येव स्वमतेषु विपरिवर्त्य निर्मितवन्तः, नेपालादिदेशेष्वद्यापि नूतनास्तन्त्रग्रन्था विरच्यन्त इति ज्ञायते, प्रमाणत्वेनोपस्थाप्यन्ते च तैर्यदस्माकं प्राचीनस्मृतिसंहितासु तन्त्रस्योल्लेखो नास्ति, तन्त्रोक्तबीजानां मन्त्राणाञ्च प्रणाली विभिन्नैव प्राचीनशास्त्रशैलीत इति, रामायणे महाभारते च तन्त्रमन्त्राणां नास्ति प्रभावः; किं बहुनाऽष्टादशमहापुराणेष्वपि वार्तैव नास्ति शिववक्त्रविनिर्गतशास्त्रस्येति। उपपुराणादिषु केष्वपि स्मृतिनिबन्धकाराणामाधुनिकानां रघुनन्दनादीनां निबन्धेषु च बहूनि नाम्ना धृतानि तन्त्राणि प्रमाणत्वेनापि गृहीतानीत्यनेनैवं प्रतीयते यत् तन्त्राणि नवीनान्येव न प्राचीनानीति, रामायणभारतादियुगे तन्त्रस्यास्तितास्वीकारेऽपि प्रभावशून्यत्वमपरेऽनुमिमते। यथा पूर्वम् ऋक्सामयजुषां त्रयी वेदशब्दव्यपदिष्टा सती परतोऽथर्ववेदमप्यात्मन्यन्तर्भावितवती, तथा अथर्ववेदोक्ताभिचारादिमूलमुररीकृत्य तन्त्रशास्त्रमप्याविर्भूतं बहोः कालादनन्तरं स्वप्रतिष्ठां विरचयामासेत्यादि बहु प्रलपन्ति। वयं पुनस्तान् कुशलमुखरान् दूरादेव प्रणम्यानादिसंस्कारपरम्परागतं महादेववक्त्रविनिर्गतं तन्त्रशास्त्रं वेदवद् अनादीति सर्वथा सविश्रम्भं स्वीकुर्वन्तो न खलु वात्याहततृणामिवेतस्ततो विक्षिप्ततामाश्रयेमेति।

तन्त्रेषु बहवो विषया उपदिष्टाः । तत्र सृष्टि-स्थिति-लयप्रक्रिया-ज्ञान-विज्ञान-छन्दः-कोश-व्याकरण-चिकित्सा-ज्यौतिष-शाकुन-मन्त्र-पूजा-षट्कर्म-राजधर्म-युगधर्मादीनामुत्कर्षेण बहुशो विधानादस्माकमतीवावश्यकानि तन्त्राणि संसारिणां मुमुक्षूणाञ्चोत्तमर्णतामेव भेजिरे इति सर्वैरेव स्वीकार्यम् । तन्त्रशास्त्रन्तु प्रधानतस्त्रिधा विभक्तम्, (१) आगम(२)यामल(३)तन्त्रभेदतः ।

आगमशब्दनिरुक्तिस्तु—

आगतं शिववक्त्रेभ्यो गतञ्च गिरिजाश्रुतौ ।
मतञ्च वासुदेवस्य तस्मादागममुच्यते ॥ इति ।

आगमलक्षणञ्च—

सृष्टिश्च प्रलयश्चैव देवतानां तथाऽर्चनम् ।
साधनञ्चैव सर्वेषां पुरश्चरणमेव च ॥
षट्कर्मसाधनञ्चैव ध्यानयोगश्चतुर्विधः ।
सप्तभिर्लक्षणैर्युक्तमागमं तद् विदुर्बुधाः ॥ इति वाराहीतन्त्रे ।

यामललक्षणञ्च—

सृष्टिश्च ज्यौतिषाख्यानं नित्यकृत्यप्रदीपनम् ।
क्रमसूत्रं वर्णभेदो जातिभेदस्तथैव च ॥
युगधर्मश्च संख्यातो यामलस्याष्टलक्षणम् ॥

तन्त्रस्य लक्षणमपि—

सर्गश्च प्रतिसर्गश्च मन्त्रनिर्णय एव च ।
देवतानाञ्च संस्थानं तीर्थानाञ्चैव वर्णनम् ॥
तथैवाऽऽश्रमधर्मश्च विप्रसंस्थानमेव च ।
संस्थानञ्चैव भूतानां यन्त्राणाञ्चैव निर्णयः ॥
उत्पत्तिर्विबुधानाञ्च तरूणां कल्पसंज्ञिनाम् ।
संस्थानं ज्योतिषाञ्चैव पुराणाख्यानमेव च ॥
कोशस्य कथनञ्चैव व्रतानां परिभाषणम् ।
शौचाशौचस्य चाऽऽख्यानं नरकाणाञ्च वर्णनम् ॥
हरचक्रस्य चाऽऽख्यानं स्त्रीपुंसोश्चैव लक्षणम् ।
राजधर्मो दानधर्मो युगधर्मस्तथैव च ॥
व्यवहारः कथ्यते च तथा चाध्यात्मवर्णनम् ।
इत्यादिलक्षणैर्युक्तं तन्त्रमित्यभिधीयते ॥ इति वाराहीतन्त्रे ।

आगमादीनामपि भेदबाहुल्यं वर्तते—

आगमं त्रिविधं प्रोक्तं चतुर्थमैश्वरं स्मृतम् ।

कल्पश्चतुर्विधः प्रोक्त आगमो डामरस्तथा ।

यामलश्च तथा तन्त्रं तेषां भेदाः पृथक् पृथक् ॥ इत्यादि ।

तन्त्राणि प्रधानतश्चतुःषष्टिसंख्याकानि—

'चतुःषष्टिश्च तन्त्राणि यामलादीनि पार्वति ।'

इति वाराहीतन्त्रवचनात्, सन्ति च पुराणानामुपपुराणानीव तन्त्राणामप्युपतन्त्राणि भूयांसि । तन्त्राणामप्युपतन्त्राणि ।

उपतन्त्रविषये त्वेवमुक्तम्—

सिद्धोक्तान्युपतन्त्राणि कपिलोक्तानि यानि च ।

अद्भुतानि च एतानि जैमिन्युक्तानि यानि च ॥

वशिष्ठः कपिलश्चैव नारदो गर्ग एव च ।

पुलस्त्यो भार्गवः सिद्धो याज्ञवल्क्यो भृगुस्तथा ॥

शुक्रो बृहस्पतिश्चैव अन्ये ये मुनिसत्तमाः ।

एभिः प्रणीतान्यन्यानि उपतन्त्राणि यानि च ॥

न संख्यातानि तान्यत्र धर्मवद्भिर्महात्मभिः ।

सरित्सारतराण्येव संख्यातानि निबोधत ॥ वाराहीतन्त्रे ।

कानिचित् पुनस्तन्त्राण्यनुपादेयानीति कथितं महाविश्वसारतन्त्रे—

कल्पभेदेन तन्त्राणि कथितानि च यानि च ।

पाषण्डमोहनायैव विफलानीह सुन्दरि ॥ इति ।

एवञ्च उपादेयमनुपादेयञ्च तन्त्रं विशिष्य ज्ञातुमुचितम् । यद्यपि तत्र चतुःषष्टिसंख्या समुल्लसिता तथाऽपि तान्त्रिकसम्प्रदायानुसारेण कानिचिदुपतन्त्राण्यपि प्रमाणत्वेन गृहीतानि कानिचिच्च तन्त्राण्यपि कल्पभेदवृत्त्या परिहृतानीति सम्प्रदाय एवात्र प्रमाणम् । एवमपि कानि सम्प्रदायपरिगृहीतानि कानि च नेति न कैरपि प्रकाश्यते यतस्तन्त्राणां तन्त्रविषयाणाञ्च गोपनीयत्व एव वैशिष्ट्यमिति तन्त्रनिष्णाताः सर्वथा सर्वदैवेदं प्रमाणवचनं समामनन्ति—

गोपनीयं प्रयत्नेन न देयं यस्य कस्यचित् ।

गोप्यं गोप्यं पुनर्गोप्यं जननीजारगर्भवत् ॥ इति ।

विषयेऽस्मिन्नेवं छगुसे कल्पेऽस्मिन् कानि तन्त्राणि प्रमाणानीति विवेचयन्तो वयं तन्त्रसारप्राणतोषणीकारादिपरिगृहीतान्येव तन्त्राणि प्रमाणत्वेन स्वीकुर्म इत्यत्र किं बहु वक्तव्यम् ।

शिवोक्ततन्त्राणि तावत् शाक्त-शैव-वैष्णवभेदेन त्रिधा विभक्तानि । साधकाः पुनः स्वस्वगुरुपरम्परागतसम्प्रदायानुसारेणैव तेषामेकतमे वर्तन्त इति ।

तन्त्रेषु तावन्महापुराणादिष्विव श्लोकसंख्यानिर्देशोऽपि वर्तते—

न शक्यं विस्तराद् वक्तुमपि वर्षशतैरपि ।

संक्षेपाद् वै प्रवक्ष्यामि लोककल्पोक्तवर्त्मना ॥

त्रिवि देवे नवलक्षं पाताले ब्रह्मशासने ।

लक्षमात्रं भारते च क्षितौ तन्त्राणि यानि च ॥ इति वाराहीतन्त्रे ।

तान्त्रिकनये तु कलौ देवतार्चनं तन्त्रोक्तरीत्यैव कर्तव्यमिति निश्चयः, अन्यथा सर्वमेव निष्फलं भवति । तथा च—

कृते श्रुत्युक्त आचारस्त्रेतायां स्मृतिसम्भवः ।

द्वापरे तु पुराणोक्तः कलावागमकेवलम् ।

आगमोक्तविधानेन कलौ देवान् यजेत् सुधीः ।

न हि देवाः प्रसीदन्ति कलौ चान्यविधानतः ॥

वेदोक्तं चैव स्मृत्युक्तं मन्त्रं न योजयेत् कलौ ॥ इति वाराहीतन्त्रे ।

प्रमाणमिदमूरीकृत्यैव सम्प्रदायविदो देवीपुराण-कालिकापुराणाद्युक्तश्रीभगवद्दुर्गामहापूजादिष्वपि मातृकान्यासादिकमाचरन्त्येवेति नाविदितं विदुषाम् ।

दीक्षाग्रहणानन्तरमेव तन्त्रोक्तेषु कार्येष्वधिकारिणो भवन्ति नान्यथेति ब्राह्मणादिसर्ववर्णेष्वयं विधिः । अनन्तरं च पूर्णाभिषिक्ता भवन्ति, पूर्णाभिषेकानन्तरमेव ते सर्वेष्वेवाऽऽत्मोत्कर्षसाधकेषु क्रमदीक्षादिषु कर्मसु समर्था भवन्तीति । एवञ्च दीक्षाग्रहणार्थं गुरोरावश्यकता वर्तते । गुरुलक्षणेऽपि विशेषविधिरवगन्तव्यः । शिष्यस्य लक्षणमपि बहु विचार्य कृतम्, तत्र तिथिनक्षत्रादिविचारो मन्त्रविचारश्च वर्तते । सर्वथैवेयं शैली वेदग्रहणशैलीतो नितरां विभिन्नेति दीक्षाविषयेऽपि किञ्चिदुच्यते—

वैदिकाचारेषु दीक्षाशब्दव्यवहारो नास्ति, तत्र तु संस्कार एव, तत्र च दीक्षास्थानीय उपनयनाख्यः संस्कारो ब्राह्मणादीनाम्, तत्र प्रधाना ऋग् गायत्री, सा च सर्वेषामेव ब्राह्मणानामेकैव । एवं यथा तान्त्रिकदीक्षायां दातव्यो मन्त्रः शिष्यनामानुसारेण विचार्य यो यस्योपयुज्यते स एव तस्मै दीयते नान्य इति नियमः ; न खल्वेवं गायत्री विचार्यते शिष्यनाम्ना, आचार्यस्तु पिता तदन्यो वा । परमत्र तान्त्रिकाचारेषु—

'पितुर्मन्त्रं न गृह्णीयात् तथा मातामहस्य च'

इति निषेधादन्य एव गुरुः कर्तव्यः, स च कुलगुरुर्गुरुपुत्रस्तत्पुत्रो वेति कुलमधिकृत्य तेषां गुरुशिष्यसम्बन्धः । तत्र शूद्राणां नास्ति वैदिकी दीक्षा गायत्र्यामनधिकारात्, परमत्र तान्त्रिकी दीक्षा चतुर्णामेव वर्णानां भवतीति । गायत्री तु सम्यगुच्चारयितव्या, तान्त्रिकमन्त्राणां तूपांशुजप एव श्रेयान्, मन्त्रस्तु शिष्यकर्ण एव दातव्यः—

'दक्षकर्णे वदेन्मन्त्रं त्रिवारं पूर्णमानसः' इति ।

वैदिकाचारे तु पितुरभावे—

उपनीय तु यः शिष्यं वेदमध्यापयेद् गुरुः ।

सकल्पं सरहस्यञ्च तमाचार्यं विदुर्बुधाः ॥

इति वचनात् कल्परहस्यसहितवेदज्ञानवतः सकाशाद् गायत्रीग्रहणे प्राशस्त्यमात्रमवगम्यते, तस्य कुलगुरुत्वमस्तु मा वेति न विचार्यते। अत्र तु—

पैत्र्यं कुलगुरुं यस्तु त्यजेद् वै पापमोहितः।
स याति नरकं घोरं यावच्चन्द्रार्कतारकम्॥

इति वचनात् कुलगुरोरेव मन्त्रो ग्रहीतव्य इति। विशेषशिक्षार्थं तु गुर्वन्तरमपि वृणुयादित्यप्युक्तम्—

मधुलोभाद् यथा भृङ्गः पुष्पात् पुष्पान्तरं व्रजेत्।
ज्ञानलुब्धस्तथा शिष्यो गुरोर्गुर्वन्तरं व्रजेत्॥ इति।

यथा स्मार्ताचारेषु—

'न चातिसृष्टो गुरुणा स्वान् गुरून् न नमेत् क्वचित्'

इत्यादिमनुस्मृतिबलाद् गुरुः पूजनीयो विशिष्टश्च तथा तत्सदृशस्तदतिरिक्तो वा गुरुस्तान्त्रिकाचारेषु। तथा च गुरुलक्षणम्—

'गु'कारस्त्वन्धकारः स्याद् 'रु'कारस्तन्निरोधकः।
अन्धकारनिरोधित्वाद् गुरुरित्यभिधीयते॥

शिष्यलक्षणञ्च—

शरीरमर्थं प्राणांश्च स्वगुरुभ्यो निवेद्य यः।
गुरुभ्यः शिष्यतायोगं शिष्य इत्यभिधीयते॥ इति।

तान्त्रिकाचारेषु गुरुरेव सर्वस्वम्—

गुरुर्ब्रह्मा गुरुर्विष्णुर्गुरुर्देवो महेश्वरः।
गुरुस्तीर्थं गुरुर्यज्ञो गुरुर्दानं गुरुस्तपः॥
गुरुरग्निर्गुरुः सूर्यः सर्वं गुरुमयं जगत्।
गुरुमूलं जगत् सर्वं गुरुमूलं परन्तपः॥
गुरुः कर्ता गुरुर्हर्ता गुरुः पाता महीतले।
गुरुसन्तोषमात्रेण तुष्टाः स्युः सर्वदेवताः॥

गुरोरसन्तोषे तु शिष्यस्य महाननर्थो भवतीत्यपि ज्ञायते—

गुरुः पिता गुरुर्माता गुरुर्देवो गुरुर्गतिः।
शिवे रुष्टे गुरुस्त्राता गुरौ रुष्टे न कश्चन॥

इत्यादिवचनशतेन। सर्वदैव सर्वास्ववस्थासु गुरोराज्ञाचारी स्यादेव—

न लङ्घयेद् गुरोराज्ञामुत्तरं न वदेत् तथा।
दिवा रात्रौ गुरोराज्ञां दासवत् परिपालयेत्॥
उक्तानुक्तेषु कार्येषु नापेक्षां कारयेद् बुधः।
गच्छतः प्रयतो गच्छेद् गुरोराज्ञां न लङ्घयेत्॥

न श्रृणोति गुरोर्वाक्यं श्रृणुयाद् वा पराङ्मुखः ।
अहितं वा हितं वाऽपि रौरवं नरकं व्रजेत् ॥
गुर्वर्थं धारयेद् देहं गुर्वर्थं धनमर्जयेत् ।
निजप्राणान् परित्यज्य गुरुकार्यं समाचरेत् ॥ इति ।

गृही एव गुरुर्भवितुमर्हति न सन्न्यासीति, तदाह—

पुत्रदारैश्च सम्पन्नो गुरुरागमसम्मतः ।

दीक्षाशिक्षाभेदेन गुरोर्द्वैविध्यमप्युक्तम्—

गुरुस्तु द्विविधः प्रोक्तो दीक्षा-शिक्षाप्रभेदतः ।
आदौ दीक्षागुरुः प्रोक्तः शेषे शिक्षागुरुर्मतः ॥ इति ।

तन्त्रेषु प्रधानत आचारनिर्णयः कृत इति, स चायं सप्तविधः—

सर्वेभ्यश्चोत्तमा वेदा वेदेभ्यो वैष्णवं महत् ।
वैष्णवादुत्तमं शैवं शैवाद् दक्षिणमुत्तमम् ॥
दक्षिणादुत्तमं वामं वामात् सिद्धान्तमुत्तमम् ।
सिद्धान्तादुत्तमं कौलं कौलात् परतरं न हि ॥ इति ।

तदेवं सप्तस्वाचारेषु शैव-दक्षिण-वाम-सिद्धान्त-कौलाचाराः पञ्च तान्त्रिकप्रसिद्धाः । तत्र पुनः पञ्चस्वाचारेषु द्वैविध्यमाचारस्य प्रकटितम्—

आचारो द्विविधो देवि वाम-दक्षिणभेदतः ।
जन्ममात्रं दक्षिणं हि अभिषेकेण वामकम् ॥ इति ।

एवमेतेष्वप्याचारेषु कौलाचारो गूढतरः, ये खलु कौलास्ते कथमपि नात्मानमन्येभ्यः प्रकटयन्ति, गुप्तभावेनैव समाजेषु विचरन्तीति प्रसिद्धिः—

अन्तःशाक्ता बहिःशैवाः सभायां वैष्णवास्तथा ।
नानावेशधराः कौला विचरन्ति महीतले ॥ इति ।

एवंरूपाः खलु कौलाः प्रच्छन्नवेशत्व एव स्वात्मनां वैशिष्ट्यं मन्यन्ते ।

एषाञ्चाऽऽचाराणां मध्ये भावशब्दवाच्यो विशेषो वर्तते, स पुनस्त्रिविधः, पशुभाव-वीरभाव-दिव्यभावभेदतः—

'भावश्च त्रिविधो देवि दिव्य-वीर-पशुक्रमात्' इति ।

तन्त्रान्तरेऽपि वर्णितं मनुजानां जन्मावधि षोडशाब्दं यावत् पशुभावः, ततः पञ्चाशदन्तं वीरभावः, ततश्च जीवनान्तं यावद् दिव्यभाव इति ।

भावेष्वेतेषु पशुभावं हीनत्वेन प्रकटयन्ति तदितरं भावमवलम्बमानास्तान्त्रिकाः—

दिव्य-वीरौ महाभावावधमः पशुभावकः ।
वैष्णवः पशुभावेन पूजयेत् परमेश्वरि ॥

शक्तिमन्त्रे वरारोहे पशुभावो भयानकः । इति ।

दिव्यवीरभावायुत्कर्षमप्युद्घोषयन्ति—

दिव्यैर्वीरैर्महेशानि जायते सिद्धिरुत्तमा ।
दिव्ये वीरे न भेदोऽस्ति भेदो वीरो महोद्धतः ॥
दिव्यवीरौ प्रवक्ष्यामि सर्वभावोत्तमोत्तमौ ॥

इत्यादिप्रमाणानामुपन्यासेनेति । तान्त्रिकाणां साधनमार्गे पञ्चमकारापरनामधेयानां पञ्चतत्त्वानां व्यवहारस्यैव वैशिष्ट्यम् । एतेषाञ्च—

'मत्स्यं मांसं तथा मद्यं मुद्रा मैथुनमेव च'

इति साधारणी संज्ञा । पशुभावाधिकारिणस्तु एतेषां साक्षादभिधाबोधितमर्थं परिहाय रूपककल्पितमर्थान्तरं गृह्णन्ति ।

वीराचारिणस्तु साक्षादर्थमेव गृह्णन्ति, उदाहरन्ति च—

ज्यौतिषे मन्त्रवादे च वैदिके वेदकर्मणि ।
अर्थमात्रन्तु गृह्णीयान्नापशब्दं विचारयेत् ॥
मन्त्रस्य वादो यत्रेति मन्त्रवादस्तन्त्रमिति ॥

ते तावत् पञ्चतत्त्वानि मन्त्रप्रयोगेण शोधयित्वा व्यवहरन्ति शोधनेनैव तेषाममेध्यत्वमपसरतीति तत्सम्प्रदायविदो वदन्ति च, शास्त्रेष्वशोधितानामेव मद्यादीनां व्यवहारे दोष उक्त इति च तेषां निर्णयः ।

आम्रेडयन्ति च निरुत्तरतन्त्रप्रमाणम्—

'आगमः पञ्चमो वेदः कौलस्तु पञ्चमाश्रमः' इति ।

तदेवमाचाराणां भावानाञ्च विशिष्य स्वरूपवर्णनमतिविस्तृतं स्यादिति संक्षेपत एव तानुल्लिख्य विरता भवामः, अत्र विशेषस्तु पण्डितशौण्डैरस्मत्सहकर्मिभिः श्रीमद्भिर्नरेन्द्रनाथवेदान्ततीर्थैराङ्गलभाषालिखितभूमिकायां विनिवेशित इति तत्र द्रष्टव्यः ।

अथ मातृकाभेदपदेन मातृकाया भेदो वा मातृकाया भेदो यस्मिन्निति वा व्यासार्थस्य बोधो यदि भवेत्, यदि वा मातृकापदेनाष्टमातृकाषोडशमातृकाऽक्षरमातृकादीनां बोधो भवेत्; अथवा "मातृकावर्णभेदेभ्यः सर्वे मन्त्राः प्रजज्ञिरे" इति वचनान्मन्त्राणां भेद इत्यर्थोऽवगम्येत तथाऽपि ग्रन्थवर्णितविषयैः सह नाम्नोऽस्य कोऽपि सम्बन्धो वर्तत इति न निर्णेतुं प्रभूयते, अतोऽस्य ग्रन्थस्य कथं मातृकाभेदपदेन व्यपदेश इति जानाति भगवान् स्वयमेव ग्रन्थवक्ता महेश्वरः । अत्र च पुष्पिकायां मातृकाभेदशब्दमपहाय ग्रन्थस्यास्य तथाविधनामविधाने बीजं नास्माकमर्वाग्दृशां प्रत्यक्षमिति सलज्जमावेदयामः । षष्टिपटलात्मकं सर्वं तन्त्रमिति मते त्वनुपलब्धेषु पटलेषु नामोषितः कोऽपि विषयो वर्त्तते न वेति कथं महेश्वरादन्यो जानीयात् ।

अत्र यदुक्तं तन्त्रेषु दिव्यवीरपशुभेदाद् भावानां त्रित्वम्, तत्र—

मातृ—२

"प्रथमे पशुभावश्च द्वितीये वीरभावकम् ।
तृतीये दिव्यभावश्च... ... ... ॥
दिव्यं विवेकजं प्रोक्तं सर्वसिद्धिप्रदायकम् ।
उत्तमं तद् विजानीयादानन्दरससागरम् ॥
मध्यमं चाऽऽत्मोल्लासं वीरभावं क्रियान्वितम् ।
वेदोद्भवं फलार्थञ्च पशुभावं हि चाधमम् ॥
सर्वनिन्दासमाख्यातं भावानामधमं पशोः ।" इति

अत्र तु दिव्याचारो वीराचारश्च समजातीयः, पशुभावश्च भिन्नजातीय इति । तत्र तावद् दिव्यो वीरभावश्च वामाचारः, पशुभावश्च दक्षिणाचारः । तत्रापि वामाचारदक्षिणाचारयोर्विरोधस्तयोः साधकबाधकप्रमाणानि च बहुषु तन्त्रेषु पृथक् पृथगुपपादितानि । अत्र च बहुभिः पण्डितैर्निबन्धकारैश्च कल्पभेदेन मूलभेदेनाधिकारिभेदेन च कदाचित् कस्यचिदाचारस्य हेयत्वं कदाचिद् वोपादेयत्वमिति निरणायि । परमत्र पशुभावे स्मृतिपुराणादिसमाहृतः सात्त्विकाचाराविरुद्धः पन्थाः परिगृहीत इति सर्वे समामनन्ति । वामाचारश्च प्रधानतो भोगमार्गसाध्य इति । भोगवैशिष्ट्यञ्च स्मृतिपुराणादिवचनप्रमाणं विधूय स्वतन्त्रतामापद्यते । सोऽयमाचारोऽस्मिंस्तन्त्रे समर्थित इति वीराचारिणामुपकारकः प्राधान्येन समर्थकश्च । तथा हि—श्रीदेव्युवाच

सर्वत्राहं श्रुता नाथ भोगं चेन्द्रियपुष्टिदम् ।
भोगेन मोक्षमाप्नोति कथं वदसि योगभृत् ॥

श्रीशङ्कर उवाच— भोगेन लभते योगं भोगेन कुलसाधनम् ।
भोगे स सिद्धिमाप्नोति भोगेन मोक्षमाप्नुयात् ॥ तृतीयपटले ।

अनन्तरञ्च कुलकुण्डलिन्या एव भोगो भवति न तु मनुजानामिति भङ्ग्या यदुक्तमत्र महादेवेन, तयोक्तियुक्त्या कदाचिद् ग्रन्थोऽयं पश्वाचारिणां वा ब्रह्मार्पणज्ञानवतां लिङ्गभेदेऽप्यभिन्नानां वैदान्तिकानां वेति न भ्रमितव्यमित्यनुपदमेवोदाहृतं देव्या—

मद्यपाने महापुण्यं सर्वतन्त्रे श्रुतं मया ।
जातिभेदं न कथितमिदानीं तत् प्रकाशय ॥ इत्यादि तृतीयपटले ।

महादेवेन च यथायथमुत्तरं दत्तम्—

निर्वाणविषये देवि मद्यं परमकारणम् ।
मद्यपानं विना देवि महामोक्षो न लभ्यते ॥
कारणेन विना देवि मोक्षज्ञानादिकं न हि ।
कारणं देवदेवेशि मोक्षदं सर्वजातिषु ॥ इति चतुर्थपटले ।

ततश्च स्वयम्भूकुसुमादिलक्षणकथनेन महाशङ्खमालानिरूपणेन च प्रकटितमत्र वीराचारप्राधान्यम् । किं बहुना वीराचारललामभूतेन वीरिकाया लक्षणस्य साधनस्य च प्रकारकथनेनान्तिमपटले

प्रकटितमनेन तन्त्रेणात्मनो वीराचारप्रधानतमत्वमिति सुव्यक्तमेव भवति वाचकानाम्। तन्त्रेऽस्मिन् बहवो विषया वर्णिताः, परं तेषां विन्याससौन्दर्यन्तु न तथोपलभ्यते, एकस्यापि विषयस्य भागशः कथनेन तत्त्वमिष्णातानामेव भावस्फूर्तिर्भवति नेतरेषामिति। यथा प्रथमपटले स्वर्णरजतनिर्माणप्रश्ने रजतनिर्माणमेव कथितम्, तदनुविषयान्तरमुपपाद्य पुनः पञ्चमपटले स्वर्ण-निर्माणप्रकारः कथित इत्यादि।

अथ मातृकाभेदतन्त्रस्थविषयानवलम्ब्य किञ्चिद्विद्योपस्थापयामः—

मातृकाभेदतन्त्रमिदं चतुर्दशस्वध्यायेषु विभक्तम्। यद्यपि सर्वेषामेव तन्त्राणां चतुःषष्ट्या पटलै-र्विभक्तिरङ्गीकृता कैश्चित् सम्प्रदायविद्भिरिति मतम्, तथाऽपि तदौपलभ्यमानतापरमिति तीर्थानामनु-मोदः। अत्राध्यायाः पुनः पटलशब्देनैवोल्लिखिताः, सेयं शैली तन्त्रशास्त्रस्य। अत्र मुद्रितादर्श-पुस्तकयोस्तु पञ्चदशाध्यायाः परिदृश्यन्ते, तत्र च हस्तलिखितपुस्तकेषु योऽयं द्वादशः पटलः स एव मुद्रितयोर्द्वादशत्रयोदशरूपत्वेन निरूपित इति ग्रन्थमध्ये स्पष्टम्।

तन्त्रेऽस्मिन् दृश्यते केषाञ्चिद् विलक्षणवस्तूनां कथोपन्यासः। तथा च—

'यन्नोक्तं सर्वतन्त्रेषु तद् वदस्व दयानिधे'

इति पार्वतीवाक्यादनन्तरं महादेवेन पारदभस्मनिर्माणम्, रौप्यनिर्माणम्, स्वर्णनिर्माणम्, पारद-शिवनिर्माणम् इत्यादि यथायथमुल्लिखितं दृश्यते। महादेव एव धातुघटितानामौषधादीनां निर्माणविधिं तन्त्रेषूक्तवानिति विशेषतो रसचिकित्सा विषचिकित्सा च तेनैवोक्ता। बहवः खलु कृतिनो बहुकालं यावत् कृत्रिमेणोपायेन स्वर्णरूप्याद्युत्पादनार्थं यतमाना आसत एव। तन्त्रेऽस्मिन् मद्यस्य गन्धहीनताकरणं दुग्धरूपताकरणमित्याद्यैन्द्रजालिकप्रक्रियाऽपि वर्त्तते। द्वितीयपटले च पुत्रोत्पत्तिविषये जिज्ञासायां येनोपायेन यया च प्रणाल्या सन्ततिरुत्पद्यते, यथा वा सन्ततिनाशो न भवतीत्यादि ग्रन्थेऽस्मिन् महादेवेन प्रतिपादितम्। श्रूयते यद्यत्वेऽपि शर्मण्यदेशीयाः सन्तानोत्पत्तौ शतशो विरुद्धानि मतानि सहेतुवादं निराकृत्य सुप्राचीनमेनमेव मतवादं निर्भरं प्रतिपन्ना इति।

अत्र च चण्डीपाठविषयमधिकृत्य येयं प्रणाली प्रकटीकृता श्रीमता भवभारहारिणा सा तु सद्यः फलप्रसूरिति विज्ञा वीराचारपरायणाः सघण्टाघोषमुद्घोषयन्तीति।

इतः प्रागस्य ग्रन्थस्य वङ्गदेशे वङ्गाक्षरैर्द्विर्मुद्रणं जातम्, वङ्गेतरविषयवासिनां दुर्ग्राह्यास्ते ग्रन्थाः साम्प्रतमप्युलभा इति सर्वदेशसाधारणीकरणेच्छया यावच्छक्यं विशुद्धादर्शपुस्तकसाहाय्येन देवनागराक्षरैरस्य मुद्रणार्थमस्मदीयसहायकसुहृद्भिरनुल्लानामस्माकमयं समुद्यमः।

तन्त्रस्यास्यानतिविस्तृततया विषयान् बुभुत्सवस्तावदाद्यन्तवाचनेनैव सर्वमनवद्यं ज्ञास्यन्तीति न तानुपादायाधिकं वक्तुमुचितं मन्यामहे। तत्र तत्र च संवादिविसंवादिप्रमाणोप-न्यासेन विषयबोधसौकर्यार्थमपि यतितमस्माभिः पादटीकायामिति।

तन्त्रस्यास्य प्रकाशनार्थमुद्युञ्जानैः पञ्च पुस्तकानि संगृहीतान्यस्माभिः। तत्र (१) संस्कृत-

साहित्य-परिषद्ग्रन्थागारतो हस्तलिखितमेकं ग्रन्थागारिकस्य श्रीमतो जानकीनाथसाहित्यशास्त्रिणः सुजनतया प्राप्तमर्वाग् वर्षशतद्वयाल्लिखितं नातिशुद्धं 'क'नाम्नाऽत्र निर्दिष्टम् ।

(२) अस्मद्गृहस्थितं वर्षशतादूर्ध्वं मुद्रितमेकं पुस्तकं 'ख'नाम्नाऽत्र निर्दिष्टम् ।

(३) श्रीमता रसिकचट्टोपाध्यायेन पञ्चाशतो वर्षेभ्यः प्राङ् मुद्रितमद्यत्वे दुष्प्रापं (out of print) पुस्तकमेकं 'ग'नाम्नाऽत्र निर्दिष्टम् ।

(४) एसियाटिक्सोसाइटीसंगृहीतम् अर्वाचीनं द्वादशपटलान्तमेकमत्यशुद्धं 'घ'नाम्नाऽत्र निर्दिष्टम् ।

(५) राजकीयग्रन्थसङ्कलनविभागसंगृहीतं प्रदर्शनी(musium)गृहपुस्तकालयतः प्राप्तमतिशुद्धमतिप्राचीनं पुस्तकमेकं स्थानविशेषेषु टिप्पणीयुतं 'ङ'नाम्नाऽत्र निर्दिष्टम् । यद्यप्यत्र मुद्रणे पञ्च पुस्तकानि संगृहीतानि तेषां च पाठभेदानुपादाय पाणिनिविरुद्धभाषासंयोजनादिदोषपरिहाराय यत्नः कृतस्तथाऽपि येषु येषु स्थानेषु पञ्चस्वपि पुस्तकेषु वैयाकरणाननुमोदितोऽप्येक एव पाठः स्वीकृतः, स महादेवोक्त इत्येव मत्वा तथैव संरक्षित इति द्रष्टव्यम् ।

श्रीमता हरतत्त्वदीधितिकृता हरकुमारठाकुरेण स्वीये निबन्धे सन्ध्यायाः कर्तव्यत्वविचारे यदिदं प्रमाणमुक्तं 'सन्ध्या सायन्तनी कार्या द्वादश्यादिष्वपि प्रिये' इति । आकरत्वेन च मातृकाभेदतन्त्रे द्वादशपटले इत्युक्तम्, तत्तु नैषु पञ्चसु पुस्तकेषु वर्तते । तादृशपाठसम्बलितो ग्रन्थस्तेषां पुस्तकागारे कदाचित् स्यादिति मन्यमानैरस्माभिस्तद्ग्रन्थसंग्रहे भूयान् यत्नः कृतः । परमस्माकमधन्यतया बहुधा यतमानैरप्यस्माभिः स ग्रन्थो नाधिगत इति सखेदमावेदयामः ।

श्रीमद्गुरुपादुकास्तोत्रं यद्यपि नैतत्तन्त्रान्तर्गतमिति ज्ञायते, न लभ्यते च त्रिष्वपि हस्तलिखितेषु पुस्तकेषु तथाऽपि मुद्रितपुस्तकयोः सत्त्वादत्युपादेयत्वाच्च तदन्ते सन्निवेशितम् ।

अत्राऽऽस्माकीनाद् दृष्टिदोषाद् वा विषयविमर्शापाटवाद् वा सीसकाक्षरसंयोजकप्रमादाद् वा विशेषनिरीक्षकावेक्षणोपेक्षया वा मुद्रायन्त्रसङ्घर्षभङ्गिभङ्गाद् वा ये भ्रमाः समुल्लसितास्तानुपेक्ष्य गुणैकपक्षपातिभिः प्रेक्षावद्भिर्वाचकैरनुकम्पा विधातव्येति साञ्जलिबन्धमसकृत् प्रार्थयते ।

मातृनवमी
शकातीताब्दाः १८९९ ।

एकान्तानुगतः
श्रीचिन्तामणिदेवशर्मा
वाराणसेयः ।

INTRODUCTION

In Sanskrit Literature various meanings are given to the word Tantra. Jagadīśa Tarkālaṅkāra, the reputed author of the Śabdaśaktiprakāśikā[1] uses this word in the sense of the science of argument. In the Pañcatantra[2], a book of fables by Viṣṇuśarman, the word is used in the sense of a chapter. Kālidāsa, in his well-known drama[3] Śakuntalā uses the word in the sense of administration. The word is used by Jayadeva in his Gītagovinda[4] in the sense of the principal doctrine. Kātyāyana[5] uses the word in the sense of the regular order of ceremonies and rites.

It has various other meanings also and they are not less than twentyfive. The Tantra as a śāstra denotes 'that body of religious scripture' which is revealed by Śiva to Pārvatī for the good of all people living in this wicked Iron (Kali) age. In this sense is the word most widely known.

The religious śāstras of the Hindus are classed under four well-marked heads—(i) the Śruti, (ii) the Smṛti, (iii) the Purāṇa and (iv) the Tantra. There are four ages or yugas—(i) Satya, (ii) Tretā, (iii) Dvāpara and (iv) Kali. Each of these ages has its appropriate śāstra or scripture which is designed to meet the requirements of the people living therein. The Kulārṇava Tantra says, 'a suitable

---

1. *Tarkaṃ tantrañca viduṣā viduṣāṃ toṣakārikā |*
kriyate jagadīśena śabdaśaktiprakāśikā ||

2. *Tantraiḥ pañcabhir etac cakāra sumonoharaṃ kāvyam |*
Mitrabhedamitraprāptikākolūkīyalabdhapraṇāśāparīkṣitakārakāṇi ceti pañca tantrāṇi racayitvā pāṭhitāste rājaputrāḥ |

3. *Lokatantrādhikāraḥ*—Act. v.

4. *Jitamanasijatantravicāram*—Gīt. II.

5. *Karmaṇāṃ yugapadbhāvas tantram—Kāty.* (Apte).

śāstra is given to each age or yuga: Śruti to Satya, Smṛti to Tretā, Purāṇa to Dvāpara and Tantra to Kali[6].' The truth to be taught ever remains the same, only the method of its realisation and teaching varies with the ages. Śruti is the original and highest source of dharma, as it is the Divine Revelation. The Ṛṣis are only seers and not authors of the Śrutis[7] which, according to the school of extreme orthodoxy, are co-eternal with God and independent of even Divine Causality (*apauruṣeya*). Smṛti, Purāṇa and Tantra, all assume Śruti as their basis and are, in fact, merely special presentments of the same truths for the respective ages. The term Śruti[8] is often used in reference to Tantra and it is said to be the fifth Veda[9] by the devoted tāntrikas. Thus they place Śruti and Tantra on the same footing. They even go further and opine that, for practical application the teachings of Tantra are to be preferred in this Kali yuga to the *ācāras* dictated in the Veda. 'The relation of the Veda to the Tantra may be well-compared with that of the Individual Soul (Jīvātmā) to the Absolute (Paramātmā).'

The Tantras are very often referred to as Āgamas and Nigamas. 'An Āgama is so called because it proceeds *(āgacchati)* from the mouth of Śambhu (Śiva) and goes to Girijā (Pārvati), being approved by Vāsudeva (Viṣṇu), and a Nigama is so called because it emanates *(nirgacchati)* from the mouth of Girijā to enter the ear of Giriśa (Śiva), being approved by Vāsudeva[10].' Thus a

6. *Kṛte śrutyuktamārgaḥ syāt tretāyāṃ smṛtisambhavaḥ !*
dvāpare tu purāṇoktaḥ kalāvāgamasammataḥ ||

7. *Svayambhūr eṣa bhagavān vedo gītas tvayā purā |*
śivādyā ṛṣiparyantāḥ smartāro'sya na kārakāḥ ||

8. *Vaidikī tāntrikī caiva dvividhā kīrtitā śrutiḥ |*
[Manusaṃhitā, Kulluka Bhaṭṭa's Com.]

9. Beveridge, 'History of India' ii. 77. as mentioned by Arthur Avalon in his Introduction to the Principles of Tantra, xxi f. n.

10. *Āgataṃ śambhuvaktrebhyo*
GAtañca girijāmukhe |
MAtañca vāsudevena
tasmād āgama ucyate ||

Tantra is called an Āgama where questions are put by Pārvatī as disciple and answers thereto are given by Śiva as preceptor, and a Nigama where Pārvatī is herself the teacher. It should be noted in this connection that the above is the special meaning of these two terms, both of which also denote the Veda. It may also be noted that devoted adherents have raised the Tantra to the status of the Veda itself not because they like to popularize it but because they really believe that it emanated from the Highest Soul (Śiva or Pārvatī).

The Tantras are so many encyclopaedias of the knowledge of their time. "The Tantra deals with all matters of common belief and interest from the doctrine of the origin of the world to the laws which govern kings and the societies which they have been divinely appointed to rule, medicine and science generally. The Tantra is not only the basis of popular Hindu practice, on which account it is known as the sādhana-śāstra, but is the repository of esoteric belief and practices, particularly those relating to Yoga and mantra-tattva. Indeed, as regards the last, which is one of the most peculiar, and at the same time, most profound aspects of Hindu teaching, the Tantra is to such an extent the acknowledged repository of this spiritual science that its other name is the mantra-śāstra. Its claims to such a name could not have been made good were there not some ground for its assertion that it is a Yoga-śāstra for the Kali age. As to which Tantras, however, are authoritative there appear to be differences of opinion, such differences being due either to a mistaken sectarianism, or possibly to real divergences as regards doctrinal thought and historical descent".

"In short, it is considered an error to regard the Tantra as the petty śāstra of any religious sect only, and a still greater mistake

---

NIrgato girijāvaktrād
GAtaśca giriśaśrutim |
MAtaśca vāsudevasya
nigamaḥ parikathyate ||

Āgamadvaitanirṇaya.

to limit its operation to that which is but one only of its particular methods or divisions of worshippers (ācāras).[11]"

We actually find in the Tantras description of the Supreme Being, the creation and destruction of the universe, classification of creatures, the origin and worship of the gods, the heavenly bodies, different worlds and hells, man and woman, cakra (centre) of the human body, dharma, āśramas and the sacraments, mantra, yantra (magic diagram on which to worship), various forms of spiritual training, japa, vrata, worship external and internal, medicine, science and many other things.

The general characteristics of the Tantra are unique as compared with those of the other śāstras. In the first place, the Tantra contains provisions of sādhana for all irrespective of caste, creed or sex. The Veda, on the other hand, does not provide for those who do not belong to the superior castes. Śūdras and women are excluded from the vedic study as they are not initiated with the sacred thread (yajñopavīta) and hence the way to Self-knowledge to be acquired by studying the Vedas is fully barred to them. There are some who question the utility of the Tantra. But they do not realise that but for the Tantra there would have been no sādhana on the part of those who stand at a lower cultural status in the Kali age. Even for those who claim superior culture and education, it may be noted, vaidika sādhana is impossible as there is almost none who can lead the life of a Brāhmaṇa, Kṣatriya or Vaiśya of the vedic age, for want of equipments that could make the vedic rituals practicable with so many of the hard and fast rules relating to them. The Gautamīya Tantra[12] aptly remarks that people of all castes, men or women whatever the case may be, may have access to the tantric rituals or in other words, may be initiated in the line of the Tantra. The Mahānirvāṇa Tantra says, 'A low kaula[13] who refuses to initiate a caṇḍāla, one belonging

11. Arthur Avalon's Introduction *(P. xxix)* to the Principles of Tantra.

12. *Sarvavarṇādhikaraśca narīṇāṃ yogyam eva ca*—chap. I.

13. *Kaula*, as an adjective, literally means relating to a family,

to the lowest and most unclean caste, or a yavana, a non-Hindu into the kaula dharma, considering them to be inferior, or a woman, out of disrespect towards her, goes the downward way[14]. All two-footed beings in this world, from the vipra (Brāhmaṇa) to the caṇḍāla are quite competent for kulācāra[15]'.

In the next place, the Tantra is above all a practical śāstra primarily concerned with action (kriyā) and ritual. In this connection it is to be understood that the Hindus establish a relation between kriyā (action) and jñāna (liberating knowledge). Although action cannot directly secure knowledge that leads to liberation, still it does not follow except through right action which consists in nothing but certain exercises physical, mental and spiritual, generically termed sādhana.

Sādhana has its own history and it has varied with race and creed. The Hindu has everything regarding sādhana in the Tantra which, on this account, is called the sādhana-śāstra. Sādhana includes in itself both worship (pūjā) and all its rituals. The Tantra is thus a practical or pratyakṣa śāstra as it affords the direct proof of experience. Thus in the spiritual sphere, the necessity of the Tantra must be admitted on all hands. The study of the Vedānta may produce big intellectual giants and may help its students to formulate philosophical theories but practically it has no value if it is not accompanied by sādhana. One may idly suppose that the nirguṇa Brahman can be realised by the mere closing of the eyes and through vedantic talk, and scholarly disputations but it should be remembered that to the sādhaka, philosophical and

ancestral, hereditary, of a noble family, well born. Here, it is a noun in the masculine gender and means a worshipper of *Śakti* according to the left-hand ritual *(vāmācāra)*, the word in the neuter gender *(kaulam)* meaning the doctrine and practices of left-hand *śāktas*.

14. *Caṇḍālaṃ yavanaṃ nīcaṃ matvā striyam avajñayā |*
kaulaṃ na kuryāt yaḥ kaulaḥ so'dhamo yāty adhogatim ||

M. N. Chap. XIV, 187.

15. *Viprādy antyajaparyantā dvipadā ye'tra bhūtale |*
te sarve'smin kulācāre bhaveyur adhikāriṇaḥ ||

M. N. Chap. XIV, 184.

scientific disputations are like the cawing of crows, closing of the eyes in pious pose is a fancy and vedantic talk is but a fashion. Mere sastric speculations cannot secure liberating knowledge. Both theory and practice are of utmost importance to reach the Highest Goal. They should go together. 'Whereas other śāstras are concerned with speculation only, the art of medicine and Tantra are practical, self-evident and prove themselves at every step.'

The Tantra is not only practical and all-embracing but also fundamentally rational. Want of reasoning involves loss of dharma. In India, religious views are diverse and many and it is said, 'there is no sage who has not a doctrine of his own'. To find out, therefore, which doctrine best suits one's capacity, one should possess an amount of intelligence and reasoning power. The more a man possesses these qualities the more competent he will be in the realm of religion, and it is well known that the efficacy of the sastric mantra very much depends on the competence (adhikāra) of the recepient.

There are some people, who in their zeal for the Vedānta speak ill of the karmakāṇḍa relating to worship and ritual practices. Of course, to one who has attained liberating knowledge the portion of the śāstra relating to worship and ritual practices is useless. It should be remembered, however, that the mastery of the arguments and language of the Vedānta does not necessarily lead to Real Knowledge. A jñānī is one who not merely knows theories of Self but at the same time practically realises it. Real Knowledge consists in spiritual experience *(anubhūti)* that can liberate the Soul from eternal bondage. Karmakāṇḍa helps the attainment of spiritual experience and therefore it is interrelated with jñāna-kāṇḍa.

The Tantra does not teach Absolute Monism. It embraces both Dualism and Monism ; for, worship (upāsanā) advocated by the Tantra, involves the dualistic idea, and spiritual experience gained through upāsanā, merging the Individual Soul into the Absolute, involves the idea of one-ness between the worshipper and the worshipped. This is, in short, the philosophy of the Tantra. 'It seeks to attain liberation for the jīvas through enjoyment of worldly objects, presenting themselves before them[16]'.

It is often whispered in some quarters, that the Tantra śāstra is of recent origin and further that it is the creation of the people of Eastern India where it largely prevails. But the antiquity of the Tantra may be proved by facts and figures, and it is not Eastern India alone where it holds its ground but the upper classes of Hindu community throughout the whole of India are ruled by the Tantra, so far as initiation (dīkṣā) is concerned. There are śāktas, vaiṣṇavas and śaivas among the Bengali Hindus of the higher class. The śāktas are initiated by the Śakti-mantra, the vaiṣṇavas by the Viṣṇu-mantra and the śaivas by the Śiva-mantra. All these mantras are the exclusive properties of the Tantra. Like Bengal, Madras, Bombay, Behar, Benares, Kashmere, Assam and almost every other notable place of India have śāktas, vaiṣṇavas and śaivas initiated by Śakti, Viṣṇu or Śiva mantra, as the case may be, and thus follow the tantric order. So it is but idle to suppose that the Tantra is the creation of people of Eastern India and that it exerts its influence here alone. Of course, the Bengalis rightly boast of their tantric sādhakas like Pūrṇānanda, Sarvānanda, Brahmānanda, Rāmaprasāda, Sadāśiva and Thākuravāṇī and tantric scholars like Kālīcaraṇa, Raghunātha and others. Nevertheless, the Tantra śāstra is not their own making. The Bengali sādhakas and paṇdits like those of other provinces have only prepared compendia and developed the practical side of it to a considerable extent for the benefit of humanity.

Some people are inclined to believe that the Tantra has come out of the Mahāyāna doctrine of the Buddhists who worship Tārā, Vajrayoginī, Kṣetrapāla and use mantra, bīja and japa in the cult of such devatās. But this is also a faulty notion, not at all well-founded. There is similarity of doctrines and practices, no doubt, in the two systems but such similarity can hardly be a proof of one borrowing from the other. As a matter of fact, we shall presently

16. *Bhogena mokṣam āpnoti* etc.—Mātṛkābheda-Tantra, iii. 1.

see that the Cina-Tantra is the originator of the worship of Tārā (Tārā is referred to in the Ṛgveda also) and that this Tantra existed in India much earlier than the Mahāyāna Buddhism made its appearance in the field. Minor similarities, here and there, are indeed outweighed by a great dissimilarity, viz., the practice of animal sacrifice. It is a known fact that the tāntrikas advocate animal sacrifice in Pañcatattvasādhana[17] while the Buddhists hold quite an opposite view.

Some are so very daring that they do not hesitate to assert that the presence of Śakti-worship in the Tantra which, according to them, has been borrowed by its Eastern authors from the aborigines is an evidence of its recent origin. But they do not see that Śakti-devatā is worshipped and Śakti-pīṭhas are established in almost all parts of India. In Benares, there is Annapūrṇā, in Kāmarūpa, there is Kāmākhyā, in Calcutta, there is Jayakālī and so on. No one

---

17. *Pañcatattva* generally means the five elements taken collectively i. e., earth *(kṣiti)*, water *(ap)*, fire *(tejas)* air *(marut)*, and ether *(vyoman)* ; but in the Tantras it means the five essentials of the tāntrikas, also called *pañcamakāra* because they all begin with the letter *M* ; i. e., *madya* (wine), *māṃsa* (meat), *matsya* (fish), *mudrā* (grain) and *maithuna* (woman).

'This is the term used by tāntrikas themselves in speaking of the conjoined elements. Vulgarly, they are called the five M's (pañcamakāra), because each of the ordinary names of the elements commences with that letter (madya, māṃsa, matsya, mudrā, maithuna). Some of these have, however, esoteric names used by tāntrikas amongst themselves. "Latā-sādhana" is a better and in some cases more accurate description of the fifth tattva than the word "maithuna" with its vulgar implications.' [Principles of Tantra, Intro. P. xxvi F. N.]

'The use of the rājasika pañcatattva is prescribed for Śāktas initiate in vāmācāra. This is overlooked in the common, though erroneous appellation —"right hand" (dakṣiṇa) and "left hand" (vāma) worship, used in a sense as if the two had no sastric connection with one another. The worship is not "right" and "left" in the sense of "proper" and "improper", orthodox and heterodox. Each is a recognized form of worship, presented by the "Tantra" for differing grades of its sādhakas. Each has a common authority. Therefore, no follower of the Tantra which prescribes these two ācāras thus speaks of them.' [Principles of Tantra, Intro. P. xxviii-xxix.]

knows when all these devīs were established in those places. If it be argued that the worship of the Śakti-devatā, provided for in the Tantra, proves that it is of recent origin, then the same thing must be said of the Purāṇas, the Mahābhārata and the Veda which bear evidence of such worship. Mādhavācārya, Vācaspati Miśra and even Śaṅkarācārya have admitted the authority of the Tantra in explaining philosophical doctrines. There were many compilers of tantric treatises like Rāghava Bhaṭṭa, Govinda Bhaṭṭa, Rāghavānanda and Virūpākṣa. They all flourished before Kṛṣṇānanda the reputed author of the Tantrasāra. Therefore, it should not be fancied that the Tantra originated two or three hundred years ago and that its development is due to Kṛṣṇānanda alone.

References, both direct and indirect, to Śiva and Śakti in the Vedas, Upaniṣads etc., may be cited to prove a great antiquity for these deities who play the most prominent part in all Tantras. The Tantras maintain that the universe is the outcome of the interaction between Śiva and Śakti. They may be identified with Puruṣa and Prakṛti of the Sāṅkhyas with this difference that Prakṛti is held to be unconscious. This Śakti is referred to in the Ṛgveda in her eight different attributes as Kālī, Tārā etc. Māyā is another name for Śakti. In the Śvetāśvataropaniṣad Māyā is said to be Prakṛti and Māyin is said to be Parameśvara [*māyāṃ tu prakṛtiṃ vidyān māyinaṃ tu maheśvaram*]. The Devīsūkta [ṚV. 10—125] of the Ṛgveda like the Devīmāhātmya (Caṇḍī) of the Mārkaṇḍeya-Purāṇa eulogizes the Śakti-devatā. The various names of Śakti such as Kālī, Karālī, Durgā, Annapūrṇā, Haimavatī, Umā, Ambā, Ambikā and Ambālikā are to be noticed in Devyupaniṣad, Tripuropaniṣad, Annapūrnopaniṣad and Dakṣiṇāmūrtyupaniṣad. Ambikā is said to be the sister of Rudra in the Taittirīya Brāhmaṇa [T. Br. 1.6.10.4]. This universe is said to be nothing but an energy (the Śakti-devatā) which may be equally proved by modern science [*Śaktimātrā-samūhasya viśvasyānekavartmanaḥ*--Vākyapadīya, 3.2]. In the Vājasaneyi-saṃhitā of the Yajur-veda (3.60—63) we find Śiva, Tryambaka, Kṛttivāsas and Pinākahasta as the names of Śiva.

M—2

In the Śatapatha Brāhmaṇa [6.1.3.18] we come across eight names of Śiva as Paśupati, Bhava, Mahān deva etc. In the Atharva-veda [11.1.22] also we find Paśupati, Bhūtapati, Bhava, Śarva as the names of Śiva.* The Kulārṇava[18] Tantra aptly remarks that the Tantra-śastra is vedātmaka and not vedabāhya.

Sir Arthur Avalon's remarks[19] on the antiquity of the Tantra literature are so illuminating that we make no apology for reproducing them here. "Whatever be the date of the first appearance of specifically tantric doctrines, which, owing to the progressive nature of its developments, may never be ascertained, it will be probably found, upon a profounder inquiry into the subject than has been hitherto made, that the antiquity of the Tantra has been much underestimated. This, however, does not mean that all the current Tantras, or all their contents, are of great antiquity. Comparatively modern Tantras may, however, be based on older versions now lost. On the orthodox hypothesis, moreover, there is no reason why new śāstra should not even now appear in the world. The work of Śiva has not come to an end with the inception of the Kali-yuga. In this, as in other matters, Indian traditions, when rightly understood, may perhaps be found to largely justify itself. The following remarks of Professor Hayman Wilson have a bearing on this point, both on the general question of the antiquity of the Hindu śāstras and that of the Tantra, if, as is commonly done, the date of the latter is to be fixed with reference to the alleged date of the paurāṇik period, which, according to general European views, precedes them : 'It is, therefore, as idle as it is irrational to dispute the antiquity or authenticity of the great portion

---

* Vide : 'Tantratattva' by late Pandit Śivacandra Vidyārṇava, '*Tantrer prācīnatva*' by late M. M. Yādaveśvara Tarkaratna in the Sāhityasaṃhitā of Āśvina, 1317 B.S., and '*Tantrasya prācīnatā*' (Sanskrit Sāhityapariṣat-Patrikā, March, 1933) by Dr. Prabhat Chandra Chakravarty.

18. *Tasmād vedātmakaṃ śāstraṃ viddhi kaulātmakaṃ priye* |
[Kulārṇava, 2. 85]

19. Introduction (*P. Lix—Lxi*) to the Principles of Tantra, Part I.

of the contents of the Purāṇas in the face of abundant positive and circumstantial evidence of the prevalence of the doctrines which they teach, the currency of the legends which they narrate, and the integrity of the institutions which they describe at least three centuries before the Christian Era. But the origin and development of these doctrines, traditions and institutions were not the work of a day, and the testimony which establishes their existence three centuries before Christianity carries it back to a much more remote antiquity—to an antiquity that is probably not surpassed by any of the prevailing fictions, institutions, or beliefs of the ancient world.' "

He adds further (*p. lxxxi*):

"But want of faith in the śāstra is becoming deeply rooted in people's minds by the troubles into which they fall through failure to realize the truth, *and by the exposition to vulgar gaze of things a proper understanding of which can be acquired from Gurus only.* ...Want of understanding of the śāstra, together with actual abuses of its injunctions by some of its adherents, have led to the insults now levelled at it. Discussion and agitation and insult have, ... to such an extent and with such constancy persecuted and wounded the community of sādhakas that no one who is a son with a body of flesh and blood and strength can bear to see the sacred names of the Mother and Father of the universe slandered and abused in such manner". (Ś. C. Vidyārṇava's Tantratattva, P. 14, translated.)

The Mātṛkābheda is an alchemical Tantra. In chapters I and V are elaborately explained the processes[20] of preparing gold, silver, gem and mercury[21]. Śaṅkara (Śiva) speaks of *pārada* (mercury) as his generative principle[22]. It is curious to note that in a Buddhist Tantra also exactly a similar statement occurs. It is well-known that alchemy is a subject for the Buddhistic Tantras which

---

20. Kenopāyena deveśa svarṇarūpyādi labhyate—1.3.

21. Mattejasā pāradena kiṃ ratnaṃ na hi labhyate—1. 5.

22. Madvīryaḥ pārado......sphuṭitaṃ maṇiḥ /

MS. belonging to the Durbar Library, Nepal for the industry and courtesy of Pandit H. P Śāstrī, who has wended his way through the bulky MS.

are comparatively modern. Mātṛkābheda is unique in that it is the first, if not the only orthodox Tantra, to deal with this subject.

As to the date of this Tantra as of all other Tantras, it is very difficult to arrive at any definite conclusion. Tantras are believed to be eternal (anādi) and emanating from Śiva himself. There being no human author named, we are left to rely on internal evidences only, for ascertaining their dates.

In the Introduction I. xxxiii—xliii to his History of Hindu Chemistry Vol. II, Sir P. C. Roy observes,—"By the second century A.D. we find the leading beliefs and ideas as crystallised in the Mahāyāna literature fully in vogue. Thus we come across in the 'Buddha-carita' of Aśvaghoṣa, who is admitted on all hands to be a contemporary of Kaniṣka such a passage as this: 'This, Sirs, is the Mahāyāna, the instrument of the law of the perfect Buddha, which is the establisher of the welfare of all beings, set forth by all the Buddhas.'[23] The "Lotus of good Law" was translated into Chinese at the close of the second century A.D[24].

Side by side with the growth of the scriptures another class of literature was called into being by the exigencies of the times—we mean the Tantras, the necessity for which has been hinted at in the first volume[25]. However esoteric may be the doctrines sought to be conveyed through the medium of these productions, it would be idle to deny that there is much in them which is calculated to pander to the baser instincts of frail humanity. At what particular time these Tantras appeared on the scene is yet a matter of conjecture, but the views of Wilson which held the ground for more than 30 years have now been found to be erroneous. Evidence is now forthcoming from quite an unexpected source, which goes to prove that Buddhist Tantras existed as early as the fifth or sixth century

---

23. Cowell's trans. p. 184. S. B. E. Series, Vol. xlix.

24. Edkin's "Chinese Buddhism," p. 89. There were several versions of this sacred book—*Vide* Kern's Intro. p. xxiii (S. B. E. Series).

25. Vol. I. Intro. lxx.

A.D., if not earlier[26]. If Buddhist Tantras, again, presuppose the existence of Hindu Tantras, one need not be considered as rash in assigning an earlier age to the latter[27].

The Tantras found a congenial home in China. Amoghavajra, a śramaṇa of northern India and a brahmin by caste resided in the celestial empire for several years between 746 and 771 A.D. and under his influence the tantric doctrines dealing with talismanic forms and professions of supernatural power first gained currency there[28]. Hence, long before his time Tantra must have been popular in India. From the eighth to the eleventh century A.D. we are in possession of authentic records as regards the prevalence of Tantras in northern India, as it was about this period that several of these were gradually imported into Tibet by Indian Pandits, but they must have been composed much earlier.[29]

---

26. *Vide :* the Palm-leaf Mss. discovered in the monastery of Hcriuzi in Japan and carried from Central India. One of these is in the hand-writing of a famous Chinese priest, named Kanshin, who came to Japan in A. D. 753. The MS. contains besides a Dhāraṇī, five Tantras —"Bud. Texts from Japan," ed. by Max Müller, Vol. i, pt. i, Intro. pp. 6-8. It is fair to conclude that these Tantras existed in the land of their birth at least two centuries earlier.

27. Waddel says :—"No one has yet realised the vast extent to which Mahāyāna and tantric Buddhist remains cover India, nor sufficiently realised the leading part played by the Mahāyāna in Indian Buddhism during its popular period."

Journal of the Roy. As. Soc. (1894).

28. Bun. Nanjio's Cata. App. ii, p. 445. Amoghavajra translated 77 works including Uṣṇṣīa-cakravarti-tantra, Garuḍagarbhaga-tantra and Vajrakumāra-tantra.

Cf.—Also "the existence of the Tantra Śāstras may thus apparently be traced at least as far back as the 6th century A. D." *Vide* "Annual Report," As. Soc. Beng. 1906.

29. In the first part of the eighth century two eminent pandits of Bengal visited Tibet at the invitation of its king and formally introduced there Buddhism ; these pandits were Śānti Rakṣita, high priest of the monastery of Nālenda and his co-adjutor Padma Sambhava, a native of Udyāna, who took charge of the tantric part of the Buddhist liturgy. They were

Atisa gave a fresh impetus to Tāntrism in the land of snow. From the analysis of Mds by Csoma we also come to know in detail the names with the dates of the Indian scholars who with the aid of the local interpreters (*lo-charas*) rendered into Tibetan the various Sanskrit Tantras.

Some of these Tantras deal with alchemy and their contents reveal to us the knowledge of chemical processes in India from about the sixth to the eighth century A.D.[30]

Fortunately we are not dependent upon the Tibetan Tantras alone for gaining an insight into this dark recess in the history of Hindu intellectual activity. In the course of our search for Mss.

---

followed by the sage Dīpaṅkara-Śrījñāna (Atisa)—b. A. D. 980, d. 1053. He acquired proficiency in the three piṭakas of the four classes of the Hīnayāna Śrāvakas, in the Vaiśeṣika philosophy, in the three piṭakas of the Mahāyāna doctrine, the Metaphysics of the Mādhyamika and the Yogācāra schools and the four classes of the Tantras. At the request of king Naya Pāla he accepted the post of high priest of the monastery of Vikramaśilā—*Vide* S. C. Dās, Journal of the Buddhist Text Soc. Pt. i.

30. Analysis of the contents of the Mds (Sūtra) by Csoma de Korosi : Asiatic Researches, xx (1836), p. 583. "A work on preparing quick-silver, the most powerful for subduing every sickness and for improving the vigor of the body."—"A work on turning base metals into gold". We are thus reminded of the contents of the Rasārṇava and the Rasaratnākara.

'What wonder is it that yellow sulphur, purified with the juice of *Butea frondośa*, converts silver into gold when roasted thrice over the fire of cow-dung cakes' ?—2.

[Kimatra citraṃ yadi pītagandhakaḥ
palāśaniryāsarasena śodhitaḥ /
āraṇyakair utpalakais tu pācitaḥ
karoti tāraṃ triputena kāñcanam //
Rasaratnākara—2.]

'What wonder is it that Calamine......roasted thrice with copper converts the latter into gold ?—3.

Hindu Chemistry, Vol. II, p. 2.

[Kimatra citraṃ rasako rasena.................. /
krameṇa kṛtvāmbudhareṇa rañjitaḥ
karoti śulvaṃ triputena kāñcanam //
Rasaratnākara—3.]

of alchemical Tantras we have come upon a precious find, in the shape of a Buddhist Tantra (Rasaratnākara) with Nāgārjuna as its reputed author. It is a Tantra of the Mahāyānist school and as such its invocations are addressed to all the Buddhas[31], and in one place there is a pointed reference to prajñā-pāramitā[32] (perfection of wisdom) appearing before Nāgārjuna in a dream and revealing to him the chemical knowledge[33].

A noteworthy feature of this work is that some chemical processes are discussed in the form of a dialogue between Śālivāhana and Nāgārjuna, and Ratnaghoṣa and Maṇḍavya.[34] These last two names are held equally in veneration with Nāgārjuna and grateful acknowledgments to their services occur in some later chemical treatises.[35]

Rasaratnākara, in short, seems to us to be a typical production representing the Mahāyānist period of intellectual activity and we may not be wide of the mark if we put down 7th or 8th century A.D. as its latest date.

The existence of a vast ancient tantric literature with alchemy as a component part has now been placed beyond doubt, thanks to the searching examination of the Maharaja's collection of valuable

---

31. Praṇipatya sarva-buddhān / Cf. the opening invocation in the Sukhāvatī Vyūha : Oṃ namaḥ śrīsarva-buddha-bodhisattvebhyaḥ / Also, namaḥ pratyeka-buddha ārya-śrāvakāṇāṃ namo bodhisattvānāṃ, in Ārya Mañjuśrīmūla Tantra.—*Vide* As. Res. xx, p. 512.

32. Cf. the invocation in Vajracchedikā—
namo bhagavatyā āryaprajñāpāramitāyai /

33. Prajñāpāramitā niśīthasamaye svapne prasādikṛtam /
nāmnā tīkṣṇamukhaṃ rasendramamalaṃ nāgārjunaproditam //

[Prajñāpāramitā (perfection of wisdom) appeared before Nāgārjuna at midnight in a dream and revealed to him the ingredients of a recipe (consisting of steel, copper, mica, pyrites, &c.).

Rasaratnākara—III. 4.]

34. Śrī-nāgārjuna uvāca—pp. 12---14.
Śālivāhana uvāca.—P. 13.
Ratnaghoṣa uvāca.—P. 14.

Vide Sans. Texts, p.p. 12---14, also Trans. p.p. 6--8 (Hindu Chemistry) .

35. Cf. Vol. I. p. 77.

MSS. of Nepal by the eminent scholars Bendall, H. P. Śāstrī and S. Lévi. Of surpassing interest is the Kubjikāmata, written in Gupta character and copied about the sixth century A.D. This school, though itself very ancient, presupposes the existence of other schools and we have distinct mention of the Mahāyāna.[36] We now learn that the gradual fusion and amalgamation of Sivaite and Buddhist Tantras had begun even anterior to the sixth century. The Kubjikātantra was evidently composed outside India proper, probably in Nepal. The Goddess Pārvatī encourages her consort to proceed to the continent for the spread of the tenets propounded by it[37]".

From these valuable accounts about the Buddhist alchemical Tantras we may readily conclude that the Mātṛkābheda-tantra, being a Sivaite Tantra alchemical in character, must belong to a period anterior to the fourth century A.D., as according to Sir P. C. Roy the Hindu Tantras should have belonged to a period at least two centuries earlier than the Buddhist alchemical Tantras. The parallel passages in the Mātṛkābheda and another Buddhist alchemical Tantra ('mattejasā pāradena' and 'madvīryaḥ pāradaḥ') cited above tend to show that the former was looked upon as an authoritative work. In the Mātṛikābheda there is a reference to the 'Cīna-tantra' [Cīnatantrānusāreṇa pūjayet siddhakālikām—1.7] which introduced the worship of Tārā for the first time and which was afterwards popularized amongst the Buddhists. We should not labour under a misconception that it was the Buddhists who first introduced the worship of Tārā and that 'Cīna-tantra' is a Tantra imported to India from China, for the fact is that no Tantra, Hindu or Buddhist, was imported from China or Tibet to India but it was the Indian scholars who carried the Buddhist Tantras to China and Tibet.

---

36. Catalogue of Palm-leaf and selected paper MSS. belonging to the Durbar Library, Nepal, by H. P. Śāstrī (1905). lxxviii, *et. seq.*

Dakṣiṇe devayānan tu pitṛyānas tathottare /
madhyame tu mahāyānaṃ śiva-saṃjñā prajīyate //

37. Gaccha tvaṃ bhārate varṣe'dhikārāya ca sarvataḥ /

The Mātṛkābheda-Tantra is divided into fourteen paṭalas or chapters. Like the other Tantras it is also presented in the form of dialogues between Śaṅkara (Śiva) and Caṇḍikā (Śakti).

Chapter I* raises two questions; one, of alchemic interest i. e., of the preparation of gold, silver, gem etc., and the other, regarding wine, technically called kāraṇa. At the very beginning of the chapter the preparation of silver is spoken of. After worshipping Siddha-Kālikā, according to the directions of the Cīna-tantra or Dakṣiṇā Kālikā, according to the directions of the Kālī-tantra, an amount of sambala, *(viaticum)* should be heated with milk for some time; then it should be taken out and thrown into water; afterwards it should be placed on fire with an amount of copper, with mystical formulas uttered over it. Some time hence it will be found that the alloy, so made, is silver and nothing else.[38]

The chapter ends with an elaborate discussion of Caṇḍikā's question how wine is turned into milk[39] and how it may be free from its unwelcome odour[40]. There are twenty-three verses in this chapter.

Chapter II deals with the general process of creation, especially the birth of children out of the mother's womb. This chapter is but the sum and substance of the Garbhopaniṣad, so to speak. Its importance lies in that it has a bearing upon the science of embryology. This chapter contains twenty-two verses.

Chapter III discusses a very important question wherein lies the peculiarity of the Tantra. Every other Hindu Scripture dissuades men from the enjoyment of pleasures and persuades them to attain

---

* The questions discussed in this chapter are historically of great value. We have hinted at this in some previous paragraphs.

38. *Satyaṃ satyaṃ hi Girije raupyaṃ bhavati niścitam—I. 16.*

39. *Kāraṇaṃ dugdharūpaṃ vā kena rūpeṇa śaṅkara,*
tatprakāraṃ mahādeva kṛpayā vada śaṅkara—I. 17.

40. *Gandhahīnaṃ bhaven madyaṃ kenopāyena śaṅkara,*
tatsarvaṃ śrotum icchāmi yadi sneho'sti māṃ prati—I. 21.

M—3

salvation through abstention but the Tantra is just the reverse: it teaches that salvation can be attained through enjoyment. Accordingly, here also the question how salvation may be attained by enjoyment[41] is incidentally discussed. It is said that when a sādhaka is not attached to the things of enjoyment but thinks that they are for the satisfaction of Kuṇḍalī Devī (inner guiding Principle) then he does not get entangled. Then follows a description of the Homa-kuṇḍa for the performance of inner sacrifice which leads to salvation. Then another question of tantric importance is raised i.e., the non-observance of caste distinction[42]. Then is described the efficacy of wine. Wine, if taken according to the dictates of the Tantra-śāstra, leads to liberating knowledge. Wine is called surā because it imparts divinity (suratva) as soon as it is enjoyed[43]. There are forty-five verses in this chapter.

Chapter IV discusses the merits of wine called kāraṇa. The acceptance of the nirmālya of Śiva and kāraṇa is sometimes prohibited. So, Caṇḍikā raises this question and Śiva in the course of his answers says that wine is the most potent cause of nirvāṇa (self-realisation). It is purer than the water of the Ganges itself. But the character of it should not be disclosed to the Paśu-sādhakas even at the risk of one's life[44]. This chapter contains thirty verses.

Chapter V discusses at length the processes of preparing mercury. According to the rules dictated in the Toḍala Tantra, worship of the Devī is necessary and then japa should be done over the thing heated for the purpose[45]. This chapter has some importance from the chemical point of view. Then, how a sādhaka may attain siddhi with the help of an unmarried or a married girl

---

41. *Bhogena mokṣam āpnoti katham vadasi yogabhṛt ?—iii. 1.*
42. *Madyapāne mahāpuṇyam sarvatantre śrutam mayā, jātibhedam na kathitam...... iii. 30.*
43. *Suratvam bhogamātreṇa surā tena prakīrtitā—iii. 40.*
44. *Gaṅgā tu kāraṇam vāri madyam paramakāraṇam—iv. 19. No vaktavyam paśor agre prāṇānte parameśvari—iv. 30.*
45. *Evam kṛte vahniyoge bhasmasāj jāyate kila, bhasmayoge bhavet svarṇam dhanadāyāḥ prasādataḥ—v. 25.*

has been fully described. This chapter contains altogether forty-three verses.

Chapter VI relates that everything of this earth may be attained by the grace of Cāmuṇḍā Kālī if the process of her worship is rightly looked into and that nobody can do any harm to her worshipper. It also describes the Solar and the Lunar eclipses and asserts that an eclipse is nothing but the contact of Śiva and Śakti ; so the time when an eclipse occurs is said to be very auspicious. Then the procedure of the worship and the mantras of Cāmuṇḍā are also described in this chapter very elaborately by means of which a sādhaka may attain siddhi. This chapter is made up of sixty-nine verses.

Chapter VII is divided into three parts. The first part explains the morning duties with some hymns about Śrīvidyā (Tripurasundarī). Part II describes the kavaca of Tripurā. Part III describes the nature of Sandhyā, its dhyāna and the place in which Śiva (Śambhu) should be worshipped, there being different results attributed to the different places of worship. Lastly, the dimension of Śivaliṅga and its worship are spoken of. There are sixty-nine verses in this chapter.

Chapter VIII describes the characteristic glory of Śiva-liṅga. Viśveśvara of Benares is said to be the sixteenth part of the complete liṅga of Śiva in Kailāsa. Lakṣmī and Nārāyaṇa are said to be not even a hundredth part of the Pārada liṅga of Śiva. p indicates Viṣṇu, ā indicates Kālikā, r indicates Śiva, and d indicates Brahmā. So, Pārada alone is the soul of Brahmā, Viṣṇu and Śiva ; and one who worships the Pārada liṅga attains to the position of the undying Śambhu Himself. There are various obstacles in making a Pārada Śiva for which śānti, svastyayana etc. are necessary at the very outset. Twelve earthen liṅgas should be first worshipped with sixteen upacāras for the purpose according to the dictates of the Toḍala Tantra[46]. There are thirty-four verses in this chapter.

---

46. *Pāradaṃ parameśāni brahmaviṣṇuśivatmakam—7.*
Yo yajet pāradaṃ liṅgaṃ sa eva śambhur avyayaḥ—8.
[*Vide : also, śl. 4, 5, 6, 14, 15, 16, 17, 18.*

Chapter IX describes the processes how minerals are reduced to ashes and the efficacy of these ashes as drugs[47]. The chapter contains only thirty-one verses.

Chapter X is very important from the tantric point of view. It proves how the Guru (Preceptor), the Mantra and the Devatā (Deity) are practically identical, they being the manifestations or attributes of one and the same Principle. The best of the sādhakas gain the Mahāmantra from the mouth of the Guru and the body of the Deity develops from the Bīja or seed which is nothing but the mantra itself. By meditating conjointly on the Guru, Mantra and Devatā the sādhaka attains siddhi, i.e., arrives at the principle towards salvation; so these three are said to be inseparable from one another. It should be noted in this connection that according to the philosophy and religion of the Tantras the Guru is the Śiva himself, the Mantra is his Bīja or liṅga and the Devatā is the agency through which the Bīja* is manifested into a Principle leading finally to Emancipation. The sacrifice of animals like the goat, buffalo etc. is then highly spoken of. In the Kali age, one attains the merit derived from a horse-sacrifice by sacrificing the goat and other smaller animals. Then follows the eulogy of this Tantra. It is said that this Tantra is Brahman Itself[48]. Hearing of this Tantra is more fruitful than that of the eighteen Purāṇas and the four Vedas with all the Aṅgas. There are twenty-four verses in this chapter.

---

47. *Kṛṣṇavarṇaṃ reṇuyutaṃ dṛṣṭvā utthāpya sundari |*
rattipramāṇaṃ tad dravyaṃ bhakṣayed yadi sundari ||
satyaṃ satyaṃ sarvakuṣṭhaṃ bhakṣaṇān nāsām āpnuyāt |
anupānam ūṣṇatoyaṃ matsyādīn parivarjayet ||
—*Sl. 27—28.*

* According to the Nityā Tantra, *Mantras* are of four kinds—*Piṇḍa*, *Kartarī*, *Bīja* and *Mālā* according to the number of syllables.

[*Vide*, as to Bīja, A. Avalon's 'Garland of Letters.

48. *Balidānaṃ mahāyajñaṃ kali-kāle ca caṇḍike |*
aśvamedhādikaṃ yajñaṃ kalau nāsti sureśvari ||—16.
Kevalaṃ śravaṇenaiva sa siddho nātra saṃśayaḥ—22.
Brahmarūpam idaṃ tantraṃ sārāt sāraṃ parāt param—24.
[*Vide : also, śl. 11. 13. 23.*

Chapter XI describes in the beginning the procedure relating to the offering of wells, palaces etc., to the Devī, with the glory thereof and the merits to be attained thereby. Then the description as to the respective dimension of the yajñasūtra (sacred thread worn by the Brahmin) is given according to the respective Veda by which the individual brahmin swears. A brahmin who puts on a sacred thread without knowing the technicality of its dimension is like a caṇḍāla, indeed, however great he may be, no matter if he be as great as Vyāsa himself[49]. This chapter contains forty-four verses.

In chapter XII the ādhāras for worshipping are described with the respective results to be obtained therefrom. Śālagrāma, maṇi (gem), yantra (diagram), pratimā (image), ghaṭa (jar), jala (water), pustikā (book), Gangā (the Ganges), Śiva-linga and prasūna (flower) are the chief ādhāras on which a deity may be worshipped. Mahāvidyā is only one in reality ; simply there is a difference in names[50]. One who is not faithful to the mantra does not attain siddhi. Then the sādhana on a cremation ground[51] is described in a few lines. There are seventy-nine verses in this chapter.

---

49. *Etat saṅketam ajñātvā yaḥ kuryāt sūtradhāraṇam |*
sa caṇḍālasama devi yadi vyāsasamo bhavet ||—44.
[*Vide : also, śl. 1, 2, 36, 37.*

50. *Ekaiva hi mahāvidyā nāmamātram pṛthak pṛthak—40.*

'In Mathematics zero has no value and is merely an empty formless (Nirākāra) thing, indicative of infinity until it is joined to an integer. But when joined to the figure 1, it converts it into 10. Similarly when she who is formless Brahman is joined to Her own Prakṛti, consisting of the three Guṇas, spoken of in Śruti as 'the unborn one, red, black and white', then she assumes for the fruition of the sādhaka's desires ten different forms (Daśamahāvidyā) whose variety is due to difference in the proportions of the three Guṇas. There are the ten Mahāvidyās who are Śiva and Śakti (Śivaśaktimayī).' See A. Avalon's Introduction to Tāntrik Texts, Vol. IX.

51. 'In every cremation ground (śmaśana where tantric rites are practised) in India the refulgent and divine halo of Bhairavas and Bhairavīs (adept tantric men and women) is yet to be seen mingling with the light of the flames of funeral pyres, rending apart the waves of nocturnal darkness

Chapter XIII deals with the japa (recitation) with mālā (beads) and describes the nature of the beads with reference to the particular Deity (Devatā) worshipped by the sādhaka. The mahāśaṅkhamālā is the best of all. The mantra of any Vidyā (female Deity) may be uttered on the mahāśaṅkhamālā and the sādhaka may attain siddhi thereby[52]. The mantra should be recited every

---

and illuminating the wide expanse of Heaven. Dead and putrefying corpses submerged (before and whilst awaiting burning, the corpse is placed in the sacred stream) near cremation grounds are still brought to life by the force of the sādhakas' mantras, and made to render aid to sādhana and siddhi. Whilst still living in this mortal world Tāntrik Yogīs even now obtain, through the potency of mantras, direct vision of the supersensual activities of the world of Devas : She, with dishevelled hair, the dispeller of fear from the hearts of Her devotees, still appears in great cremation grounds (mahāśmaśānas, where some of the most difficult forms of Tāntrik Sādhanā are practised. The auspicious Kālikā is thought of as with dishevelled hair—*vigalitacikurā*,—and so is the hair of the devotee—Karpūrādistotra, 3, 10), to give liberation to Her devoted sādhakas who, made afraid by the fear of this existence, make obeisance to and supplicate Her. Sādhakas still merge themselves in the Self of Brahman by laying their Brahmarandhra (the cavity of Brahman at the top of the head, here used for the head generally) at those lotus feet of Brahmamayī (the Devī), which are adored by Brahmā and other Devas. The throne of the daughter of the mountain (the Devī as daughter of Himavat) is still moved by the wondrous, attractive force of mantras. This, in the eyes of sādhakas, is the ever broad and royal road upon which they travel untiring to the city of liberation.

The same forces, however, against which this book, as also other orthodoxies, protest, are in conflict both with Hinduism in its present Tāntrik form and with Christianity of the older type. In the present mingling of East and West, each is providing a ferment for the other, which, when all is said, is as much a divine product as the Revelations which it sometimes appears to threaten. The embodied Ātmā, however, *must* ever seek itself revealing its search to us in that which we call the "religious spirit," clothed though It must also be in forms new or renewed—its changing expression in a world of unceasing change.'

[Principles of Tantra, Intro. PP. XII—XIII.

52. *Akasmād vai mahāsiddhir mahāśaṅkhākhyamālayā |*
tathaiva sakalā vidyā mahāśaṅkhe vaset sadā ||—4.

[*Vide : also, śl. 1, 3, 22.*

day and sacrifices of animals, too, should be daily made. There are forty-five verses in this chapter.

Chapter XIV describes three kinds of bhoga (enjoyment)—divya-bhoga, vīra-bhoga and the paśu-bhoga. The vīra is then defined and very highly spoken of. Surā (wine) is said to be urgently necessary in the vīra-bhāva (kulācara*). It is Brahman Itself. Being cursed it became surā and as soon as the curse is removed it becomes sudhā (nectar) indeed. The Guru (preceptor) should be worshipped by a sādhaka and his wife together. The wife and the son of the preceptor are also to be respected like the preceptor himself as they are no other than his own selves[53], so to speak.

At the end of the chapter we find some hymns about the pādukā of the preceptor. The last chapter contains forty-two verses and the hymns on the pādukā of the preceptor at the end are seven in number.

Thus ends the Mātṛkābheda-Tantra in fourteen paṭalas (chapters).

* 'The Kaulopaniṣad is, as it were, the seed of the Kaula doctrine and form of worship which is amplified in the Kulārṇava and other Tantras and Saṃhitās. There appear to have been differing forms of Kaula worship as evidenced by the commentary of Lakṣmīdhara on the Saundaryalaharī who was himself a Kaula and a man of great learning but spoke with severe condemnation of some of the practices of what he calls the Uttara or Northern Kaulas. Bhāskararāya, a man of considerable breadth of view and tolerance, condemns any depreciation of the faiths and rites of others'—Tāntrik Texts Vol. XI, Intro. P. 4.

53. *Bhogas tu trividho devi divya-vīra-paśukramāt—3.*
Gurupatnī guruḥ sākṣād guruputro na saṃśayaḥ—35.
[*Vide : also, śl. 3, 11, 12, 33.*

मातृकाभेदतन्त्रस्य विषयसूची

प्रथमपटलस्य १—४ पृ०

द्वितीयपटलस्य ५—८ पृ०

तृतीयपटलस्य ९—१५ पृ०

चतुर्थपटलस्य १६—२१ पृ०

पञ्चमपटलस्य २२—२८ पृ०

दशमपटलस्य ५९—६२ पृ०

एकादशपटलस्य ६३—६९ पृ०

द्वादशपटलस्य ७०—८० पृ०

त्रयोदशपटलस्य ८१—८६ पृ०

चतुर्दशपटलस्य ८७—९२ पृ०

मातृकाभेदतन्त्रम्

प्रथमः पटलः

ॐ [1]नमो देव्यै

[2]कैलासशिखरे रम्ये नानारत्नोपशोभिते ।
पप्रच्छ परया भक्त्या भैरवं परमेश्वरम् ॥ १ ॥

श्रीचण्डिकोवाच—

त्रिपुरापूजनं नाथ [3]स्वर्णरत्नैर्विशेषतः[4] ।
कलिकाले [5]स्वर्णरूप्यं गुप्तभावं तथा मणिम् [:] ॥ २ ॥
केनोपायेन देवेश स्वर्णरूप्यादि[6] लभ्यते ।
तद् वदस्व विशेषेण यथा रत्नादिकं भवेत् ॥ ३ ॥
यन्नोक्तं सर्व्वतन्त्रेषु तद् वदस्व दयानिधे ॥ ४ ॥

श्रीशङ्कर उवाच—

शृणु देवि प्रवक्ष्यामि यथा रत्नादिकं भवेत् ।
मत्तेजसा [7]पारदेन किं रत्नं न हि लभ्यते ॥ ५ ॥
तथा सामुद्रकेणैव सुशुभ्रलवणेन[8] च ।
[9]सम्बलस्य प्रकारं हि [10]शृणु देवि प्रयत्नतः ॥ ६ ॥

---

६ । सम्बलस्येति । 'दारमुच्'इति यस्य प्रसिद्धिरिति ङ-पुस्तकटिप्पन्याम् ।

---

1. 'नमः परदेवतायै' घ । 2. 'कैलाश-' घ ङ । 3. 'सर्व-' घ ङ । 4. '-विभूषणैः' ख-ग । 5. 'स्वर्णरत्नस्तप्तभावस्तथा मणिः' ख-ग, 'सर्वरत्न' ङ । 6. '-रत्नादि' ख-ग-घ-ङ । 7. पारकेण ङ । 8. 'शुद्धसामुद्रके तथा' ख-ग, 'शुभ्रसम्बलकेन' घ-ङ । 9. 'सामुद्रस्य' ख-ग । 10. 'तच्छृणुष्व प्रियंवदे' ख-ग ।

चीनतन्त्रानुसारेण पूजयेत् [1]सिद्धकालिकाम् ।
[2]अथवा पूजयेद् देवीं दक्षिणां[3] कालिकां पराम् ।
कालीतन्त्रोक्तविधिना सप्ताहं जपपूजनम् ॥ ७ ॥
सत्ये चैकन्तु त्रेतायां द्विगुणं द्वापरे त्रयम् ।
एवं सर्व्वत्र जानीयाच्चतुर्गुणजपः कलौ ॥ ८ ॥

७। कालीतन्त्रेति। अत्र संक्षेपतः कालीतन्त्रोक्ता पूजा निरूप्यते—अथार्च्चनविधिं वक्ष्ये देव्याः सर्वसमृद्धिदम्। येनानुष्ठितमात्रेण स्वयं भैरवरूपवान् ॥ ... ... आदौ यन्त्रं प्रवक्ष्यामि यज्ज्ञात्वाऽमरतां व्रजेत् ॥ आदौ त्रिकोणं विन्यस्य त्रिकोणं तद्बहिर्न्यसेत्। ततो वै विलिखेन्मन्त्री त्रिकोणत्रयमुत्तमम् ॥ वृत्तं विलिख्य विधिवल्लिखेत् पद्मं सुलक्षणम्। ततो वृत्तं विलिख्यैव लिखेद् भूपुरमेककम ॥ चतुरस्रं चतुर्द्वारमेवं मण्डलमालिखेत्। पीठपूजां ततः कृत्वा स्ववामेऽर्घ्यं न्यसेत् प्रिये ॥ मूलविद्यां षडङ्गेन मूलमन्त्रेण चार्च्चयेत्। ततो हृदयपद्मान्तः स्फुरन्तीं परमां कलाम् ॥ यन्त्रमध्ये समावाह्य न्यासजालं प्रविन्यसेत्। ततो ध्यात्वा महादेवीमुपचारान् प्रकल्पयेत् ॥ नमस्कृत्य महादेवीं तत आवरणं यजेत्। कालीं कपालिनीं कुल्लां कुरुकुल्लां विरोधिनीम् ॥ विप्रचित्तान्तु सम्पूज्य बहिःषट्कोणके ततः। उग्रामुग्रप्रभां दीप्तां तथा मध्यत्रिकोणके ॥ नीलां घनां बलाकाञ्च तथैवान्यत्रिकोणके। मात्रां मुद्रां मिताञ्चैव तथैवान्तस्त्रिकोणके ॥ सर्वाः श्यामा असिकरा मुण्डमालाविभूषिताः। तर्जनीं वामहस्तेन धारयन्त्यः शुचिस्मिताः ॥ ततो वै मातरः पूज्या ब्राह्मी नारायणी तथा। माहेश्वरी च चामुण्डा कौमारी चापराजिता ॥ वाराही च तथा पूज्या नारसिंही तथैव च ॥ सर्वासामपि देवीनां बलिः पूजा तथैव च। अनुलेपनकं गन्धो धूपदीपौ तथैव च ॥ त्रिभिः पूजा प्रकर्त्तव्या सर्वासामपि साधकैः। गुरुपङ्क्तिं षडङ्गञ्च दिक्पालांश्च ततोऽर्च्चयेत ॥ एवं पूजां पुरा कृत्वा मूलेनैव यथाविधि। नैवेद्यादीन् यथाशक्त्या दद्याद् देव्यै पुनः पुनः ॥ ततो वै दश वारांस्तु दीपं दद्यात् तु साधकः। पुष्पादिकं पुनर्दद्यान्मूलेनैव यथाविधि ॥ ततः सावहितो मन्त्री गुरुं नत्वा शिरःस्थितम्। देवीं ध्यात्वा चाष्टोत्तरसहस्रं प्रजपेन्मनुम् ॥ तेजोमयं जपफलं देव्या हस्ते समर्पयेत्। गुह्यातिगुह्यगोप्त्री त्वमिति मन्त्रेण मन्त्रवित् ॥ ततः शिरसि वै पुष्पं दत्वाष्टाङ्गं प्रणम्य च। विसृज्य परया भक्त्या संहारेणैव भक्तितः ॥ उद्वास्य हृदये देवीं तन्मयो भवति ध्रुवम्। *

1. 'कालिकां पराम्' ख-ग, 'सिद्धि-' घ। 2. श्लोकार्द्धमिदं नास्ति ख-ग। 3. 'दक्षिणा-का' क-ख-ग-घ।

* संस्कृत-साहित्यपरिषत्-प्रकाशित-कालीतन्त्रम्, १म प: २५-५८।
मन्त्रन्यासादिकन्तु तत्रैव प्रथमपटलेऽनुसन्धेयम्।

आनीय बहुयत्नेन सम्बलं तोलकद्वयम् ।
वसुराद्यं शिवं चाद्यं[1] मायाबिन्दुविभूषितम्[2] ।
बीजत्रयं चाष्टशतं प्रजपेत्[3] सम्बलोपरि ॥ ६ ॥
अशीतितोलकं मानं [4]कृष्णधेनुसमुद्भवम् ।
दुग्धमानीय यत्नेन चाष्टोत्तरशतं[5] जपेत् ॥ १० ॥
वस्त्रयुक्तेन सूत्रेण दुग्धमध्ये विनिक्षिपेत् ।
उत्तापं जनयेद्धीमान् मन्दमन्देन वह्निना ॥ ११ ॥
बिन्दु[6]वेदान्तपर्य्यन्तमर्द्धशोषं[7] भवेद् यदा ।
तदैवोत्तोल्य[8] तद्द्रव्यं तोयमध्ये[9] विनिक्षिपेत् ॥ १२ ॥
ततः परीक्षा कर्त्तव्या प्रदद्यात् पावकोपरि ।
निर्धूमं[10] पावके द्रव्यं दृष्ट्वा उत्थाप्य यत्नतः ॥ १३ ॥
तत्रैव प्रजपेन्मन्त्रं [11]सर्व्वबन्धनवात्मकम्[12] ।
[13]आनीय बहुयत्नेन शुद्धं ताम्रं मनोहरम् ॥ १४ ॥
सार्द्धेन तोलकं ताम्रं वह्निमध्ये विनिक्षिपेत् ।
यथा [14]वह्निस्तथा ताम्रं दृष्ट्वा उत्थाप्य यत्नतः ॥ १५ ॥
गुञ्जाप्रमाणं [15]तद्द्रव्यं तत्क्षणाद्[16] यदि योजयेत् ।
सत्यं सत्यं हि गिरिजे रौप्यं भवति निश्चितम् ॥ १६ ॥

---

६ । वसुराद्यमित्यादि । क-पुस्तक-टिप्पन्यां 'क्रीँ ह्रीँ क्रीँ' इत्येवं मन्त्रो दृश्यते ।
११ । वस्त्रयुक्तेन 'रक्तवस्त्रयुक्तेन' इति ङ-पुस्तकटिप्पन्याम् ।
१२ । क-पुस्तकटिप्पन्यां बिन्दुवेदान्तशब्दस्य चत्वारिंशदित्यर्थो दृश्यते ।

---

1. 'चाद्यां' क । 2. 'ताम्' क-ख-ग । 3. 'जपेत' घ । 4. 'कृष्णा-धे'- ङ । 5. 'अष्टोत्तर'- क-ख-ग । 6. 'वेदाङ्ग' ख-ग, 'वेदाग्नि-' घ, 'वेदाह्न'-ङ । 7. '-मर्द्ध शेषं' ख-ग-घ । 8. 'तदैवोत्तुल्यते द्रव्यं' घ । 9. 'दुग्धतोये' घ । 10. 'निधूमं' घ । 11. 'सर्वबन्ध-' क-ख-ग । 12. '-मयात्मकम्' 'ख-ग, सर्व्वबन्धनरात्मकम्' ङ । 13. क-ङ-पुस्तकयोरिदमर्द्धं नास्ति । 14. 'वह्नि तथा' क-ङ । 15. 'तं द्रव्यं' क । 16 '-क्षणे' क ।

[1]श्रीचण्डिकोवाच—

[2]कारणं दुग्धरूपं वा केन रूपेण शङ्कर ।
तत्प्रकारं महादेव कृपया वद शङ्कर ॥ १७ ॥

श्रीशङ्कर उवाच—

टङ्कनम् आनयेद्धीमान् तोलकन्तु चतुष्टयम् ।
वह्नियोगेन गिरिजे [3]लाजरूपञ्चकारह ॥ १८ ॥
आम्रपुष्पं तद्द्विगुणं पिष्ट्वा मिलनमाचरेत् ।
तस्योपरि जपेन्मन्त्रं महामायां हि चण्डिके ॥ १९ ॥
एतत्[4] तु गुटिकां कृत्वा [5]मेलनं कारयेद् यदि ।
तदैव दुग्धरूपं स्यात् सत्यं सत्यं हि शैलजे ॥ २० ॥

श्रीचण्डिकोवाच—

गन्धहीनं भवेन्मद्यं केनोपायेन शङ्कर ।
तत् सर्व्वं श्रोतुमिच्छामि यदि स्नेहोऽस्ति मां प्रति ॥२१॥

श्रीशङ्कर उवाच—

शिवं वह्निसमारूढं वामनेत्रविभूषितम् ।
बिन्दुनादसमायुक्तं[6] गन्धमादाय संलिखेत् ॥ २२ ॥
उह्यतां[7] पदमुच्चार्य्य चाष्टोत्तरशतं यदि ।
प्रजपेत् साधकश्रेष्ठो दुर्गन्धादिविनाशनम् ॥ २३ ॥

इति श्रीमातृकाभेदतन्त्रे शिवपार्व्वतीसंवादे प्रथमः पटलः ॥ १ ॥

---

१८ । टङ्कनं 'सोयागा' इति भाषेति ङ-पुस्तकटिप्पन्याम् ।

१९ । महामायां ह्रीँ इत्यर्थः ।

२२ । शिवमित्यादि । तेन 'ह्रीँ गन्ध उह्यताम' इति मन्त्रेण भवितव्यमिति प्रतीयते ।

२३ । 'उह्यता'मित्यत्र 'उज्भ्यता'मिति पाठः समीचीनतया प्रतिभाति, किन्तु आदर्शपुस्तकेषु तथाऽदर्शनात् 'उह्यता'मिति पाठ एव मूले सन्निवेशितः ।

---

1. घ-पुस्तके 'श्री' नास्ति । 2. कारणमित्याद्यारभ्य शैलजे इत्यन्ता श्लोकचतुष्टयी ख-ग-पुस्तकयोर्नास्ति । 3. 'राजरूपं' क-ख-ग-घ । 4 'तत्र' घ, 'ततस्तु' ङ । 5. 'मीलनं' ङ । 6. '-दं 'कलायुक्त'' ख-ग, -'द्-कलायुक्त'' घ-ङ । 7. 'उष्णतां पर-' ख-ग, 'ऊह्यताम्' क-ख-ग-घ ।

द्वितीयः पटलः

श्रीदेव्युवाच—

वद ईशान सर्व्वज्ञ सर्व्वतत्त्वविदां वर ।
यत् त्वया कथितं [1]नाथ मम सङ्गे विहारतः ॥ १ ॥
कथं वा जायते पुत्रः शुक्रस्य[2] कुत्र संस्थितिः ।
वर्द्धमानं[3] सदा[4] लिङ्गं प्रवेशो[5] वा कथं भवेत् ॥ २ ॥
भीतियुक्ता ह्यहं नाथ त्राहि मां [6]दुःखसङ्कटात् ॥ ३ ॥

[7]श्रीशङ्कर उवाच—

मणिपूरं महापद्मं सुषुम्णामध्यसंस्थितम् ।
तस्य[8] नालेन देवेशि नाभिपद्मं मनोहरम् ॥ ४ ॥
[9]वक्रत्रयसमायुक्तं सदा शुक्रविभूषितम् ।
ऊर्द्ध्वं[10] नालं सहस्रारे अतः शुक्रविभूषितम् ॥ ५ ॥
तस्मादेव स्तनद्वन्द्वं वर्द्धमानं[11] दिने दिने ॥ ६ ॥
मध्यनालं सुषुम्णान्तं वृन्ताकारं[12] सुशीतलम् ।
[13]आयोन्यग्र-मधोनालं[14] सदानन्दमयि शिवे[15] ॥७॥
श्रृणु चार्वङ्गि सुभगे तन्मध्ये लिङ्गताडनात्[16] ।
यद्रूपं परमानन्दं तन्नास्ति भुवनत्रये ॥ ८ ॥

---

1. 'देव' ङ । 2. 'कथं वा शुक्र-' घ-प्रा । 3. 'वर्द्धमानस्य लिङ्गस्य प्रवेशो वा कथं भवेत्' प्रा- । 4. 'महालिङ्गं' ख-ग । 5. 'प्रवेशं' क-घ । 6. 'भयसागरात्' ख-ग । 7. घ-पुस्तके 'श्रीशङ्कर उवाच' इत्यंशो नास्ति, 'महादेव उवाच' प्रा । 8. 'तस्मान्नालेन' घ-प्रा । 9. 'रक्तत्रय-' ख-ग, 'वक्र' ङ, 'नालत्रय-' प्रा । 10. 'ऊर्द्ध्वं नालं' ख-ग-घ । 11. 'वर्द्धते च' ख-ग । 12 'वृत्ताकारं' ख-ग । 13. 'आयोन्यन्त-' घ । 14 '-नाले सदानन्दमयं' ख-ग, '-मयं' ङ-प्रा । 15. '-नन्दममी शिवे' घ, 'शिवम्' ङ । 16. '-ताडनम्' ख-ग ।

नाभिपद्मन्तु यद्रूपं तच्छृणुष्व समाहितः (ता)[1] ।
[2]बिन्दुस्थानं मध्यदेशे सदा पद्मविराजितम् ॥ ९ ॥
बाह्यदेशे चाष्टपत्रं[3] चतुरस्रं तु[4] तद्बहिः ।
चतुर्द्वारसमायुक्तं सुवर्णाभं सवृत्तकम्[5] ॥ १० ॥
तत्पत्रेण[6] भवेत् पुष्पं वृन्तयुक्तं त्रिपत्रकम् ।
प्रफुल्ले तु त्रिपत्रारे[7] बाह्ये[8] [9]रुधिरदर्शनम् ॥ ११ ॥
एतन्मध्ये[10] महेशानि यदि स्याल्लिङ्गताडनम् ।
पद्ममध्ये गते शुक्रे सन्ततिस्तेन जायते ॥ १२ ॥

---

१२ । एतन्मध्य इत्यादि । तत्रापि कालादिनियममाह—शाक्तानन्दतरङ्गिणी-प्रथमपरिच्छेदधृतज्ञानभाष्ये—रजस्वला च या नारी विशुद्धा पञ्चमे दिने । पीडिता कामबाणेन ततः पुरुषमीहते ॥ भगलिङ्गसमायोगान्मैथुनं स्यात् तदा तयोः । अन्योऽन्य-स्पर्शनादेव जायते च महासुखम् ॥ क्षरते च यदा रेतः प्राणापानविसंश्रितम् । क्षिति-रापस्तथा तेजो वायुराकाशमेव च ॥ सर्वेषां तत्र तत्त्वं स्याद् देहस्थरक्तबीजयोः ॥ इति ।

पद्ममध्य इत्यादि । पद्ममध्ये शुक्रगमनप्रकारस्तु प्रपञ्चसारे—स्वस्थानतश्च्युता-च्छुक्राद् बिन्दुमादाय मारुतः । गर्भाशयं प्रविशति यदा तुल्यं तदापरः ॥ आर्त्तवात् परमं बीजमादायास्याश्च मूलतः । यदा गर्भाशयं नेष्यत्यथ सं मिश्रयेन्मरुत् ॥ संक्षोभ्य संवर्द्धयति तन्मलं शोणिताधिकम् । स्त्री स्याच्छुक्राधिकं ना स्यात् समेन च नपुंसकम् ॥ वायुवह्न्यम्भसां योगे गर्भवृद्धिः प्रजायते । तथा ज्ञानभाष्ये—नाभिपद्मे महादेवि भ्राम्यते च समीरणैः । कुम्भकारो यथा चक्रे घटते च घटादिकम् ॥ तथा समीरणो गर्भे घटते प्राणिनां तनुम् ।

वीर्यवद्गर्भकारणमुक्तं राघवभट्टधृताध्यात्मविवेके—पूर्णषोडशवर्षा स्त्री पूर्ण-विंशेन सङ्गता । शुद्धगर्भाशये मार्गे रक्ते शुक्रेऽनिले हृदि ॥ वीर्यवन्तं सुतं सूते ततो न्यूनाब्दयोः पुनः । रोगाल्पायुरधन्यो वा गर्भो भवति नैव वा ॥ इति ।

---

1. '-हिता' प्रा । 2 'बिन्दु-नालं' ख-ग, 'व-[व] स्थानं मध्यदेशेऽस्य' प्रा । 3. 'चाष्टशतं' ख-ग । 4. 'च' प्रा । 5. 'सुवृन्तकम्' ख-ग, 'सवृन्तकम्' ङ-प्रा । 6. '-पद्मेन' घ-ङ-प्रा । 7. 'त्रिपत्रे वै' प्रा । 8. 'बाह्ये' ख-ग । 9. 'शोणित-' प्रा । 10 'तन्मध्ये च' ख-ग ।

पुरुषस्य तु यच्छुक्रं शक्ते[1]रक्ताधिको भवेत् ।
तदा कन्या[2] भवेद्देवि विपरीतः[3] पुमान् भवेत् ॥ १३ ॥
उभयोस्तुल्यशुक्रेण क्लीवं भवति निश्चितम् ॥ १४ ॥
शृणु चार्व्वङ्गि सुभगे पुष्पमाहात्म्यमुत्तमम् ।
मध्ये[4] तच्छुक्रसंयोगे[5] वर्द्धते तद्[6] दिने दिने ।
एवं दिङ्मासंप्राप्ते[7] तत्[8] पुष्पं वृन्तसंयुतम् ॥ १५ ॥
गलिते[9] परमेशानि व्यक्तो[10] भवति सन्ततिः ॥ १६ ॥

श्रीदेव्युवाच[11]—

किञ्चिद्रोगादिसम्भूते कृमिकीटादिसम्भवे ।
तस्माज्जीवं[12] प्रणश्यन्ति सा[13] नारी जीव्यते[14] कथम् ॥१७॥

श्रीशङ्कर उवाच[15]—

अस्य[16] पुष्पस्य माहात्म्यं किं वक्तुं शक्यते मया ।
बिन्दुस्थानं[17] सहस्रन्तु पुष्पमध्ये प्रियंवदे ॥ १८ ॥

---

१३ । पुरुषस्येत्यादि । शारदातिलकेऽप्युक्तम्—रक्ताधिका भवेन्नारी भवेद्रेतोऽधिकः पुमान् । उभयोः समतायान्तु नपंसकमिति स्थितिः ॥

१४ । उभयोरित्यादि । तत्राधिकतुल्यतादिकं प्रमाणीकृतं राघवभट्टेन—द्वाविंशती रजोभागाः शुक्रमात्राश्चतुर्द्दश । गर्भसञ्जनने काले पुंस्त्रियोः सम्भवन्ति हि ॥ नारी रजोऽधिकांशे स्यान्नरः शुक्राधिकांशके । उभयोरुक्तसङ्ख्यायां स्यान्नपुंसकसम्भवः ॥ इति ।

---

1. 'शक्तिर्व्वा चाधिका' घ, 'शुक्रं वा चाधिकं' ख-ग, 'सक्तेरत्रा-' ङ, 'शक्तेस्तस्याधिकं यदि' प्रा । 2. 'कन्यां विजानीयाद्' प्रा । 3. 'विपरीतात्' ख-ग, 'विपरीते' घ-ङ प्रा । 4. 'मेध्यं' प्रा । 5. '-योगेन' ख-ग । 6. 'च' घ-प्रा । 7. 'संप्राप्तौ' प्रा । 8. 'तत्पुष्पे वृन्तसंयुते' घ-प्रा, 'तत्पुष्पं वृत्तसंयुते' ङ । 9. 'गणिते' ख-ग । 10. 'व्यक्ता' प्रा । 11. श्रीनास्ति क-ख, 'श्रीशिव उवाच' ख-ग ? । 12. 'तस्या जीवं' ख-ग, '-जीवे' घ, 'तस्या जीवः' ङ, '-जीवाः' प्रा, । 13. 'निनरी' ? घ 14. 'जीवते' प्रा । 15. क-ख-ग-पुस्तकेषु 'श्री' नास्ति । 16. 'तस्य' ख-ग-घ-ङ-प्रा । 17. 'बिन्दुस्थान-स-' घ-प्रा ।

बुद्बुदा यत्र[1] तिष्ठन्ति तत्रैव सन्ततिर्भवेत् ।
एवंक्रमेण देवेशि सहस्रं सन्ततिर्यदि[2] ।
वर्द्धमानं [3]महापुष्पं पीडा किञ्चिन्न जायते ॥ १६ ॥
[4]मया सार्द्धं महेशानि विहारं कुरु यत्नतः ।
विहारे यो भवेत् पुत्रो गणेशः [5]स च कीर्त्तितः ॥ २० ॥
अपरे परमेशानि तव पुत्रप्रसादतः ।
पृथिव्यां जायते सृष्टिर्न्निर्व्विघ्नेन यथोचितम् ॥ २१ ॥
[6]एतच् श्रुत्वा ततो देवी मदनानलविह्वला ।
शिवेनालिङ्गिता देवी शिवाकारेण वै तदा॥ २२ ॥

इति श्रीमातृकाभेदतन्त्रे शिवपार्वतीसंवादे द्वितीयः पटलः ॥ २ ॥

---

1. 'येऽत्र' प्रा । 2. '-र्यदा' ख-ग । 3. 'तदा' प्रा । 4. 'मम क-घ-ङ ।
5. 'सैव' ङ । 6. क-ख-ग-घ-पुस्तकेषु इदमर्द्धं नास्ति ।

तृतीयः पटलः

श्रीदेव्युवाच—

सर्व्वलाहं[1] श्रुता नाथ भोगं [2]चेन्द्रियपुष्टिदम् ।
भोगेन मोक्षमाप्नोति कथं वदसि योगभृत् ॥ १ ॥

श्रीशङ्कर उवाच—

भोगेन लभते योगं भोगेन कुलसाधनम् ।
भोगेन सिद्धिमाप्नोति भोगेन मोक्षमाप्नुयात् ॥ २ ॥
तस्माद् भोगं सदा कार्य्यं बाह्यपूजा यथेच्छया[3] ।
भोजनस्य विधानं[4] यत् तच्छृणुष्व प्रियंवदे ॥ ३ ॥
मूलाधारे तु या शक्तिर्भुजगाकाररूपिणी ।
जीवात्मा परमेशानि तन्मध्ये वर्त्तते सदा ॥ ४ ॥
भोजनेच्छा[5] भवेत् तस्मान्निर्लिप्तो जीवसंज्ञकः ।
सैव साक्षाद् गुणमयी निर्गुणो जीव उच्यते ॥ ५ ॥
जीवस्य भोजनं देवि भ्रान्तिरेव[6] न संशयः ।
गुणयुक्ता कुण्डलिनी चन्द्रसूर्य्याग्निरूपिणी ॥ ६ ॥
मूलाधाराच्च तां[7] देवीमाजिह्वान्तां[8] विभावयेत् ।
शोधितान् मत्स्यमांसादीन् सम्मुखे स्थापयेद् बुधः ॥७॥

७। शोधितानित्यादि। मत्स्यमांसादिशोधनमाह महानिर्वाणतन्त्रे पञ्चमोल्लासे—
मांसमानीय पुरतस्त्रिकोणमण्डलोपरि। फटाभ्युक्ष्य वायुवह्निबीजाभ्यां मन्त्रयेत् त्रिधा ॥
कवचेनावगुण्ठ्याथ संरक्षेच्चास्त्रमन्त्रतः। धेन्वा वममृतीकृत्य मन्त्रमेतमुदीरयेत् ॥

---

1. 'सर्वत्रैव श्रुतं' ख-ग। 2. 'च श्रिय-' ? घ। 3. 'यदेच्छया' क। 4. 'यद्‌विधानं' क। 5. 'भोजनेषु भवेत् तस्य नि-' ख-ग, 'भोजनेच्छा भवेत्तस्या नि-' घ। 6. 'भ्रान्तिः केवलसंशयः' क-ख-ग। 7. '-धारस्थितां' क। 8. '-ह्वां तां' क, '-ह्वान्तं' घ-ङ।

२

मूलमन्त्रं समुच्चार्य्य जुहोमि कुण्डलीमुखे ।
अनेन मनुना देवि [1]प्रतिग्रासं [2]समाहरेत् ॥ ८ ॥
प्रतिग्रासे [3]परेशानि एवं कुर्य्याद्विचक्षणः ।
तदैव ब्रह्मरूपोऽसौ सत्यं सत्यं सुरेश्वरि ॥ ९ ॥
[4]भुज्यते कुण्डली देवी इति चिन्तापरो हि[5] यः ।
मन्त्रसिद्धिर्भवेत्तस्य ज्ञानसिद्धिर्न चान्यथा ॥ १० ॥
एवं कृते ब्रह्मरूपः शिवरूपः स्वयं हरिः ।
योगसिद्धिर्भवेत्तस्य चाष्टसिद्धिर्भविष्यति ॥ ११ ॥
शत्रुभिर्दीयते यत्[6] तु कृत्रिमं दारुणं विषम् ।
भक्षणात् तत्क्षणे[7] देवि ह्यमृतं नात्र संशयः ॥ १२ ॥
मन्त्रेण [8]शोधितं द्रव्यं भक्षणादमृतं भवेत् ।
यदैव[9] कालकूटन्तु[10] समुद्रमथने प्रिये ॥ १३ ॥
तदा चानेन[11] मनुना[12] तत्क्षणात् खादितं मया ॥ १४ ॥
सर्पाकारा कुण्डलिनी या देवी परमा कला ।
भुज्यते सर्परूपेण तत्रैव[13] दारुणं विषम् ॥ १५ ॥
इति ते कथितं कान्ते भोजनस्य विधानकम् ।
एतत् सर्व्वं महेशानि गोप्तव्यं पशुसङ्कटे ॥ १६ ॥

विष्णोर्व्वक्षसि या देवी या देवी शङ्करस्य च । मांसं मे पवित्रीकुरु कुरु तद्विष्णोः परमं पदम् ॥ इत्थं मीनं समानीय प्रोक्तमन्त्रेण संस्कृतम् । मन्त्रेणानेन मतिमांस्तं मीनमभिमन्त्रयेत् ॥ "ॐ त्र्यम्बकं यजामहे सुगन्धि पुष्टिवर्धनम् । उर्वारुकमिव बन्धनान्मृत्योर्मुक्षीय मामृतात् ॥ अथवा सर्व्वतत्त्वानि मूलेनैव विशोधयेत् । केवलं मूलमन्त्रेण यद्द्रव्यं शोधितं भवेत् ॥ तदेव देवताप्रीत्यै सुप्रशस्तं मयोच्यते ॥ इति । [महानिर्व्वाणतन्त्रम्, पञ्चमोल्लासः, २०६–२१०, २३१–२३४]

1.'सर्व ग्रासं' घ-ङ। 2. 'समुद्धरेत्' क-ख-ग। 3.'महेशानि' ङ। 4.'पूज्यते' क । 5. 'भवेत्' घ । 6. 'यस्मै' ख-ग, 'देवि' घ । 7. 'तत्क्षणात्' ख-ग । 8. 'पुटितं' घ । 9.'तदेव' ख-ग, 'यदैक-' घ । 10. '-टं हि' ख-ग । 11. 'चारेण' क-ख-ग-ङ । 12. 'मधुना' क । 13. 'तत्तत्रैवोरगे' घ ।

श्रीदेव्युवाच—

शृणु नाथ परानन्द[1] परापरकुलात्मक[2]।
वद मे परमेशान होमकुण्डन्तु कीदृशम् ॥ १७ ॥

श्रीशिव उवाच—

मणिपूरस्य बाह्ये तु नाभिपद्मं मनोहरम्।
अष्टपत्रं तथा वृत्तं तन्मध्ये कुण्डदुर्लभम् ॥ १८ ॥
[3]चतुरस्रादिकं देवि तत् कुण्डं कामरूपकम्।
सर्व्वकुण्डस्य देवेशि विप्रः[4] कर्त्ता विधीयते ॥ १९ ॥
वर्त्तुलं बाहुजातस्य वैश्यस्य [5]चार्द्धचन्द्रकम् ॥ २० ॥
त्रिकोणं पादजातस्य होमकुण्डं सुरेश्वरि।
एवं कुण्डं महेशानि नालत्रयविभूषितम् ॥ २१ ॥
ऊर्द्ध्वं नालं सहस्रारे[6] [7]परामृतविभूषितम्।
[8]मध्यनालं [9]नाभिपद्मे मूलाधारे च सुन्दरि ॥ २२ ॥
आलिङ्गाग्रमधोनालं सदानन्दमयं शिवे।
होमकुण्डमिदं देवि सर्व्वतन्त्रे[10] परिष्कृतम् ॥ २३ ॥
येन होमप्रसादेन साक्षाद्ब्रह्ममयो भवेत्।
विप्रस्य [11]चाहुतिर्होमं विज्ञातव्यं चतुष्टयम् ॥ २४ ॥

१९। चतुरस्र इत्यादि। अत्र संवादि प्रमाणमुक्तं तन्त्रान्तरतन्त्रेऽपि—विप्राणां चतुरस्रं स्याद् राज्ञां वर्त्तुलमिष्यते। वैश्यानामर्द्धचन्द्राभं शूद्राणां त्र्यस्रमीरितम् ॥ इति।

---

1. '···'नन्द' घ। 2. 'परमेश कुलान्तक' ख-ग, '-कुलान्तकम्' घ, 'कुलात्मकम्' ङ। 3. '-चतुर्व्वर्णा-' क, '-चतुर्हस्ता-' ख-ग। 4. 'विप्रकर्त्ता' क। 5. 'अर्द्ध-' ख-ग। 6. 'सहस्रारामृतबिन्दुविभूषितम्' ख-ग। 7. 'परमामृतविभूषितम्' क। 8. 'मध्ये नालं' ख-ग। 9. '-नाभिमध्ये' ख-ग। 10. '-तन्त्रपरि-' ख-ग-घ। 11. 'चाहुतीं होमो' क, 'चाहुतिं होमे' घ।

क्षत्रियस्य[1] त्रयं देवि वैश्यस्य चाहुतिद्वयम् ।
[2]शूद्रस्यैकाहुतिर्देवि[3] [4]मुक्तिश्चापि चतुर्विधा ॥ २५ ॥
महामोक्षं ब्राह्मणस्य सायुज्यं क्षत्रियस्य च ।
सारूप्यञ्चोरुजातस्य सालोक्यं [5]शूद्रजातिषु ॥ २६ ॥
बाह्यकुण्डं[6] बाह्यहोमे[7] एवं हि सुरवन्दिते ।
जातिभेदे[8] कुण्डभेदं कुर्य्यात् साधकसत्तमः ॥ २७ ॥
बाह्यहोमे[9] [10]काम्यसिद्धिर्भविष्यति न संशयः ।
ज्ञानहोमे मोक्षसिद्धिर्लभते नात्र संशयः ॥ २८ ॥
इति ते कथितं कान्त तन्त्राणां सारमुत्तमम् ।
न वक्तव्यं पशोरग्रे शपथो[11] मे त्वयि प्रिये ॥ २९ ॥

श्रीदेव्युवाच—

मद्यपाने[12] महापुण्यं सर्व्वतन्त्रे श्रुतं मया ।
जातिभेदं[13] न कथितमिदानीं तत् प्रकाशय ॥ ३० ॥

[14]श्रीशङ्कर उवाच—

सर्व्वयज्ञाधिपो विप्रः संशयो नास्ति पार्व्वति ।
[15]सौत्रामण्यां कुलाचारे[16] चत्वारो[17] ब्राह्मणादयः ॥३१॥

---

२६ । महामोक्षमित्यादि । अत्र संवादि प्रमाणन्तु निर्वाणतन्त्रे द्वितीयपटले—ब्राह्मणस्य महामोक्षं सायुज्यं क्षत्रियस्य च । सारूप्यञ्चोरुजातस्य शूद्रस्य सहलोकताम् ॥ इति ।

---

1. 'बाहुजातस्य' क, 'राजन्यस्य' घ-ङ । 2. 'पादजातस्य होमे तु दद्यादेकाहुतिं शिवे । चतुर्वर्णस्य होमेषु' ख-ग । 3. '-हुतिं देवि' घ-ङ । 4. 'मुक्तिश्चापि चतुर्विधाम्' घ-ङ । 5. 'पाद-' क-घ-ङ । 6. 'बाह्यं कुण्डं' ख-ग-घ । 7. '-होमो' क । 8. '-भेदं' क । 9. 'अस्य श्लोकस्य स्थाने ख-ग-पुस्तकयोः 'सन्न्यासमग्निहोमञ्च तावदेव कलौ युगे' अयं पाठः— । 10 'कार्य्य-' घ-ङ । 11. 'संशयो' ख-ग । 12. '-दाने' ख-ग । 13. '-भेदे' घ-ङ । 14. 'महादेव' ख-ग । 15. 'शौत्रामिण्यां' ङ, 'संयामिन्यां कुलाचारे' ङ पुस्तक-टिप्पनीपाठः । 16. 'महे यज्ञे' ख-ग, 'महायज्ञे' घ-ङ-प्रा । 17. 'तत्त्वज्ञा' ख-ग ।

ब्राह्मणस्य महामोक्षं मद्यपाने[1] प्रियंवदे ।
ब्राह्मणः परमेशानि यदि पानादिकञ्चरेत् ॥ ३२ ॥
तत्क्षणा[2]-च्छिवरूपोऽसौ सत्यं सत्यं हि शैलजे ॥३३॥
तोये[3] तोयं यथा लीनं यथा[4] तेजसि तेजसम् ।
घटे भग्ने[5] यथाऽऽकाशं वायौ [6]वायुर्यथा प्रिये ॥ ३४ ॥
तथैव मद्यपानेन ब्राह्मणो ब्रह्मणि[7] प्रिये ।
लीयते नाऽत्र सन्देहः परमात्मनि शैलजे ॥ ३५ ॥
सायुज्यादि महामोक्षं नियुक्तं क्षत्रियादिषु ।
सा[8] नारी मानवी [9]मद्यपाने देवी न संशयः ॥ ३६ ॥
सूक्ष्मसूत्रे यथा वह्निर्देहमध्ये तथा[10] शिवा ।
[11]तपोरूपं बृहत् सूत्रं पूजारूपं तथा हरिः[12] ॥ ३७ ॥
संयुक्तं कुरुते[13] यत्र वर्द्धमानो[14] महाङ्कुशः ।
मद्यपानं विना देवि तज्ज्ञानं[15] न हि लभ्यते ।
अत एव हि विप्रेण[16] मद्यपानं सदा[17] चरेत् ॥ ३८ ॥

---

३२ । ब्राह्मणस्येत्यादि । अत्र संवादि प्रमाणमुक्तं गुप्तसाधनतन्त्रे सप्तमपटले— यदि विप्रो भवेद्देवि पञ्चतत्त्वपरायणः । सत्यं सत्यं महेशानि परतत्त्वे प्रलीयते ॥ यथा जलं तोयमध्ये लीयते परमेश्वरि । तथैव तत्त्वसेवायां लीयते परमात्मनि ॥ क्षत्रियः परमेशानि सहयोगे वसेद् ध्रुवम् । वैश्यस्तु लभते देवि स्वरूपं नात्र संशयः ॥ शूद्रस्तु परमेशानि सहलोके सदा वसेत् । एतदन्यो महेशानि यदि तत्त्वपरायणः ॥ सत्यं सत्यं महेशानि मुक्तिफलमखण्डितम् । सेनानीः परमेशानि देवीदेहे प्रलीयते ॥ शोधनञ्च मया प्रोक्तं नीलतन्त्रादियामले । न कस्मैचित् प्रवक्तव्यं प्रकाशाच्छिवहा भवेत् ॥ इति ।

---

1 '-दाने' क । 2. 'तत्क्षणे शिव-' क-घ-ङ । 3. 'तोयं तोये' घ । 4. 'तेजसि तेजसं तथा' ख-ग, 'तेजसं तेजसि यथा' क, 'तेजसं तैजसे यथा' प्रा । 5. 'भग्नं' ख-ग-प्रा । 6. 'वायुं यथा भवेत्' घ-ङ । 7. 'ब्राह्मणि' क । 8. 'सा नारी मद्यपानेन तत्तद्देवी' क-ङ । 9. 'उक्तं देवि' ख-ग । 10. 'यथा शिवः' ख-ग । 11. 'ततो रूपं' क । 12. 'हविः' घ । 13. 'कारयेदत्र' ख-ग । 14. '-न-उपर्बुधः' क-ङ । 15. 'तत्त्वज्ञानं न लभ्यते' ख-ग-प्रा । 16. 'विप्रस्तु' प्रा । 17. 'समा-' प्रा ।

वेदमाताजपेनैव ब्राह्मणो न हि शैलजे ।
ब्रह्मज्ञानं यदा देवि तदा ब्राह्मण उच्यते ॥ ३९ ॥
[1]देवानाममृतं ब्रह्म तदियं[2] [3]लौकिकी सुरा ।
सुरत्वं[4] भोगमात्रेण सुरा तेन प्रकीर्त्तिता ॥ ४० ॥
मन्त्रत्रयं सदा[5] पाठ्यं ब्रह्मशापादिमोचनम् ।
प्रकुर्य्यात्तु [6]द्विजेनैव तदा ब्रह्ममयी सुरा ॥ ४१ ॥

---

३९ । वेदमातेति । प्रकरणेऽस्मिन् "ब्राह्मणस्य मद्यपानविधायकवचनम्···अभिषिक्तब्राह्मणपरमिति ज्ञातव्यम् । नन्वभिषेके—स्वस्ववर्णं परित्यज्य शिवत्वं लभते ध्रुवमिति वचनादभिषिक्तस्य जातिविचाराभावात् कथमभिषिक्तपरमिति चेत्, सत्यं स्वजातिचिह्नरक्षकस्य ज्ञानदुर्बलस्य पानार्थमेतद्वचनमित्यवेहि । अथवाऽभिशप्तसुरापाननिषेधार्थं सुरापाननिषेधकवचनम् । सुरा तु चतुर्युग एव पवित्रकारिणी केवलमभिशापेनैवापेया, अतः शापमोचनपूर्व्वरूपतया पेयैवे"ति प्राणतोषिणी । तन्त्रसारकारास्तु तत्त्वशोधनप्रकारमुक्त्वा "एतद्द्रव्यदानन्तु शूद्रस्यैव ··· ···। एतद् द्रव्यन्तु शूद्रस्य नान्येषान्तु कदाचन ॥ ··· ··· तदभावेऽनुकल्पविधानम् । तथा च गोक्षीरं ब्राह्मणो दद्याद् गव्यमाज्यञ्च बाहुजः ॥ ··· तेन क्षत्रियादीनां मुख्यस्य दानेऽधिकारो न पाने । यत्तु पीत्वा पीत्वा पुनः पीत्वा पतित्वा च महीतले । उत्थाय च पुनः पीत्वा पुनर्जन्म न विद्यते॥ भैरवीतन्त्रे—पाने भ्रान्तिर्भवेद् यस्य घृणा स्याद्रक्तरेतसोः। शुचौ चाशुद्धताभ्रान्तिः पापाशङ्का च मैथुने ॥ स भ्रष्टः पूजयेद् देवीं चण्डीमन्त्रं कथं जपेत् । तथा मदिरायां मैथुने च जातिवृत्तिं न चाचरेत् । एतत् तु चतुर्थाश्रमिपरम्" इत्युक्तवन्तः । अनयोः पर्य्यालोचनया "ब्राह्मणैः पीयते मद्यं न मद्यं द्विजपुङ्गवैः" इति निरुत्तरतन्त्रपञ्चमपटलीयप्रमाणैकवाक्यतया च एवमेव प्रतीयते यद् एतादृशस्यैव ब्राह्मणस्य मद्यादावधिकारिता न तु केवलं जात्या ब्राह्मणस्य । एवञ्च मद्यपानविधायकवचनेषु ब्राह्मणशब्दस्य विशेषार्थपरत्वे न काचिदनुपपत्तिः स्यादिति सुधीभिश्चिन्त्यम् । कारणस्याग्राह्यत्वविषयकवचनानि तु चतुर्थपटले द्वितीयश्लोकटिप्पन्याम् निवेदयिष्यन्ते ।

४१ । मन्त्रत्रयमित्यादि । संक्षेपतो यत् सुराशोधनमुक्तं तन्त्रसारे तदेवोपस्थाप्यते—

---

1. 'वेदाना-' ङ । 2. 'तदिदं' क-घ-ङ, 'तदेव' प्रा । 3. 'कौलिकी' ख-ग । 4. 'चत्वारिंशश्लोकपरार्द्धमारभ्य द्विचत्वारिंशश्लोकपूर्व्वार्द्धस्य स्थाने ख-ग-पुस्तकयोः 'सुरान्नं भोगमात्रेण वह्निर्दीप्तो भवेन्नरः । अयं पाठः । 5, 'तदा पाठ्यं' घ । 6. 'हि येनैव' प्रा ।

हविरारोपमात्रेण वह्निर्दीप्तो यथा भवेत् ।
शापमोचनमात्रेण सुरा मुक्तिप्रदायिनी ॥ ४२ ॥
अत एव हि देवेशि ब्राह्मणः पानमाचरेत् ।
स ब्राह्मणः स वेदज्ञः सोऽग्निहोत्री स दीक्षितः ॥४३॥
बहु किं कथ्यते देवि स एव [1]त्रिगुणात्मकः ॥ ४४ ॥
मुक्तिमार्गमिदं देवि गोप्तव्यं पशुसङ्कटे[2] ।
प्रकाशात् कार्य्यहानिः स्यान् निन्दनीयो न चान्यथा ॥४५

इति श्रीमातृकाभेदतन्त्रे हरगौरीसंवादे तृतीयः पटलः ॥ ३ ॥

यथा सुराभाण्डं धृत्वा पठेत्—एकमेव परं ब्रह्म स्थूलसूक्ष्ममयं ध्रुवम् । कचोद्भवां ब्रह्महत्यां तेन ते नाशयाम्यहम ॥ सूर्य्यमण्डलसम्भूते वरुणालयसम्भवे । अमाबीजमये देवि शुक्रशापाद्विमुच्यताम् ॥ वेदानां प्रणवो बीजं ब्रह्मानन्दमयं यदि । तेन सत्येन ते देवि ब्रह्महत्यां व्यपोहतु ॥ ततः ॐ वां वीं वूं वैं वौं वः ब्रह्मशापविमोचितायै सुरादेव्यै नमः । इति तदुपरि दशधा जपेत् । ततः ॐ शां शीं शूं शैं शौं शः शुक्रशाप-विमोचितायै सुधादेव्यै नमः । इति तदुपरि दशधा जपेत् । एवं ह्रीं श्रीं क्रां क्रीं क्रूं क्रैं क्रौं क्रः कृष्णशापं विमोचयामृतं स्रावय स्वाहेति दशधा जपेत् । ततो मूलमन्त्रं तदुपरि अष्टधा जप्त्वा देवतामयं विभावयेदिति द्रव्यशुद्धिः ।

---

1. 'निर्गुणात्मकः' प्रा । 2. '-सन्निधौ' घ ।

चतुर्थः पटलः

[1]श्रीचण्डिकोवाच—

कारणेन महामोक्षं[2] निर्म्माल्येन शिवस्य च ।
श्रुतं वेदे[3] पुराणे च[4] तव वक्त्रे[5] सुरेश्वर ॥ १ ॥
अग्राह्यं तव निर्म्माल्यमग्राह्यं कारणं विभो ।
मृषा वाक्यं महादेव कथं वदसि योगभृत् ॥ २ ॥

१ । निर्म्माल्येनेत्यादि । अत्र संवादि प्रमाणम्—शिवदत्तं विष्णुदत्तं गिरिजादत्तमेव च । नैवेद्यमुदरे कृत्वा नरः सायुज्यमाप्नुयात् ॥ इति । तथा—रोगं हरति निर्म्माल्यं शोकन्तु चरणोदकम् । नैवेद्यं सर्व्वपापानि शम्भोर्द्दहति निश्चितम् ॥ इति हरतत्त्वदीधितिधृततन्त्रकौमुदीवचनद्वयम् ।

२ । अग्राह्यमित्यादि । शिवनिर्म्माल्यस्याग्राह्यतोक्ता कालिकापुराणे—अग्राह्यं शिवनिर्माल्यं पत्रं पुष्पं फलं जलमिति । पद्मपुराणे च—द्रव्यमन्नं फलं तोयं शिवस्य न स्पृशेत् क्वचित् । न नयेच्छिवनिर्माल्यं कूपे सर्व्वं विनिक्षिपेत् ॥ मक्षिकापादमात्रं यः शिवस्वमुपजीवति । लोभान्मोहात् पतत्येव कल्पान्तं नरके नरः ॥ इति । पुराणसंग्रहेऽपि—शिव उवाच । अनर्हं मम नैवेद्यं पत्रं पुष्पं फलं जलम् । शालग्रामशिलालग्नं सर्व्वं याति पवित्रताम् ॥ नैवेद्यञ्च नरो भुक्त्वा शुद्ध्यै च चान्द्रायणञ्चरेदिति एतदेव देव्याः प्रश्ने बीजम् ।

अत्र देव्याः प्रश्ने बीजरूपेण वचनान्युच्यन्ते—तथाच रुद्रयामले—वेदत्यागान्मद्यपानाच्च शूद्रदारनिषेवणात् । तत्क्षणाज्जायते विप्रश्चण्डालादपि गर्हितः ॥ इति । कालीकुलार्णवे—सुरा वै मलमन्नानां पुरीषं मलमुच्यते । तस्माद् ब्राह्मणराजन्यौ वैश्यश्च न सुरां पिबेत् ॥ सुरादर्शनमात्रेण कुर्य्यात् सूर्य्यावलोकनम् । तत्समाघ्राणमात्रेण प्राणायामत्रयञ्चरेदिति ॥ कुब्जिकातन्त्रे च—भुक्त्वा मत्स्यञ्च मांसञ्च स्पृष्ट्वा हेतुञ्च भैरवि । त्रिरात्रोपोषितो भूत्वा पञ्चगव्येन शुध्यतीति ॥ कालीकुलामृते चतुर्थपटले च—ब्राह्मणस्तु सुरां दत्त्वा ब्राह्मण्यादेव हीयते । ब्राह्मणः पशुराख्यातः

1. 'श्री नास्ति' क । 2. 'मोक्षो' प्रा । 3. 'देव' ख-ग, 'वेद-' प्रा । 4. '-णेषु' ख-ग-प्रा । 5. 'भक्तः सुरेश्वरः' ख-ग, 'वक्त्रात्' घ, 'वाक्ये महेश्वरः' प्रा ।

श्रीशङ्कर उवाच—

शृणु देवि प्रवक्ष्यामि [1]यन्मां त्वं परिपृच्छसि।
[2]तत्तत् सर्वं प्रवक्ष्यामि सावधानावधारय॥ ३॥
चतुरशीतिलक्षेषु [3]योनिगर्त्ते तथैव हि।
भ्रमणं कुरुते जीवस्ततो मोक्षस्य भाजनम्॥ ४॥
एतन्मध्ये महाज्ञानं यदि स्याद् [4]वीरवन्दिते।
[5]तदा मोक्षमवाप्नोति भ्रमणं [6]केन वा भवेत्॥ ५॥
[7]अत एव महेशानि गुप्तभावमथाकृतम्।
यस्य जन्म न [8]पूर्णत्वं स कथं मोक्षभाजनम्।
यस्य [9]पापाधिकं देवि स कथं स्वर्गभाजनम्॥ ६॥
[10]अत एव [11]महेशानि गुप्तभावं मया कृतम्।
निर्म्माल्येन [12]भवेत् स्वर्गं निर्व्वाणं सुरया भवेत्॥ ७॥
पापयुक्तो हि चाण्डालो निर्म्माल्यं गृह्यते यदा।
तदा [13]मोक्षमवाप्नोति शिवरूपी न चान्यथा॥ ८॥

पाशवं कल्पमाचरेत्॥ इति। वाराहीतन्त्रे नवमपटले च—मद्यं मांसं तथा मत्स्यं मैथुनं परमेश्वरि। मानुषेण बलिं पञ्च ब्राह्मणो न स्मरेत् क्वचित्॥ इति। श्रीक्रमे च—न दद्याद् ब्राह्मणो मद्यं महादेव्यै कथञ्चन। वामकामो ब्राह्मणोऽपि मद्यं मांसं न भक्षयेत्॥ इति। कुलचूडामणौ च—यत्रासवमवश्यन्तु ब्राह्मणस्तु विशेषतः। गुडार्द्रकं तदा दद्यात् ताम्रे वा विसृजेन्मधु॥ इति। मेरुतन्त्रे प्रथमपटले—वाममार्गेण तद्याद्यवर्णं हित्वा प्रशस्यते। ब्राह्मणस्तु सुरां पीत्वा रौरवं नरकं व्रजेत्॥ वाममार्गी ब्राह्मणोऽपि मद्यं मांसं न भक्षयेत्॥ इति।

---

1. 'निर्म्माल्यं परिपृच्छति' ख-ग, 'यन्मा त्वं' घ। 2. 'प्रतत' ख-ग। 3. 'सहस्रेषु' क-घ-ङ। 4. 'छद्र-' प्रा। 5. 'तदैव मोक्षमाप्नोति' प्रा। 6. 'कस्य' क-घ-ङ। 7. 'अयं श्लोकः क-ख-ग-ङ-पुस्तकेषु नास्ति। 8 'पूर्णन्तु' प्रा। 9. 'पापाधिकत्वञ्च' प्रा। 10 'अत्र एव' इत्यारभ्य 'सुरया भवे'दित्यन्तोंऽशः ख-ग-पुस्तकयोर्नास्ति। 11 'महादेवि' प्रा। 12. 'लभेत्' प्रा। 13 'मोक्षो भवेत सत्यं शिवरूपो' ख-ग-घ, 'मोक्षं भवेत् सत्यं शिवरूपो' ङ, 'मोक्षं लभेत् सत्यं शिवरूपो' प्रा।

३

महापातकयुक्तोऽपि[1] कारणं प्रपिबेद् यदि ।
[2]ज्ञानान्मुक्तिर्भवेत् सत्यं जातिभेदादिकं न हि ॥ ९ ॥
सर्व्वजातिषु निर्व्वाणं ज्ञानेन परमेश्वरि ।
अत एव [3]महेशानि गुप्तभावं मया कृतम् ॥ १० ॥
गुप्तभावार्थ[4]-यद्वाक्यं [5]परिहासार्थमेव च[6] ।
[7]तदर्थमेव तद् वाक्यं न मिथ्या परमेश्वरि ॥ ११ ॥
निर्वाणविषये देवि मद्यं परमकारणम् ।
मद्यपानं विना देवि [8]महामोक्षो न लभ्यते ॥ १२ ॥

श्रीचण्डिकोवाच—

गङ्गायां ज्ञानतो मोक्षं तथैव म्रियते यदि ।
गङ्गायाश्चाधिकं नाथ कारणं [9]परदुर्लभम् ॥ १३ ॥

श्रीशङ्कर उवाच—

पूर्णब्रह्ममयी [10]देवि [11]सुरादेवी न चान्यथा ।
तस्याश्च षोडशांशैका या गङ्गा [12]सुरपूजिता ॥ १४ ॥
तथैव तुलसी देवी शतांशैका [13]सुरेश्वरी ।
[14]विमोक्षार्थी च यो मर्त्त्यस्तीर्थसेवां न चाचरेत् ॥ १५ ॥
[15]यथैव मालिकामध्ये महाशङ्खं विमोक्षदम् ।
तथैव कारणं देवि [16]सदा मोक्षप्रदायकम् ॥ १६ ॥

---

१६ । महाशङ्खमित्यादि । महाशङ्खमालाया वैशिष्ट्यं तत्कारणस्यास्थ्नः पञ्चाशद्-वर्णबीजात्मकत्वकथनेनाह प्राणतोषणीधृतनित्यातन्त्रे द्वितीयपटले—भग-

---

1. '-युक्तो वा कारणं पीयते यदा' क-ङ, '-युक्तोऽपि कारणं पीयते यदा-' घ । 2. 'तदा मुक्ति-' ख-ग-प्रा । 3. 'हि देवेशि' ख-ग । 4. '-भावार्थं' ख-ग । 5. 'परिहारार्थ-' घ । 6 'हि' ख-ग । 7 'तत्तदर्थेन' घ-ङ, 'तत्तदर्थेन मद्वाक्यं' ख-ग । 8 'महामोक्षं' क-ख-ग-ङ । 9. 'देव-' ख-ग, 'परम-' ङ । 10. 'देवी' क-घ । 11 'सुधा-' घ-ङ । 12. 'भुवि दुर्लभा' क-टिप्पनी । 13. 'न संशयः' ख-ग । 14. 'विमूढो हि' ख-ग । 15. 'तथैव' ङ । 16. 'महामोक्ष-' ख-ग ।

कारणेन विना देवि मोक्षज्ञानादिकं न हि ।
महाशङ्खं विना देवि न मन्त्रः सिद्धिदायकः ॥ १७ ॥
साक्षाद् ब्रह्ममयी माला महाशङ्खाख्यया[1] पुनः ।
शिलायन्त्रे[2] च वृन्दायां गङ्गायां सुरपूजिते[3] ।
[4]नैव स्पृशेन्महाशङ्खं स्पर्शनात् काष्ठवद् भवेत् ॥ १८ ॥

रूपा महामाया शुक्र-तर्पणतत्परा । जगदाकर्षिणी विद्या जगद्गुह्या वरानने ॥ तत्रैव गृह्यते सारं जगतां बीजरूपकम् । तद्बीजं परमेशानि पञ्चाशद्वर्णरूपकम् ॥ गर्भं प्राप्य भवेदस्थि शिशोर्मज्जासमन्वितम् । तदस्थि त्वद्धमप्यस्ति पञ्चाशद्वर्णरूपकम् ॥

महाशङ्खस्वरूपमाह ताराकल्पे—नृललाटास्थिखण्डेन रचिता जपमालिका । महाशङ्खमयी माला । इति । कर्णनेत्रान्तरस्थास्थिमहाशङ्खः प्रकीर्त्तितः । इति च । बृहन्नीलतन्त्रे चतुर्थपटलेऽपि—युद्धे मृतस्य देवेशि चण्डालस्यास्थिकेन च । मस्तकस्य विशेषेण महाशङ्खः प्रकीर्त्तितः ॥ इति । मुण्डमालातन्त्रे द्वितीयपटलेऽपि—नराङ्गुल्यस्थिभिर्माला ग्रथिता पर्वभेदतः । सर्वसिद्धिप्रदा मोक्षदायिनी वरवर्णिनि ॥ नाड्या संग्रथिता माला कार्या रक्तेन वाससा । नाडीभिर्ग्रथिता माला महासिद्धिप्रदा प्रिये ॥ इति । महाशङ्खविशेषस्य वर्जनीयत्वमाह नित्यातन्त्रे—स्वेच्छामृतं स्त्रियं विप्रं तिर्य्यगयोनिगतं तथा । रोगिणं यवनं वृद्धं दीक्षितञ्चापि वर्जयेत् ॥ ग्राह्यत्वमप्याह तत्रैव—वज्राहतं सर्पदष्टं पतित्वा वा जले मृतम् । व्याघ्रादिनिहतं वापि सम्मुखे वा रणे मृतम् ॥ चण्डालाद्याः प्रधानास्ते अधमाः शूद्रजातयः । इति ।

१८ । शिलायन्त्र इत्यादि । उक्तमेतत् स्वतन्त्रतन्त्रेऽपि—आनीय च्छिन्नशीर्षस्य नरस्य पतितस्य च । तुलसीगोमयास्पृष्टं तथा गङ्गोदकेन च ॥ यवनब्राह्मणास्यस्य तत्कार्य्यं साधकैर्जनैः । अस्पृश्यं तच्च जानीयाच्छालग्रामशिलादिभिः ॥ इति ।

---

1. '-ख्यमेव च' ङ । 2. '-यन्त्रेषु' ख-ग, '-मन्त्रे च' घ । 3. '-पूजिताम्' घ । 4. 'नैवं स्पृश-' ख-ग ।

[1]श्रीचण्डिकोवाच—

गङ्गा [2]तु कारणं वारि मद्यं परमकारणम् ।
कारणस्पर्शमात्रेण [3]मालाः शुद्धा भवन्ति हि ॥ १९ ॥
[4]गङ्गास्पर्शेन देवेश काष्ठवन्मालिका कथम् ।
वद मे परमेशान इति मे संशयो हृदि ॥ ॥ २० ॥

श्रीशङ्कर उवाच—

कारणं देवदेवेशि मोक्षदं सर्व्वजातिषु ।
तथा स्वर्गादिजनकं गङ्गातोयं न संशयः ॥ २१ ॥
कारणे निवसेद् देवि महाकाली परा कला ।
[5]महाविद्या वसेन्नित्यं [6]सुरायां परमेश्वरि ॥ २२ ॥
महाशङ्खे वसेन्नित्यं पञ्चाशद्वर्णरूपिणी ।
महाविद्या वसेन्नित्यं महाशङ्खे च सर्व्वदा ॥ २३ ॥
गङ्गास्पर्शनमात्रेण गङ्गायां लीयते [7]प्रिये ।
[8]काष्ठस्पर्शनमात्रेण काष्ठे वह्निस्तृणे[9] यथा ॥ २४ ॥
गङ्गास्पर्शे तथा देवि गङ्गायां लीयते प्रिये ।
तत्क्षणे च [10]महाशङ्खः काष्ठवन्नात्र संशयः ॥ २५ ॥
शिलायन्त्रे तुलस्यादौ तथैव परमेश्वरि ॥ २६ ॥
[11]महाशङ्खाख्यमालायां यो जपेत् साधकोत्तमः ।
अष्टसिद्धिः करे तस्य स एव शम्भुरव्ययः ।
मौलौ गङ्गा स्थिता यस्य गङ्गास्नानेन तस्य किम् ॥ २७ ॥

---

1. 'श्रीपार्व्वत्युवाच' ख-ग । 2. 'कारणवारि च' घ, 'गङ्गा कारणवाची च' क । 3. 'माला' इत्यारभ्य 'देवेश' इत्यन्तोंऽशः ख-ग-पुस्तकयोर्नास्ति, 'मालास्तुष्टा' घ, 'माला तुष्टा' ङ । 4. 'गङ्गायाः स्पर्शमात्रेण' ङ । 5. अयं श्लोकः ख-ग-पुस्तकयोर्नास्ति । 6. 'सुरया' घ । 7. 'ध्रुवम्' ख-ग । 8. 'काष्ठे'त्यादि 'प्रिये' इत्यन्तोऽशः ख-ग-पुस्तकयोर्नास्ति । 9. '-स्तृणां' क, '-स्तृणं' ङ । 10. 'महाशङ्ख' क-घ-ङ । 11. 'महाशङ्खे च' ख-ग ।

वाराणसी कामरूपं हरिद्वारं प्रयागकम् ।
गण्डकीं वदरिकां देवि गङ्गासागरसङ्गमम् ॥ २८ ॥
यस्य भक्तिर्महाशङ्के तस्य दर्शनमात्रतः ।
तीर्थस्नानफलं सर्व्वं लभते नात्र संशयः ॥ २९ ॥
इति ते कथितं [1]कान्ते [2]सर्व्वं परमदुर्लभम् ।
[3]न वक्तव्यं पशोरग्रे प्राणान्ते[4] परमेश्वरि[5] ॥ ३० ॥

इति श्रीमातृकाभेदतन्त्रे [6]हरगौरीसंवादे चतुर्थः पटलः ॥ ४ ॥

---

1. 'सर्व्वं' घ । 2. 'सारं' घ, 'सारात् सारं सुदुर्लभम्' ख-ग । 3. 'पशोरग्रे न वक्तव्यं' ङ । 4 '-न्तेऽपि कदाचन' ख-ग । 5. एतदनन्तरं 'इति ते कथितं देवि रहस्यं सर्व्वकामदम्' इत्यधिकः पाठः घ-ङ-पुस्तकयोः । 6. 'चण्डिकाशङ्करसंवादे' घ ।

पञ्चमः पटलः

श्रीचण्डिकोवाच—

पारदं भस्मनिर्माणं केनोपायेन शङ्कर ।
तदहं श्रोतुमिच्छामि [1]यदि तेऽस्ति कृपा मयि ॥ १ ॥

श्रीशङ्कर उवाच—

पारदे भस्मनिर्माणे नानाविघ्नानि[2] पार्व्वति ।
अत एव हि तत्रादौ शान्तिं कुर्य्याद् द्विजोत्तमः ॥ २ ॥
वरयेत् कर्म्मकर्त्तारं वक्ष्यमाणविधानतः ।
पूजयेत् षोडशं लिङ्गं पार्थिवं पर्वतात्मजे ॥ ३ ॥
षोडशेनोपचारेण तोडलोक्तविधानतः ।
भोगयोग्यं प्रदातव्यं मधुपर्कं सुरेश्वरि ॥ ४ ॥
पञ्चामृतेन देवेशं स्नापयेच्छुद्धवारिणा ।
पुरुषस्य [3]यथायोग्यं युग्मवस्त्रं निवेदयेत् ॥ ५ ॥
[4]चतुरङ्गुलिविस्तारं रौप्यनिर्म्माणपीठकम् ।
अलङ्कारं यथायोग्यं [5]पुरुषस्य निवेदयेत् ॥ ६ ॥

---

४ । षोडशेनेत्यादि । षोडशोपचारा उक्ताः शिवार्च्चनचन्द्रिकायाम्—आसनं स्वागतं पाद्यमर्घ्यमाचमनीयकम् । मधुपर्काचमस्नानवसनाभरणानि च ॥ गन्धपुष्पे धूपदीपौ नैवेद्यं वन्दनं तथा । प्रयोजयेदर्च्चनायामुपचारांस्तु षोडश ॥ इति । प्रकारान्तरं यथा कृष्णार्च्चनचन्द्रिकाधृत-मन्त्ररत्नावल्याम्—पाद्यार्घ्याचमनीयञ्च स्नानं वसनभूषणे । गन्धपुष्पे धूपदीपौ नैवेद्याचमनं ततः ॥ ताम्बूलमर्चना स्तोत्रं तर्पणञ्च नमस्क्रियाम् । प्रयोजयेदर्चनायामुपचारांस्तु षोडश ॥ इति । तोडलतन्त्रोक्त-शिवपूजा तु निरूपयिष्यते सप्तमपटले ।

---

1. 'तद् वदस्व कृपानिधे' ख-ग । 2. '-विघ्नादि-' ख-ग । 3 'प्रमाणञ्च' ख-ग ।
4. 'चतुरङ्गुल-' ख-ग । 5. 'पुरुषाय' ख-ग ।

[1]अलक्तकयुतं वापि दद्यान्मलयजं शिवे ।
षडङ्गधूपं देवेशि प्रदद्याच्च पुनः पुनः ॥ ७ ॥
घृतयुक्तं तथा दीपं दद्यात् कल्याणहेतवे ।
नैवेद्यं विविधं रम्यं नानाफलसमन्वितम् ॥ ८ ॥
[2]शर्करासंयुतं कृत्वा पायसं विनिवेदयेत् ।
दद्यात् तोयं महेशानि विजयासंयुतं प्रिये ॥ ९ ॥
षडक्षरं महामन्त्रं [3]गजान्तकसहस्रकम् ।
प्रजपेत् साधकश्रेष्ठस्ततः सिद्धो भवेद् ध्रुवम् ॥ १० ॥
अथवा परमेशानि धनदां धनदायिनीम् ।
पूजयेद् बहुयत्नेन षोडशेनोपचारतः ॥ ११ ॥

७। षडङ्ग इत्यादि। षडङ्गधूपो यथा शारदायाम्—गुग्गुलु अगुरूशीरशर्करामधुचन्दनैः। धूपयेदाज्यसंमिश्रैर्नीचैर्देवस्य देशिकः॥ ४र्थः पः १०६-१०७। प्रकारान्तरमपि तत्रैव शारदातिलके—सिताज्यमधुसंमिश्रं गुग्गुल्वगुरुचन्दनम्। षडङ्गधूपमेतत्तु सर्वदेवप्रियं सदा॥

१०। षडक्षरमित्यादि। "ॐ नमः शिवाय" इति। अत्र तोडलतन्त्रोक्तप्रमाणन्तु निवेदयिष्यतेऽष्टमपटले। गजान्तकेति—अष्टोत्तरसहस्रमित्यर्थः।

११। धनदामित्यादि। धनदाप्रयोगस्तु गुप्तसाधनतन्त्रे नवमपटले—श्रीशिव उवाच। अथातः संप्रवक्ष्यामि धनदां सर्वसिद्धिदाम्। यामाराध्य महादेवि कुबेरो धननायकः॥ दान्तं बिन्दुसमारूढं महामायां हरिप्रियाम्। रतिप्रिये ततः पश्चाद् वह्निजायां ततः प्रिये॥ नवाक्षरो महामन्त्रो द्रुतं सिद्धिप्रदायकः। कुबेरोऽस्य ऋषिः प्रोक्तः पङ्क्तिश्छन्द उदाहृतम्॥ देवता धनदा देवी सर्वसिद्धिप्रदायिनी। धर्मार्थकाममोक्षाख्यचतुर्वर्गफलप्रदा॥ षड्दीर्घमायया चैव षडङ्गन्यासमाचरेत्। ध्यानमस्याः प्रवक्ष्यामि येन सिद्धो भवेन्नरः॥ ॐ देवीं काञ्चनकान्तकान्तिविमलां रक्तांशुकाच्छादितां हेमाम्भोजयुगाभयाङ्कुशकरीं रत्नोल्लसत्कुण्डलाम्। सर्वाभीष्टफलप्रदां त्रिनयनां नागेन्द्रहारो-

---

1, 'अलक्तसंयुतं' क-ख-ग, 'अलक्तं संयुतं वारि' ङ। 2. 'शर्कराज्ययुतं' क। 3. 'जपेदेक-' ख-ग।

द्वादशाहं [1]भजेद् धीमान् दिक्सहस्रं ततो जपेत् ।
तद्दशांशं महेशानि होमं [2]कुर्य्याद्विचक्षणः ॥ १२ ॥
[3]होमकर्मण्यशक्तश्चेद् द्विगुणं जपमाचरेत् ।
यदि प्रीता भवेत् [4]सा हि तदा किं वा न सिध्यति ॥१३॥
प्रत्यहं परमेशानि कुबेरो दीयते वसु ।
भस्मनिर्माणकं [5]देवि विचित्रं तस्य किं शिवे ॥ १४ ॥
गुरवे दक्षिणां दद्याद् यथाविभवविस्तरैः ।
ततः सिद्धो भवेन्मन्त्री नात्र [6]कार्य्या विचारणा ॥ १५ ॥

[7]श्रीचण्डिकोवाच—

विधानं देवदेवेश भस्मनिर्माणकर्म्मणि ।
[8]सकृत्कृते येन रूपे [9]भस्मसाज्जायते विभो ॥ १६ ॥

उज्ज्वलां वन्दे सर्वभयापहां त्रिजगतां पापापहारिणीं परम् ॥ स्वकीयात्मस्वरूपां तां भावये-च्छिवस्वरूपिणीम् । एवं ध्यात्वा महेशानि मानसैः पूजनञ्चरेत् ॥ अर्घ्यपात्रं स्थाप-यित्वा धेनुयोनिं प्रदर्शयेत् । पीठपूजां ततः कृत्वा ततः पीठमनुं जपेत् ॥ आधार-शक्तिमारभ्य यजेत् पद्मासनं प्रिये । प्रणवादिनमोऽन्तेन पूजयेत् साधकाग्रणीः ॥ पुन-र्ध्यात्वा महेशानि मूलेनावाहनञ्चरेत् । षडङ्गेन च संपूज्य जीवन्यासं समाचरेत् ॥ मूल-मन्त्रं समुच्चार्य्य ततो द्रव्यं समुच्चरेत् । देव्यायै च ततः पश्चाद् योगात्मकमनुं स्मरेत् ॥ पाद्याद्यैः पूजयेद्देवीं यथाविभवविस्तरैः । यन्त्रमस्याः प्रवक्ष्यामि तज्ज्ञात्वामृतमश्नुते ॥ नवयोन्यात्मकं चक्रं विलिखेत् कर्णिकोपरि । द्विदलं पद्ममालिख्य चतुरस्रं ततो बहिः ॥ कोणेषु वज्रं संलिख्य मध्ये बीजं समुल्लिखेत् । इदं यन्त्रं महेशानि साक्षाद् देवीस्वरू-पकम् ॥ लक्ष्मीं पद्मां पद्मालयां श्रियञ्चैव हरप्रियाम् । शवाञ्च कमलाञ्चैव अब्जाञ्च चञ्चलान्तथा ॥ लोलाञ्च प्रणवाद्येता नमोऽन्तेन प्रपूजयेत् । पुनर्मध्ये ततो देवीं पूजयेत् साधकोत्तमः ॥ प्राणायामं ततः कृत्वा यथाशक्ति जपञ्चरेत् । गुह्यातीति जपफलं देव्या हस्ते समर्पयेत् ॥ प्राणायामं ततः कृत्वा प्रणामाष्टाङ्गमाचरेत् । अथोत्थाय महेशानि विशेषार्घ्यं निवेदयेत् ॥ आत्मसमर्पणं कृत्वा विहरेच्च निजेच्छया । इति ।

---

1. 'जपेद' ख-ग । 2. 'कुर्याद् द्विजोत्तमः' घ-ङ । 3. '-होमकर्मण्यशक्त-' ख-ग । 4. 'सम्पि' ङ । 5 'कूर्म' ख-ग । 6. कार्य्यविचारणा ङ । 7 'श्री' नास्ति क-ङ । 8 'कृतेन रूपेण' ख-ग, 'कृते येन रूपेण' ङ । 9. भस्मसाद्यते' क ।

[1]श्रीशङ्कर उवाच—

आनीय पारदं देवि [2]स्थापयेत् प्रस्तरोपरि ।
तस्योपरि जपेन्मन्त्रं [3]सर्व्ववन्ध्यनवात्मकम् ॥ १७ ॥
[4]साष्टसहस्रं देवेशि प्रजपेत् साधकाग्रणीः ।
स्वयम्भुपुष्पसंयुक्ते वस्त्रे चारुणसन्निभे ॥ १८ ॥
संस्थाप्य पारदं देवि मृत्पात्रयुगले शिवे ।
पुष्पयुक्तेन सूत्रेण बध्नीयाद् बहुयत्नतः ॥ १९ ॥
[5]मुक्तिधाराजलेनैव [6]धान्यस्य परमेश्वरि ।
लेपयेद् बहुयत्नेन रौद्रे [7]शुष्कञ्च कारयेत् ॥ २० ॥
पुनश्च लेपयेद् धीमान् ततो वह्नौ विनिक्षिपेत् ।
अष्टमीनवमीरात्रौ [8]क्षिपेन्नैव सुरेश्वरि ॥ २१ ॥
अथवा परमेशानि मृत्पात्रे स्थापयेद्रसम् ।
वल्लीरसेन तद्द्रव्यं शोधयेद् बहुयत्नतः ॥ २२ ॥
[9]घृतनारीरसेनैव तथैव शोधनञ्चरेत् ।
एवं कृते तु गुटिकां यदि स्याद् दृढबन्धनम् ॥ २३ ॥
[10]धुस्तूरञ्च समानीय मध्ये शून्यञ्च कारयेत् ।
[11]कृष्णाख्यतुलसीयोगे तथा घृतकुमारिका ॥ २४ ॥

१७। सर्व्ववन्ध्येत्यादि—"ॐ ऐँ ह्रीं क्लीं ह्रूीं ह्रीं क्लीं नमः" इति नवाक्षरमन्त्र इति ङ-पुस्तक-टिप्पन्याम् ।

---

1. 'श्री' नास्ति क-ङ। 2 'स्थापये'दित्यादि 'पारदं देवी'त्यन्तोंऽशः ख-ग-पुस्तकयोर्नास्ति। 3. 'सर्व्वबन्धमयात्मकम्' क, सर्वबन्धनमात्मकम् ङ। 4. 'साष्टं' घ। 5. 'मृत्तिकया च रजसा' ख-ग, 'मृत्तिकया रजेनैव' घ-ङ। 6. 'बध्नीयात्' ङ। 7. 'शुष्काणि' क-ङ। 8. 'निक्षिपेन्नैव सुन्दरि' ख-ग। 9. 'घृतकुमारी-' घ। 10. 'धुस्तूरफल-' ङ। 1 . 'कृष्णाख्या-' क-घ।

४

एवं कृते वह्नियोगे भस्मसाज्जायते किल ।
[1]भस्मयोगे भवेत् स्वर्णं धनदायाः प्रसादतः ॥ २५ ॥
विवर्णं जायते द्रव्यं यदि पूजां न [2]चाचरेत् ॥ २६ ॥

[3]श्रीचण्डिकोवाच—

[4]स्वयम्भु कीदृशं नाथ कुण्डगोलन्तु[5] कीदृशम् ।
[6]स्वपुष्पं कीदृशं नाथ वज्रपुष्पन्तु कीदृशम् ।
सर्व्वकालोद्भवं नाथ कीदृशं वद शङ्कर ॥ २७ ॥

[7]श्रीशङ्कर उवाच—

विवाहरहिता कन्या [8]प्रथमं पुष्पसंयुता ।
तच्छोणितं महेशानि स्वयम्भु[9] नात्र संशयः ॥ २८ ॥
भर्त्तरि [10]विद्यमाने तु [11]या कन्या [12]चान्यजा शिवे ।
तदुद्भवं कुण्डपुष्पं सर्व्वकार्य्यार्थसाधकम्[13] ॥ २९ ॥
मृते भर्त्तरि [14]देवेशि या कन्या [15]अन्यजा शिवे ।
तदुद्भवं गोलपुष्पं देववश्यकरं परम् ॥ ३० ॥
[16]विवाहितायाः कन्यायाः प्रथमे ऋतुसम्भवे ।
तच्छोणितं महेशानि [17]स्वपुष्पं सर्वमोहनम् ॥ ३१ ॥
विवाहितायाः कन्यायाः पुरुषस्य [18]च ताडनात् ।
यदि पुष्पं समुद्भूतं वज्रं तत् परिकीर्त्तितम् ॥ ३२ ॥

---

1. 'भस्मयोगं' क । 2. 'चारयेत्' ङ । 3. 'श्री' नास्ति क । 4. 'स्वयम्भू' ख-ग, 'स्वयम्भुं' क-ङ । 5 '-गोलञ्च' ख-ग । 6. इदमर्द्धं क-ख-ग-पुस्तकेषु नास्ति, 'खपुष्पं' ङ । 7. 'श्री' नास्ति क-ङ । 8. 'प्रथमे ऋतुसंयुता' ख-ग, 'प्रथमा' ङ । 9. 'स्वयम्भुं' क, 'स्वयम्भू-' ख-ग । 10. 'वर्त्तते देवि' घ, 'भर्त्तते देवि' क-ङ । 11. 'कन्यायाश्चैव सुन्दरि' ख-ग । 12. 'चान्यगा' घ । 13 '-साधनम्' ख-ग, 'साधकः' क-घ । 14. 'या देवि' ख-ग । 15. 'जायते प्रिये' क-घ-ङ । 16. ख-ग-पुस्तकयोः अयं श्लोको नास्ति । 17 'ख-पुष्पं' ङ । 18. 'तु' ख-ग ।

विवाहितायाः कन्यायाः प्रतिमासे च यद् भवेत् ।
सर्व्वकालोद्भवं पुष्पं कथितं वीरवन्दिते ॥ ३३ ॥
सप्तक्रोशं वह्निमध्ये स्थापयेद् बहुयत्नतः ।
[1]तत उत्थाय [2]तद् द्रव्यं स्वर्णपात्रे निधाय च ॥ ३४ ॥
प्रजपेत् परमेशानि [3]प्रासादाख्यं महामनुम् ।
ततः सिद्धो भवेन्मन्त्री नान्यथा मम भाषितम् ॥ ३५ ॥
एतन्मन्त्रं महेशानि [4]गजान्तकसहस्त्रकम् ।
जपित्वा पूजयेत् पश्चात् पार्थिवं शिवलिङ्गकम् ॥ ३६ ॥
ततः परीक्षा कर्त्तव्या शृणु मत्प्राणवल्लभे ।
शुद्धताम्रं वह्निमध्ये मृत्पात्रे तोलकं [5]मितम् ॥ ३७ ॥
द्रवीभूते च ताम्रे च [6]गुञ्जामानं क्षिपेद् यदि ।
तत्क्षणे[7] परमेशानि स्वर्णं भवति निश्चितम् ॥ ३८ ॥
गुञ्जाप्रमाणं[8] तद् द्रव्यं भोजनं कुरुते यदि ।
[9]सर्वरोगपरित्यक्तो जायते मदनोपमः ।
मन्त्रसिद्धिर्भवेत्तस्य जायते [10]चिरजीविता ॥ ३९ ॥
प्रत्यहं परमेशानि शतनारीं[11] रमेद् यदि ।
वीर्य्यादिरहितं न स्यात् तेजोवृद्धिकरं परम्[12] ॥ ४० ॥

---

३४ । सप्तक्रोशमिति—'क्रोशं प्रहरम्' इति ङ-टिप्पन्याम् ।

३५ । प्रासादाख्यमित्यादि । 'सान्तमौकारसंयुक्तं बिन्दुभूषितमस्तकम् । प्रासादाख्यो मनुः प्रोक्तो भजतां कामदो मणिः ॥' तेन "हौँ" इति मन्त्रकोषः ।

३६ । गजान्तकसहस्त्रकम्—अष्टोत्तरसहस्रमित्यर्थः ।

---

1. 'उत्थापितं' ख-ग । 2. 'तं द्रव्यं' क-ख-ग-ङ । 3. 'प्रसादाख्यं' क । 4. 'गजाण्डक-' ख-ग । 5. 'सितं' क-घ-ङ । 6. 'शुक्रमानं' ख-ग, 'गुञ्जामात्रं' ङ । 7. '-क्षणात्' ख-ग । 8. '-मात्रं तु' ङ । 9. 'सर्वरोगैः परि-' ख-ग, 'सर्वरोगं परित्यक्त्वा' घ । 10. 'चिरजीवितः' ख-ग, 'चिरजीवता' घ । 11. '-नारी' ख-ग-घ । 12. '-वृद्धिः परस्परम्' क-ग-ङ ।

[1]मरणं नैव पश्यामि यदि [2]ध्यानयुतो भवेत् ।
तस्य वित्तं विलोक्यैव कुबेरोऽपि तिरस्कृतः ॥ ४१ ॥
गानेन तुम्बुरुः साक्षाद् दानेन वासवो यथा ।
महेश इव [3]योगीन्द्रो [4]निरृतिरिव दुर्धरः ॥ ४२ ॥
महाबलो महावीर्य्यो महासाहसिकः शुचिः ।
महास्वच्छो दयावांश्च सर्वप्राणिहिते रतः ।
बहु किं कथ्यते देवि स एव गणनायकः ॥ ४३ ॥

इति श्रीमातृकाभेदतन्त्रे [5]हरगौरीसंवादे पञ्चमः पटलः ॥ ५ ॥

---

1. 'सवर्ण' ख-ग । 2. 'व्याल-' ख-ग । 3. 'योगीशो' ख-ग । 4. 'निरृते-' ङ ।
5. 'चण्डिकाशङ्कर-' घ ।

षष्ठः पटलः

श्रीचण्डिकोवाच—

वद ईशान सर्व्वज्ञ सर्वतत्त्वविदां वर ।
महारोगे महादुःखे महादारिद्र्यसङ्कटे ॥ १ ॥
नानाव्याधिगते वापि नानापीडादिसङ्कटे ।
[1]राज्यनाशे राजभये कारागारगते पुनः ॥ २ ॥
राजदण्डे[2] च देवेश तथा च ग्रहपीडिते[3] ।
केनोपायेन[4] देवेश मुच्यते वद शङ्कर ॥ ३ ॥

[5]श्रीशङ्कर उवाच—

शृणु चार्वङ्गि सुभगे यन्मां त्वं परिपृच्छसि ।
[6]तत्तत् सर्वं प्रवक्ष्यामि सावधानावधारय ॥ ४ ॥
या चाद्या परमा विद्या चामुण्डा कालिका [7]परा ।
[8]तस्याः प्रयोगमात्रेण किं न सिध्यति भूतले ॥ ५ ॥

[9]श्रीचण्डिकोवाच—

राहुश्चाण्डालो[10] विख्यातः [11]सर्व्वत्र परमेश्वर ।
पुण्यकालः[12] कथं [13]देव तस्य स्पर्शे दिवाकरे ॥ ६ ॥
निशाकरे तथा [14]नाथ [15]इति मे संशयो हृदि ।
[16]कथयस्व [17]परानन्द पश्चादन्यत् प्रकाशय ॥ ७ ॥

---

1. 'राजध्वंसे' ख-ग । 2. 'तथा ग्रहपीडने च जलवह्निसमाकुले' ख-ग, 'राज्ञि कुण्डे च' घ, 'राज्ञः कुसे' ङ । 3. '-पीडने' ङ । 4 '-पाये द्रुतं नाथ' क-ङ, 'पायेन हे नाथ' घ । 5. 'श्री' नास्ति क, 'ईश्वर' घ । 6. 'एतत्' घ । 7. 'स्मृता' ख-ग । 8. 'योगमात्रेण सुभगे' ख-ग । 9 'श्री' नास्ति क-ङ । 10. '-ल-विख्यातः' क-घ-ङ । 11. 'सर्ववित' ख-ग । 12 '-काले' ख-ग-ङ-प्रा । 13. 'नाथ' घ । 14. 'देव' घ । 15 'चेति' क-घ-ङ । 16. 'कथमस्य' घ । 17. 'महादेव' ख-ग ।

[1]श्रीशङ्कर उवाच—

शृणु चार्वङ्गि सुभगे [2]ग्रहणञ्चोत्तमोत्तमम्[3] ।
ग्रहणं त्रिविधं देवि चन्द्रसूर्य्याग्निसंयुतम् ॥ ८ ॥
शक्तेर्ललाटके[4] नेत्रे वह्निस्तिष्ठति सर्वदा ।
वामनेत्रे तथा चन्द्रो दक्षे सूर्यः प्रतिष्ठितः ॥ ९ ॥
शम्भुनाथेन देवेशि रमणं क्रियते [5]यदा ।
तदैव[6] ग्रहणं देवि शक्तियुक्तो[7] यदा शिवः ॥ १० ॥
वामनेत्रे [8]चुम्बने तु शशाङ्कग्रहणं तदा ।
दक्षनेत्रे [9]चुम्बने च भास्करग्रहणं [10]तदा ॥ ११ ॥
ललाटे [11]चुम्बने चाग्निग्रहणं परमेश्वरि ।
शिववीर्य्यं[12] यतो वह्निरतोऽदृश्यः[13] सुरेश्वरि ॥ १२ ॥
[14]राहुः [15]शिवः समाख्यातस्त्रिगुणा शक्तिरीरिता ।
शिवशक्त्योः समायोगो[16] ग्रहणं परमेश्वरि ॥ १३ ॥
[17]शिवशक्तिसमायोगः [18]कालं ब्रह्ममयं[19] प्रिये ।
अत एव महेशानि राश्यादीन् न विचारयेत् ॥ १४ ॥
तिथिनक्षत्र[20]योगेन [21]यद्योगं परमेश्वरि ।
[22]तदैव परमेशानि राश्यादिगणनञ्चरेत् ॥ १५ ॥

---

१३ । त्रिगुणा शक्तिरिति । चन्द्रसूर्य्याग्निरूपिणीत्यर्थ इति ङ-पुस्तकटिप्पन्याम् ।

---

1. 'श्री' नास्ति क-ङ । 2. 'प्रयोग-' ख-ग-प्रा । 3 '-मोत्तमः' घ । 4. '-चक्रे च' ख-ग, '-टे नेत्रे च' घ-प्रा । 5 'यदि' प्रा । 6. 'तथैव' ख-ग, 'तदेव' घ । 7 '-युक्तः सदा' ख-ग-प्रा । 8. 'चुम्बिते च' प्रा । 9. 'चुम्बिते च' प्रा । 10 'तथा' प्रा । 11 'चुम्बिते' प्रा । 12. '-बीजं' ख-ग-ङ-प्रा । 13 '-ऽदृश्यं' ख-ग । 14. ख-ग-पुस्तकयोरयं श्लोको नास्ति । 15. 'शिवं' ङ । 16. '-योगाद्-' प्रा । 17. 'शिवशक्तेः' ख-ग, 'शिवशक्त्योः' क । 18 'कालो' प्रा । 19. '-मयः शिवे' प्रा । 20. '-योगे च' ख-ग, '-योगे तु' प्रा । 21. 'यथायोगं महेश्वरि' प्रा । 22. 'तदेव' ख-ग-प्रा ।

शिवशक्तिसमायोगात् सर्व्वं ब्रह्ममयं जगत् ।
मासपक्षतिथीनाञ्च [1]नोच्चार्य्यं परमेश्वरि ॥ १६ ॥
दृष्टिमात्रेण जप्तव्यं तदा [2]सिद्धिर्भवेद् ध्रुवम् ।
तत्कालं परमं [3]कालं विज्ञेयं वीरवन्दिते ॥ १७ ॥
तत्र यद्यत् कृतं [4]सर्व्वमनन्तफलमीरितम् ।
[5]पुरैव कथितं सर्वं बहु किं कथ्यतेऽधुना ॥ १८ ॥
एतत् सुगुप्तभेदं हि तव स्नेहात् प्रकाशितम् ।
न वक्तव्यं पशोरग्रे [6]न वक्तव्यं सुरेश्वरि ॥ १६ ॥
[7]एतत्तत्त्वं प्रयत्नेन ब्रह्मा जानाति माधवः ।
प्रगोप्तव्यं प्रयत्नेन स्वयोनिरिव [8]शैलजे ॥ २० ॥

श्रीचण्डिकोवाच—

चामुण्डाया महामन्त्रं कीदृशं [9]परमेश्वर ।
आराधनं कीदृशं वा तद् वदस्व दयानिधे ॥ २१ ॥

श्रीशङ्कर उवाच—

शृणु चार्व्वङ्गि सुभगे चामुण्डामन्त्रमुत्तमम् ।
यस्य विज्ञानमात्रेण पुनर्ज्जन्म न विद्यते ॥ २२ ॥

---

१८ । तत्र यद् यदित्यादि । "अत्रानन्तफलकीर्त्तनाद् जपदशांशहोमादिकमपि न कर्त्तव्यम् । तदुक्तं गायत्रीतन्त्रे प्रथमपटले—चन्द्रसूर्य्योपरागे च जप्त्वा ब्रह्ममयो भवेत् । मन्त्रस्य परमेशानि न च होमादिकञ्चरेत् ॥ कृते होमादिके भद्रे तज्जपं विफलं भवेत् । जपमात्रे महेशानि अनन्तस्तन्मनुर्यथा ॥ अनन्तस्य महेशानि दशांशं केन जायते । इति ।" एतत्कल्पस्तु ज्ञानिनाम् इति प्राणतोषणी ।

---

1. 'नोच्चार्य्यं' ख-ग । 2 'सिद्धो भवेत्' क-घ । 3. 'कामं' ङ । 4. 'कर्म अनन्त-' ख-ग-प्रा । 5. 'पूर्वं च' ख-ग-प्रा । 6 'प्राणान्तेऽपि' ख-ग-प्रा । 7. '-एतत् सर्वं' ङ । 8. 'पार्वति' ख-ग । 9. 'वद शङ्कर' ख-ग ।

कालीबीजयुगं देवि कूर्च्चबीजं ततः परम् ।
त्र्यक्षरी [1]परमा विद्या चामुण्डा कालिका स्वयम् ॥ २३ ॥
सप्ताहं पूजयेद् देवीमुपचारैश्च षोडशैः ।
पूजान्ते प्रजपेन्मन्त्रं त्रिसहस्रं वरानने ॥ २४ ॥
रात्रौ [2]तु पञ्चतत्त्वेन पूजयेत् परमेश्वरीम् ।
तथा रात्रौ जपेन्मन्त्रं कुलशक्तिसमन्वितम् ॥ २५ ॥
यन्त्रनिर्माणयोग्यं हि पीठं [3]दद्यात् सुविस्तरम् ।
भोगयोग्यं प्रदातव्यं मधुपर्कं यथोचितम् ॥ २६ ॥
शक्तेर्यथा विधेयं स्याद् युवत्याः परमेश्वरि ।
तथा वस्त्रं प्रदातव्यं सर्वकल्याणहेतवे ॥ २७ ॥
अलङ्कारं यथायोग्यं [4]तत्र तत्र नियोजयेत् ।
नैवेद्यं विविधं रम्यं नानाद्रव्यसमन्वितम् ॥ २८ ॥
सामिषान्नं प्रदातव्यं परमान्नं सशर्करम् ।
पूजयेत् परया भक्त्या बलिदानं ततः परम् ॥ २९ ॥

२३। कालीबीजयुगमित्यादि। तेन 'क्रीँ क्रीँ हूँ' इति मन्त्रो भवति इति ङ-पुस्तकटिप्पन्याम् ।

२५। रात्रौ तु पञ्चतत्त्वेनेति। पञ्चतत्त्वमुक्तं गुप्तसाधनतन्त्रे सप्तमपटले—श्रीशिव उवाच। शृणु देवि प्रवक्ष्यामि तत्त्वं परमदुर्लभम्। मन्त्रोद्धारक्रमेणैव तत् सर्वं कथयामि ते॥ भान्तमकारसंयुक्तं थान्तं वायुयुतं कुरु। बिन्दुयुक्तं पुनर्भान्तमाकारं बिन्दुसंयुतम् ॥ चन्द्रबीजं समुच्चार्य्य ऋंकारं तदनन्तरम्। पुनर्भान्तं तकारञ्च चन्द्रवायुयुतं शिवे ॥ पुनर्भान्तं महेशानि पञ्चमस्वरसंयुतम्। थान्तं वह्निसमारूढमाकारसंयुतं कुरु ॥ पुनर्भान्तं महेशानि सूर्य्यस्वरविभूषितम्। तान्तमुकारसंयुक्तं धान्तमबिन्दुसंयुतम् ॥ पञ्चतत्त्वमिदं देवि सर्व्वतन्त्रेषु गोपितम ॥ इति। कालीकुलार्णवे च—मद्यं मांसं तथा मत्स्यं मुद्रा मैथुनमेव च। पञ्चमात् तु परं नास्ति शाक्तानां भोगमोक्षयोः ॥ इति।

---

1. 'सा महा-' घ। 2. 'च' ङ। 3. 'कुर्य्यात्' ख-ग। 4 'तव देव्यै निवेदयेत्' घ।

प्रत्यहं परमेशानि [1]चाद्यन्ते [2]वा बलिं हरेत् ।
साङ्गे जाते महेशानि चाथवा [3]बलिमाहरेत् ॥ ३० ॥
एवं कृते [4]महासिद्धिं लभते नात्र संशयः ।
धनार्थी धनमाप्नोति पुत्रार्थी पुत्रवान् भवेत् ॥ ३१ ॥
विवादे जयमाप्नोति राजद्वारे जयी भवेत् ।
सर्वत्र विजयी भूत्वा देवीपुत्र इव क्षितौ ॥ ३२ ॥
रोगेभ्यो घोररूपेभ्यः पूजयित्वा प्रमुच्यते ।
[5]इच्छासिद्धिर्भवेत् तस्य सर्वसिद्धिर्न चान्यथा ॥ ३३ ॥
कारागारगते[6] [7]देवि मुच्यते नात्र संशयः ।
प्रयोगं परमेशानि सारं परमदुर्लभम् ॥ ३४ ॥
अतिस्नेहेन देवेशि तव स्थाने प्रकाशितम् ।
अथवा परमेशानि पठेच्चण्डीं [8]सनातनीम् ॥ ३५ ॥
[9]पूजयेच्चण्डिकां देवीं सुगन्धिपुष्पसंयुतैः ।
धूपदीपेन गन्धेन नैवेद्येन सुरेश्वरि ॥ ३६ ॥
अवश्यं पञ्चतत्त्वेन पूजयेच्चण्डिकां पराम् ॥ ३७ ॥
आदावृष्यादि-[10]सूक्तेन [11]चार्घ्यान्ते परमेश्वरि ।
पञ्चतत्त्वं समानीय शोधयेच्छास्त्रवित्तमः[12] ॥ ३८ ॥

---

३७ । पञ्चतत्त्वेनेत्यादि । तत्त्वशोधनमुक्तं महानिर्वाणतन्त्रे अष्टमोल्लासे—आसादयेत् तु तत्त्वानि स्थापयेदग्रतः शिवे । तारादिप्राणबीजान्तं शतावृत्त्या जपन् मनुम् ॥ सर्वतत्त्वेषु चक्रेश इमं मन्त्रमुदीरयेत् । "ब्रह्मार्पणं ब्रह्म हविर्ब्रह्माग्नौ ब्रह्मणा हुतम् ॥ ब्रह्मैव तेन गन्तव्यं

---

1. 'आद्यन्ते' ख-ग, 'चाद्यान्तेव' घ । 2. 'वारुणीं' ख-ग । 3. 'वारुणीं हरेत्' ख-ग । 4 'महासिद्धिर्ल-' क-घ-ङ । 5 'इति सिद्धि-' घ । 6 '-गारागते' क-घ-ङ । 7. 'चापि' ङ । 8. 'पुरा-' ख-ग । 9. 'पूजयेच्चण्डिकादेवीं' ख-ग । 10. '-सूत्रेण' क-घ-ङ । 11. 'चाद्यन्ते' ख-ग, 'चार्घ्यान्ते' क । 12. '-येन्मन्त्रवि-' ख-ग-घ-ङ ।

५

तर्पणञ्च ततः कृत्वा चार्घ्यपात्रे विनिक्षिपेत् ।
अर्घ्योदकेन संप्रोक्ष्य पूजयेत् पीठदेवताम् ॥ ३९ ॥
प्रणवञ्च समुद्धृत्य मायाबीजं ततः परम् ।
प्रभां मायां [1]जयां सूक्ष्मां विशुद्धां [2]नन्दिनीं तथा ॥ ४० ॥
सुप्रभां विजयां सर्वसिद्धिदां परिपूजयेत् ।
[3]वज्रनखदंष्ट्रायुधाय हूं फडित्यन्ततस्ततः ॥ ४१ ॥
नमोऽन्तेन[4] तु देवेशि आसनञ्च समर्च्चयेत् ।
गुरुपङ्क्तिं पूजयित्वा पुनर्ध्यानं समाचरेत् ॥ ४२ ॥
आवाहनं ततो मुद्रां जीवन्यासं प्रपूजनम् ।
[5]षडङ्गेन तु सम्पूज्य परिवारान् प्रपूजयेत् ॥ ४३ ॥
शङ्खनिधिं [6]पद्मनिधिं तथा ब्राह्म्यादिकं यजेत् ।
[7]इन्द्रादींश्चैव वज्रादीन् पूजयेत् साधकोत्तमः ॥ ४४ ॥
प्रणवादिनमोऽन्तेन पूजयेत् साधकोत्तमः ।
पुनर्देवीं महेशानि पञ्चतत्त्वेन पूजयेत् ॥ ४५ ॥

ब्रह्मकर्मसमाधिना । सप्तधा वा त्रिधा जप्त्वा तानि सर्वाणि शोधयेत् ॥ ततो ब्राह्मेण मनुना समर्प्य परमात्मने । ब्रह्मज्ञैः साधकैः सार्द्धं विदध्यात् पानभोजनम् ॥ इति । तत्रैव पञ्चमपटले—मद्यं मांसं तथा मत्स्यं मुद्रा मैथुनमेव च । शक्तिपूजाविधावाद्ये पञ्चतत्त्वं प्रकीर्त्तितम् ॥ पञ्चतत्त्वं विना पूजा अभिचाराय कल्पते । नेष्टसिद्धिर्भवेत् तस्य विघ्नस्तस्य पदे पदे ॥ शिलायां शस्यवापे च यथा नैवाङ्कुरो भवेत् । पञ्चतत्त्व-विहीनायां पूजायां न फलोद्भवः ॥ इति पञ्चतत्त्वैः पूजायाः प्राशस्त्यमुक्तम् ।

---

1. 'तमां' क। 2 'नन्दनीं' ख-ग, 'नलिनीं' क। 3. 'वज्रनख तथा दंष्ट्रायुधाय हूँ फडिति ततः' क, 'वज्रनखदंष्ट्रायुधाय हूँ फडित्यपि' ख-ग। 4. '-न्तेनैव मन्त्रेण' ख-ग, 'नम अन्तेन' घ। 5. 'षडङ्गमण्डलं पूज्य' घ। 6. 'तथा पद्मनिधिं ब्राह्मादिकं' क-घ-ङ। 7. 'इन्द्रादींश्च तथा वज्रादींश्चैव परिपूजयेत्' क-घ-ङ।

प्राणायामं ततः कृत्वा गुरुमन्त्रेष्टदेवताम् ।
ऐक्यं विभाव्य देवेशि मूलमन्त्रं [1]जपेच्छतम् ॥ ४६ ॥
प्राणायामं ततः कृत्वा कारणादीन् समाहरेत् ।
तस्यै दत्त्वा स्वयं पीत्वा पठेच्चण्डीं सुरेश्वरि[2] ॥ ४७ ॥
साङ्गे जाते तु [3]माहात्म्ये पुनः पानं समाचरेत् ।
[4]ततस्तु प्रपठेद् धीमान् क्रमेण [5]पानमाचरेत् ॥ ४८ ॥
समाप्ते तु [6]विलोमेन [7]पुनर्म्मन्त्रं शतं जपेत् ।
यदि भाग्यवशाद् देवि शक्तियोगं[8] लभेन्नरः ॥ ४९ ॥
[9]तत्क्षणे हि विजानीयात् सर्व्वसिद्धिः करे स्थिता ।
एवं कृत्वा महेशानि यदि पाठं समाचरेत् ॥ ५० ॥
माहात्म्यं तस्य पाठस्य [10]किं वक्तुं शक्यते मया ।
[11]शतवक्त्रं यदि भवेत् तदा वक्तुं न शक्यते ॥ ५१ ॥
पञ्चवक्त्रेण देवेशि किं [12]वक्तुं शक्यतेऽधुना ।
सकृत् पाठेन देवेशि किं पुनर्ब्रह्म केवलम् ॥ ५२ ॥
अवश्यं लभते शान्तिं [13]सर्व्वत्र परमेश्वरि ।
यदि शान्तिं न लभते मम वाक्यं मृषा [14]तदा ॥ ५३ ॥
षोडशेनोपचारेण प्रथमं पूजनञ्चरेत् ।
द्वितीये पञ्चतत्त्वेन पूजयेच्चण्डिकां प्रिये ॥ ५४ ॥

---

1. 'जपेत् सुधीः' ख-ग । 2. '-रीम्' ख-ग-घ । 3. 'माहात्म्यम्' ख-ग । 4. 'ततस्ततत्सत् पठेद्' घ । 5. परिपूजयेत्' ख-ग । 6. 'विरोमेण' क । 7. 'मूलमन्त्र'' क-घ-ङ । 8. '-योगो भवेन्नरः' ख-ग, '-योगो' क-ङ । 9. 'तत्क्षणाद्धि' ख-ग । 10. 'न वक्तुं' ख-ग । 11. पद्यार्द्धमिदं नास्ति ख-ग-पुस्तकयोः । 12. 'मया कथ्यतेऽ-' ख-ग-घ-ङ । 13. 'सर्व्वत्र परमेश्वरि, यदि शान्ति न लभते' इत्यंशः ख-ग-पुस्तकयोर्नास्ति । 14. 'कदा' ख-ग ।

सहस्रावृत्तिपाठेन यत् फलं लभते नरः ।
सकृत् पाठस्य देवेशि कलां नार्हति षोडशीम् ॥ ५५ ॥
ध्यानमस्याः प्रवक्ष्यामि यथा ध्यात्वा पठेन्नरः ॥ ५६ ॥
ॐ या चण्डी मधुकैटभादिदैत्यदलनी या माहिषोन्मादिनी
या धूम्रेक्षणचण्डमुण्डमथनी या रक्तबीजाशनी ।
शक्तिः शुम्भनिशुम्भदैत्यदलनी या [1]सिद्धिलक्ष्मीः परा
सा देवी [2]नवकोटिमूर्त्तिसहिता मां पातु विश्वेश्वरी ॥५७॥
[3]ध्यानमेतच्चण्डिकायाः शृणुष्व वीरवन्दिते ॥ ५८ ॥
[4]शृणु मन्त्रं [5]प्रवक्ष्यामि त्रैलोक्येषु च दुर्लभम् ।
वेदाद्यं [6]वाग्भवं [7]मायां कामबीजं ततः परम् ॥ ५९ ॥
स्थिरमायां महामायां कामबीजं[8] ततो नमः ।
नवाक्षरं महामन्त्रं जपेदादौ शतं प्रिये ॥ ६० ॥
विपरीतं महामन्त्रं पाठान्ते तु शतं जपेत् ।
शृणु देवि प्रवक्ष्यामि ऋषिच्छन्दः[9] [10]सुदुर्लभम् ॥ ६१ ॥

ॐ सप्तशतीमहास्तोत्रस्य [11]मेधातिथिर्ऋषिर्गायत्र्यनुष्टुब्-बृहतीपङ्क्तित्रिष्टुब्जगत्य[12]श्छन्दांसि महाकालीमहालक्ष्मीर्महा-

---

५९ । वेदाद्यमित्यादि । तेन "ॐ ऐँ ह्रीँ क्लीँ ह्रीँ ह्रीँ क्लीँ नमः" इति मन्त्रो भवति ।

६१ । विपरीतमित्यादि । तेन "नमः क्लीँ ह्रीँ ह्रीँ क्लीँ ह्रीँ ऐँ ॐ" इति मन्त्रो भवति ।

---

1. 'स्वर्ग-' ख-ग । 2. 'नवकोटिशक्ति-' घ- । 3. इदमर्द्धं क-घ-ङ-पुस्तकेषु नास्ति । 4. 'शृणुष्व त्वं' ख-ग । 5 'महेशानि' ख-ग-घ । 6. 'वाग्भवं बीजं मायां काममतः' ङ । 7. 'माया' घ । 8. 'काममायां' घ । 9. '-च्छन्दं' क-घ-ङ । 10. 'अनुत्तमम्' ङ । 11. 'मेध्यादि-' घ । 12. '-जगत्युष्णिङ्महत्य-' ख-ग ।

सरस्वतीदेवता-[1]स्तवकं, ऐँ ह्रीँ क्लीँ बीजानि[2] ग्लौँ[3] शक्तिः [4]ममामुककामसिद्ध्यर्थे[5] [6]विनियोगः ॥ ६२ ॥

प्रणवेन महेशानि षडङ्गन्यासमाचरेत् ।
इति ते कथितं कान्ते चण्डीपाठस्य लक्षणम् ॥ ६३ ॥
सावर्णिः सूर्य्य [7]इत्यादि सावर्णिर्भविता मनुः ।
एतन्मात्रं पठेद्देवि किञ्चिन्न्यूनाधिकं न हि ॥ ६४ ॥
वारत्रयं [8]पठेद्देवि [9]संजप्यं तु दिनत्रयम् ॥ ६५ ॥
महारोगे महादुःखे राजपीडादिदारुणे ।
नानाव्याधिगते वापि राज्यनाशे तथा भये ॥ ६६ ॥
ग्रहपीडादिसंजाते ब्रह्महत्यादिपातके ।
एवं पाठेन देवेशि मुच्यते नात्र संशयः ॥ ६७ ॥
बहु किं कथ्यते देवि सर्व्वशान्तिं[10] लभेन्नरः ।
सर्वशङ्काविनिर्मुक्तो जायते मदनोपमः ॥ ६८ ॥
एवं कृते महेशानि यदि सिद्धिर्न जायते ।
पुनस्तेनैव कर्त्तव्यं ततः सिद्धो भवेद् ध्रुवम् ॥ ६९ ॥

इति श्रीमातृकाभेदतन्त्रे[11] हरपार्व्वतीसंवादे षष्ठः पटलः ॥ ६ ॥

---

1. '[illegible]वचं' क । 2 'बीजं' क-ख-ग-घ । 3. '[illegible]' ख-ग । 4. '[illegible]-' ख-ग । 5. '-सिद्ध्यर्थे चण्डीपाठे', '-र्थपाठे' घ । 6. 'जपे विनि-' क । 7. '-तामसः' क-ख । 8. 'महा-' क । 9. 'स्थाप्यते तद्' क-ख, 'संस्थाप्यं तु' घ-ङ । 10. '-शान्तिर्भवेद् ध्रुवम्' घ । 11. '-तन्त्र सर्वतन्त्रोत्तमोत्तमे' ख-ग । '-तन्त्रे षष्ठः' घ ।

सप्तमः पटलः

[1]श्रीशिव उवाच—

अथातः संप्रवक्ष्यामि त्रिपुरामन्त्रमुत्तमम् ।
यस्य विज्ञानमात्रेण पुनर्ज्जन्म न विद्यते ॥ १ ॥
त्रिपुरा त्रिविधा देवि बाला [2]प्रोक्ता [3]पुरा शिवे ।
तथैव भैरवी देवी नित्यातन्त्रे मयोदिता ।
इदानीं [4]सुन्दरीं देवीं शृणु पार्वति सादरम् ॥ २ ॥

[5]श्रीदेव्युवाच—

महामन्त्रं श्रुतं नाथ [6]वामकेश्वरयामले ।
प्रातःकृत्यादि देवेश [7]आराधनक्रमं वद ॥ ३ ॥

[8]श्रीशिव उवाच—

[9]प्रातरुत्थाय मन्त्रज्ञः सहस्रारे निजं गुरुम् ।
पूर्वोक्तध्यानमुच्चार्य्य[10] पूजयेद् बहुयत्नतः ॥ ४ ॥
तथा च [11]श्रीगुरोर्ध्यानं गुप्तसाधनतन्त्रके ।
कथितञ्च मया पूर्वं मन्त्रं शृणु वरानने ॥ ५ ॥

---

५ । तथा चेत्यादि । श्रीगुरोर्ध्यानमुक्तं गुप्तसाधनतन्त्रे द्वितीयपटले—श्रीशङ्कर उवाच……कुलवृक्षान् नमस्कृत्य गुरुं ध्यायेत् पराम्बुजे । शरच्चन्द्रसमाभासं शरत्पङ्कज-लोचनम् ॥ ईषद्धास्यं शारदीयपूर्णेन्दुसदृशाननम । दिव्यस्रगम्बरधरं दिव्यगन्धानुलेपनम् ॥ सुरक्तशक्तिसंयुक्तवामभागमनोहरम् । वराभयकराम्भोजं सर्वलक्षणलक्षितम ॥ सहस्रारे

---

1. 'श्रीशङ्कर' ख-ग । 2. 'चोक्ता' घ-ङ । 3. 'तथा' ख-ग । 4. 'छन्दरी देवी' घ । 5. 'श्रीपार्वत्युवाच' ख-ग, 'श्री' नास्ति ङ । 6. 'वामकेशे च' ङ । 7. 'आराधनं' घ । 8. नास्ति घ-पुस्तके । 'शिव उवाच' ङ । 9. 'प्रातःकाले समुत्थाय' ङ । 10. '-माचर्य्य' ख-ग । 11. 'श्रीगुरो-' ङ ।

वाग्बीजञ्च महामायां विष्णुशक्तिं समुच्चरेत् ।
हसखफ्रें[1] तथानन्दभैरवस्य [2]मनुं ततः ॥ ६ ॥
तस्य शक्तेर्मनुं[3] पश्चात् ततश्चैवं[4] हसौः स्मृतः[5] ।
[6]श्रीगुरोश्च तथा शक्तेर्मन्त्रमेतत् सुरेश्वरि ॥ ७ ॥
[7]श्रीगुरोरानन्दनाथान्ते अथातः शक्तिरीरिता ।
[8]वाग्बीजादीन् समुच्चार्य्य अमुकानन्दनाथ च ॥ ८ ॥
श्रीपादुकां समुच्चार्य्य पूजयामि नमस्ततः ।
वाग्बीजञ्च शम्भुपत्नीं[9] तदुत्तरे[10] हरिप्रियाम् ॥ ९ ॥
भूतबीजं समुच्चार्य्य प्रवदेच्च तदात्मकम्[11] ।
समर्पयामि देवेशि पूजाविधिरिति प्रिये ॥ १० ॥
ततश्चाष्टाक्षरं मन्त्रमष्टोत्तरशतं जपेत् ।
जपं समर्पयित्वा तु[12] नमेदञ्जलिना प्रिये ॥ ११ ॥

महापद्मे गुरुं शिरसि चिन्तयेत् । एतत् ते कथितं देवि श्रीगुरोर्ध्यानमुत्तमम् ॥ इति । श्रीगुरोर्ध्यानञ्च तत्रैव—सहस्रारे महापद्मे किञ्जल्कगणशोभिते । प्रफुल्लपद्मपत्राक्षीं घनपीनपयोधराम ॥ सहस्रवदनां नित्यां क्षीणमध्यां शिवां गुरुम् । पद्मरागसमाभासां रक्तवस्त्रसुशोभनाम् ॥ रत्नकङ्कणपाणिञ्च रत्ननूपुरशोभिताम् । शरदिन्दुप्रतीकाश-वक्त्रोद्भासितकुण्डलाम् ॥ स्वनाथवामभागस्थां वराभयकराम्बुजाम् ॥ इति ।

६-७ । वाग्बीजञ्चेत्यादि । अत्र ऐँ ह्रीँ श्रीँ हंसखफ्रेँ इति मन्त्रः, इति ङ-टिप्पन्याम् । 'हसक्ष मलवरयूँ आनन्दभैरवाय वषट्' हसक्ष मलवरयीँ सुधादेव्यै वषट् इति आनन्दभैरवस्य तच्छक्तेश्च मनुरिति प्राणतोषणी ।

८ । श्रीगुरोरित्यादि । एवञ्चात्र ऐँ ह्रीँ श्रीँ अमुकानन्दनाथश्रीपादुकां पूजयामि नमः, ऐँ ह्रीँ श्रीँ हसौः तदात्मकं समर्पयामि इति मन्त्रेण पूजा कर्त्तव्येति ।

११ । ततश्चेति । ऐँ ह्रीँ श्रीँ हसखफ्रेँ हसौः इत्यष्टाक्षरो मन्त्र इति ।

---

1. 'हंसखफ्रेँ' क-घ-ङ । 2. 'मनुर्मतः' ख-ग, 'मनुस्ततः' घ । 3. 'शक्तिमनुं' क-ङ, 'शक्तेर्मनुः' ख-ग । 4. '-श्चैव' ख-ग । 5. 'हसौः' ङ । 6. 'श्रीगुरोस्तत्तथा' ख-ग । 7. 'श्रीगुर्वानन्दनाथान्तः स्वाहान्तः शक्तिरीरिता' ख-ग, 'श्रीगुरुं वन्दे नाथान्ते आद्यन्ते शक्तिरीरिता' घ, 'श्रीगुरुदेवानन्दनाथान्ते नमोऽन्तेन यजेद् गुरुम्' ङ । 8. 'वाग्बीजादि' ख-ग । 9. '-पत्नी' ख-ग-ङ । 10. 'तदुत्तर-' क-घ-ङ, 'तदुत्तरे च हरिप्रिया' ङ । 11 'तदात्मकः' ङ । 12. 'प्रणमे-' ङ ।

[1]श्रीदेव्युवाच—

स्तुतिश्च कवचं नाथ श्रोतुमिच्छामि साम्प्रतम् ।
श्रीगुरोः कवचं स्तोत्रं [2]त्वया प्रोक्तं पुरा प्रभो ॥ १२ ॥
इदानीं [3]श्रीगुरोः स्तोत्रं कवचं मयि कथ्यताम् ।
यस्य विज्ञानमात्रेण पुनर्जन्म न [4]विद्यते ॥ १३ ॥

श्रीशिव उवाच—

शृणु देवि प्रवक्ष्यामि स्तोत्रं परमगोपनम् ।
यस्य श्रवणमात्रेण संसारान्मुच्यते नरः ॥ १४ ॥
नमस्ते देवदेवेशि[5] नमस्ते हरपूजिते ।
ब्रह्मविद्यास्वरूपायै तस्यै नित्यं नमो नमः ॥ १५ ॥
अज्ञानतिमिरान्धस्य ज्ञानाञ्जनशलाकया ।
[6]यया चक्षुरुन्मीलितं [7]तस्यै [8]नित्यं नमो नमः ॥ १६ ॥
भवबन्धनपारस्य तारिणी जननी परा ।
ज्ञानदा मोक्षदा नित्या तस्यै [9]नित्यं नमो नमः ॥ १७ ॥
[10]श्रीनाथवामभागस्था [11]सदा या सुरपूजिता ।
सदा विज्ञानदात्री च तस्यै [12]नित्यं नमो नमः ॥ १८ ॥
सहस्रारे महापद्म सदानन्दस्वरूपिणी ।
महामोक्षप्रदा [13]देवी तस्यै नित्यं नमो नमः ॥ १९ ॥
ब्रह्मविष्णुस्वरूपा च महारुद्रस्वरूपिणी ।
त्रिगुणात्मस्वरूपा च तस्यै नित्यं नमो नमः ॥ २० ॥

---

1. 'श्री' नास्ति ङ । 2. 'स्वयं' घ । 3. 'श्रीगुरोः' ख-ग-घ । 4. 'जायते' प्रा । 5. 'देवेश' क । 6. 'चक्षुरुन्मीलितं येन' क-ख-ग-घ । 7. 'तस्मै' ख-ग । 8. 'श्रीगुरवे नमः' ख-ग । 9. 'श्रीगुरवे नमः' ख-ग । 10. 'अनाथ-' क, 'श्रीनाथवामोत्संस्था' घ । 11. 'सर्वदा' ख-ग, 'सदया' प्रा । 12. 'श्रीगुरवे नमः' ख-ग । 13. 'देवि' घ ।

चन्द्रसूर्य्याग्निरूपा च [1]सदाऽऽघूर्णितलोचना ।
स्वनाथश्च [2]समालिङ्ग्य तस्यै नित्यं नमो नमः ॥ २१ ॥
ब्रह्मविष्णुशिवत्वादि[3]-जीवन्मुक्तिप्रदायिनी ।
ज्ञानविज्ञानदात्री [4]च तस्यै [5]नित्यं नमो नमः ॥ २२ ॥
इदं स्तोत्रं महेशानि यः पठेद् भक्तिसंयुतः ।
स सिद्धिं लभते नित्यं सत्यं सत्यं न संशयः ॥ २३ ॥
प्रातःकाले पठेद् यस्तु गुरुपूजापुरःसरम् ।
स एव धन्यो लोकेऽस्मिन्[6] देवीपुत्र इव क्षितौ ॥ २४ ॥

7(इति श्रीमातृकाभेदतन्त्रे सर्व्वतन्त्रोत्तमोत्तमे हरगौरीसंवादे शक्तिरूपिगुरोः .
स्तोत्रं समाप्तम् ॥)

[8]श्रीशङ्कर उवाच—

स्तोत्रं समाप्तं देवेशि कवचं शृणु सादरम् ।
यस्य [9]श्रवणमात्रेण वागीशसमतां व्रजेत् ॥ २५ ॥
[10]स्त्रीगुरोः कवचस्यास्य सदाशिव ऋषिः स्मृतः ।
[11]तदाख्या देवता [12]प्रोक्ता चतुर्वर्गफलप्रदा ॥ २६ ॥
[13]क्लीँ बीजं मे शिरः पातु [14]तदाख्यातं ललाटकम् ।
क्लीँ बीजं चक्षुषोः [15]पातु सर्व्वाङ्गं मे [16]सदाऽवतु ॥ २७ ॥

---

1. 'मदाऽऽ-' प्रा । 2. 'सदालिङ्ग्य' ङ । 3. '-स्वरूपा च' ख-ग । 4. '-प्रदात्री' प्रा । 5. 'स्त्रीगुरवे' प्रा' । 6. 'लोकेशो' क-घ-ङ, 'लोकेषु प्रा' । 7. 'इति श्रीमातृकाभेदतन्त्रे' इत्यादि 'समास-' मित्यन्तोंऽशः क-घ-ङ-पुस्तकेषु नास्ति । 8 'श्री' नास्ति क-घ-ङ । 9. 'स्मरण-' प्रा । 10. 'श्रीगुरोः' घ । 11. 'ताराख्या' प्रा । 12. 'ख्याता' प्रा । 13. 'इदमर्द्धं ख-ग-पुस्तकयोर्नास्ति । 14. '-ख्यातां' घ । 15. 'मध्ये' घ-प्रा । 16. 'सदाशिवः' ॥ त०प० ।

६

[1]ऐँ बीजं मे मुखं पातु ह्रीँ [2]जङ्घां परिरक्षतु ।
श्रीँ बीजं स्कन्धदेशं मे [3]वाग्भवं मे भुजद्वयम् ॥ २८ ॥

हकारं [4]मे दक्षभुजं क्षकारं वामहस्तकम् ।
[5]क्षमर्णौं तदधः पातु [6]लकारं हृदयं मम ॥ २९ ॥

[7]रकारं पृष्ठदेशञ्च[8] रकारं[9] दक्षपार्श्वकम् ।
[10]जूङ्कारं वामपार्श्वे तु सकारं [11]मेरुमेव तु ॥ ३० ॥

मकारं[12] चाङ्गुलीः पातु [13]लकारं मे [14]नखोपरि ।
[15]वकारं मे नितम्बञ्च [16]रकारं [17]जानुयुग्मकम् ॥ ३१ ॥

[18]यीः कारं पादयुगलं ह्सौः [19]सर्व्वाङ्गमेव तु ।
ह्सौर्लिङ्गञ्च [20]लोमञ्च केशञ्च परिरक्षतु ॥ ३२ ॥

[21]ऐँ बीजं पातु पूर्व्वे [22]तु ह्रीँ बीजं दक्षिणेऽवतु ।
[23]श्रीँ बीजं पश्चिमे पातु उत्तरे भूतसम्भवम्[24] ॥ ३३ ॥

[25]श्रीँ पातु चाग्निकोणे च[26] तदाख्यां[27] नैरृते ऽवतु ।
[28]दैव्यम्बा पातु वायव्यां शम्भोः श्रीपादुकां तथा ॥ ३४ ॥

---

1. 'ऐँ' इत्यारभ्य 'नखोपरि' इत्यन्तोंऽशः ख-ग-पुस्तकयोर्नास्ति । 2. 'जिह्वां' घ-त०प०प्रा० । 3. 'हसखफ्रेँ भुजद्वयं' घ-ङ-त०प०प्रा० । 4. 'कण्ठदेशं मे सकारं षोडशं दलम्' घ-ङ-त०प०प्रा० । 5. 'क्षमनोफ्रेँ अधःपातु' घ, 'क्षमार्णं' ङ, 'क्ष-वर्णस्तदधः' त०प०प्रा० । 6 'नकारं' घ, 'ल्कारो' त०प०प्रा० । 7. 'वकारः' घ । 8. '-देशं मे' क । 9. 'वकारः' ङ त०प०, 'वकारो' त०प०प्रा । 10. 'भकारं वामपार्श्वे च' घ, 'यूँकारं' ङ, 'हुँकारो' त०प०, 'यूँकारो' प्रा । 11. 'मेरुदेशके' घ । 12. 'मकारञ्चा-' प्रा । 13. 'नकारं' क, 'ल्कारो' प्रा, 'ल्कारः पातु मे नखम्' त०प०, 'वकारो' प्रा । 14. 'नकारं मे नखं वतु' क । 15. 'वकारो' प्रा । 16. 'रकारो' त०प० । 17. 'षोरुयुग्मञ्च' ङ, 'जठरेऽवतु' घ, 'जठरं' वतु क, 'जठरं मम' त०प० । 18. 'रींकारं' ख-ग, 'वींकारं' घ, 'यीँकारं' ङ, 'यींकारः' त०प० । 19. 'सर्वाङ्गे मेऽवतु' ख-ग, 'सर्वाङ्गके' त०प० । 20. 'लोमानि' त०प०प्रा । 21. 'श्रीँ बीजं' ख-ग । 22. 'मे' त०प०प्रा । 23. 'क्लीँ' प्रा । 24. '-सम्भवम्' ख-ग । 25. 'ऐँ' त०प० । 26. 'तु' ख-ग । 27. 'वेदाद्या' त०प०, 'वेदाख्या' प्रा । 28. 'दिव्यम्बा' क-ङ, 'देवान् मां' घ ।

पूजयामि तथा चोर्द्ध्वं नमश्चाधः सदाऽवतु ।
इति ते कथितं कान्ते कवचं परमाद्भुतम् ॥ ३५ ॥
गुरुमन्त्रं [1]जपित्वा तु कवचं प्रपठेद् यदि ।
स सिद्धः [2]सगणः सोऽपि [3]शिवः साक्षान्न संशयः ॥ ३६ ॥
पूजाकाले पठेद् यस्तु कवचं मन्त्रविग्रहम् ।
पूजाफलं [4]भवेत् तस्य सत्यं सत्यं सुरेश्वरि ॥ ३७ ॥
[5]त्रिसन्ध्यं यः पठेद् देवि स सिद्धो नात्र संशयः ॥ ३८ ॥
भूर्ज्जे विलिख्य [6]गुटिकां स्वर्णस्थां धारयेद् यदि ।
तस्य दर्शनमात्रेण वादिनो निष्प्रभां[7] गताः ॥ ३९ ॥
विवादे जयमाप्नोति [8]रणे च [9]निर्ऋतिरिव ।
सभायां जयमाप्नोति मम तुल्यो न संशयः ॥ ४० ॥
सहस्रारे [10]भावयं [11]स्तां त्रिसन्ध्यं [12]प्रपठेद् यदि ।
स एव [13]सिद्धो लोकेशो[14] [15]निर्वाणपदमीहते[16] ॥ ४१ ॥
समस्तमङ्गलं नाम कवचं परमाद्भुतम् ।
यस्मै कस्मै न दातव्यं न प्रकाश्यं कदाचन ॥ ४२ ॥
देयं शिष्याय शान्ताय चान्यथा पतनं[17] भवेत् ।
अभक्तेभ्योऽपि[18]देवेशि पुत्रेभ्योऽपि न दर्शयेत् ॥ ४३ ॥

---

1. 'पठित्वा च' ख-ग । 2. 'छगुणः' ख-ग । 3. 'शिव एव न' प्रा । 4. 'लभेत्' ख-ग । 5. ख-ग-पुस्तकयोरिदमर्द्धं नास्ति । 6. 'गुलिकां' ङ-प्रा० । 7. 'निष्प्रभा मताः' । 8. 'रणे च' इत्याऽरभ्य 'जयमाप्नोति' इत्यन्तोंऽशः ख-ग-पुस्तकयोर्नास्ति । 9. 'निर्ऋतिः समः' ङ-प्रा, 'नैर्ऋते' त०प० । 10. 'भावयेतां' घ । 11. 'तं' ख-ग, 'यः' त०प०प्रा । 12. 'यः पठेत्' ख-ग । 13. 'सिद्धलो-' प्रा । 14. 'लोकेऽस्मिन्' ख-ग । 15. 'निर्वाणे नीयते तु सः' घ । 16. '-पदलीयते' क, '-मीयते' ङ-त०प०प्रा । 17. 'त्रिफलं' त०प० । 18. '-भ्यस्तु' त०प०, '-भ्यश्च' प्रा ।

इदं कवचमज्ञात्वा [1]दशविद्याश्च यो जपेत् ।
स नाप्नोति फलं तस्य [2]परे च नरकं व्रजेत् ॥ ४४ ॥

([3]इति मातृकाभेदतन्त्रे सर्व्वतन्त्रोत्तमोत्तमे हरगौरीसंवादे
श्रीगुरोः कवचं समाप्तम् ॥)

समाप्तं कवचं देवि किमन्यच् छ्रोतुमिच्छसि ।
तव स्नेहानुबन्धेन किं मया न प्रकाशितम्[4] ॥ ४५ ॥
कूर्च्चबीजं समुच्चार्य्य प्राणमन्त्रं ततः [5]प्रिये ।
अनेन वायुयोगेन [6]कुण्डलीचक्रसञ्चरेत् ॥ ४६ ॥
अष्टोत्तरशतं मूलमन्त्रं जप्त्वा नमेत् सुधीः ।
स्नानकर्म ततः कृत्वा सन्ध्यां [7]कुर्य्यात् पुरोदिताम् ॥४७॥

श्रीदेव्युवाच—

[8]सन्ध्यायाः कीदृशं ध्यानं [9]वद मे परमेश्वर ।
श्रीविद्याविषये नाथ विशेषो मयि कथ्यताम् ॥ ४८ ॥

श्रीशिव उवाच—

ध्यायेच्च सुन्दरीं देवीं त्रिविधां [10]बीजरूपिणीम् ।
प्रभाते[11]वाग्भवां देवीं मध्याह्ने[12]मदनात्मिकाम् ॥ ४९ ॥
सायाह्ने शक्तिरूपाञ्च त्रिविधां बिन्दुरूपिणीम् ।
पूजाकाले महादेवीं ध्यानानुरूपिणीं शिवाम् ॥ ५० ॥

---

४६ । कूर्च्चबीजं 'हूँ' प्राणमन्त्रो 'हंसः' इति ।

---

1. 'विद्याश्चैव च' त०प०, 'दशविद्याश्च' प्रा । 2. 'चान्ते' प्रा । 3. 'इति' इत्यादि 'समाप्त-' मित्यन्तोंऽशः' क-घ-ङ पुस्तकेषु नास्ति । 4. अतः परं 'इति मातृकाभेदतन्त्रे श्रीगुरुकवचं समाप्तम्' इत्यधिकम् प्रा । 5. 'परम्' ख-ग-ङ । 6. 'कुण्डलीं क्रमणञ्चरेत्' ख-ग । 7. 'कृत्वा' ख-ग । 8 'सन्ध्यायां' घ । 9. 'वदस्व' ख-ग । 10. बिन्दु-' ख-ग । 11. 'च गुरु' ख-ग । 12. 'च सदात्मिकाम्' ख-ग ।

वाग्भवेनेन्दुसदृशां[1] शुक्लवर्णां [2]विचिन्तयेत् ।
शक्तिबीजं[3] [4]स्वर्णवर्णं रक्तवर्णां [5]विभावयेत् ॥ ५१ ॥
प्रभाते शुक्लवर्णाभां मध्याह्ने नीलसन्निभाम् ।
सायाह्ने रक्तवर्णाभां भावयेत् साधकोत्तमः ॥ ५२ ॥
एवं ध्यात्वा महेशानि सन्ध्यां कुर्य्याद् विचक्षणः ।
शिवपूजां ततः कृत्वा [6]पूजयेत् परदेवताम् ॥ ५३ ॥
[7]ततस्तु पूजयेद्देवीं त्रिपुरां मोक्षदायिनीम् ।
[8]त्रिपुरा परमा विद्या महाविद्या पतिव्रता ॥ ५४ ॥
[9]पतिपूजां विना पूजां[10] न गृह्णाति कदाचन ।
अत एव महेशानि आदौ लिङ्गं प्रपूजयेत् ॥ ५५ ॥
पश्चात्तरं पञ्चवक्त्रं पूजयेद् बहुयत्नतः ।
ततस्तु पूजयेद् देवीं त्रिपुरां मोक्षदायिनीम् ॥ ५६ ॥

[11]श्रीदेव्युवाच—

किमाधारे [12]यजेच्छम्भुं कृपया वद शङ्कर ।
आधारभेदे देवेश साधकः फलभाग् भवेत् ॥ ५७ ॥

५२। प्रभात इत्यादि। अत्र यद् वर्णविषये विसंवादि सन्ध्याध्यानमुक्तं गायत्रीतन्त्रे प्रथमपटले—सन्ध्याध्यानं प्रवक्ष्यामि सावधानेन संशृणु। विना ध्यानं महेशानि न सन्ध्याफलमाप्नुयात् ॥ नासाग्रे लोचनं न्यस्य ध्यायेद् ब्रह्मस्वरूपिणीम्। प्रातरादित्यसङ्काशां मध्याह्ने शङ्खसन्निभाम् ॥ सायाह्ने मरकतभासां चतुर्ब्बाहुसमन्विताम् ॥ इत्यादि। तत्रैव—मध्याह्ने ······चतुर्भुजां कृष्णवर्णाम् इत्यादि, तदपि सुधीभिर्विभाव्यम्।

---

1. '-माहेशीं' ख-ग, '-सहसां-' घ। 2. अतः परं 'इन्द्रवर्णां कामबीजं नीलवर्णां विभावयेद्' इत्यधिकम्, ङ। 3. 'बीजस्वरूपाञ्च' ख-ग। 4. 'स्वर्णवर्णां' ख-ग। 5. 'विचिन्तयेत्' ङ। 6. 'पूजयेदिष्टदेवताम्' ङ। 7. इदमर्द्धं ख-ग-घ-ङ-पुस्तकेषु नास्ति। 8. 'त्रिविधा' ख-ग। 9. 'अतिपूजां' क। 10. 'देवि' ङ। 11. 'पार्वत्युवाच' ख-ग। 12. 'व्रजेत्' क।

[1]श्रीशङ्कर उवाच—

पूजयेत् पार्थिवे लिङ्गे [2]पाषाणे लिङ्गके[3] तथा ।
स्वर्णलिङ्गेऽथवा देवि[4] [5]रौप्ये ताम्रे च कांस्यके ॥ ५८ ॥
पारदे वाऽथ गङ्गायां स्फाटिके [6]मारकतेऽपि वा ।
कार्य्यभेदे लौहलिङ्गे[7] भस्मनिर्माणलिङ्गके ॥ ५६ ॥
वालुकानिर्मिते लिङ्गे गोमये वाऽथ पूजयेत् ।
पार्थिवे पूजनं देवि [8]तोडलाख्ये मयोदितम् ॥ ६० ॥

५८। पूजयेदित्यादि। लिङ्गस्य पञ्चसूत्रीकरणमुक्तं लैङ्गे तन्त्रान्तरतन्त्रे च—शिवलिङ्गस्य यन्मानं तन्मानं वृत्तसव्ययोः। योन्यग्रमपि यन्मानं तदधोऽपि तथा भवेत् ॥ लिङ्गस्य यादृग् विस्तारः परिणाहोऽपि तादृशः। लिङ्गस्य द्विगुणा देवि योनिस्तदर्धसम्मिता ॥ कुर्वीताङ्गुष्ठतो ह्रस्वं न कदाचिदपि क्वचित्। रत्नादि-शिवनिर्माणे मानमिच्छावशाद् भवेत् ॥ इति।

६०। वालुकानिर्म्मित इत्यादि। तदुक्तं तोडलतन्त्रे पञ्चमपटले—शृणु देवि प्रवक्ष्यामि पार्थिवं शिवपूजनम्। तत्रादौ परमेशानि गुरुदेवं नमेत् सुधीः ॥ ॐ हराय नमस्कारं मृत्तिकामाहरेत् सुधीः। महेश्वराय नमस्कारं लिङ्गं निर्माय यत्नतः ॥ शूलपाणे इहोच्चार्य्य सुसंप्रतिष्ठितो भव। अनेन मनुना देवि जीव-न्यासं विधीयते ॥ शकारं बिन्दुसंयुक्तं दीर्घयुक्तं षडङ्गकम्। तस्य ध्यानं प्रवक्ष्यामि शृणुष्व सुसमाहिता ॥ ॐ ध्यायेन्नित्यं महेशं रजतगिरिनिभं चारुचन्द्रा-वतंसं रत्नाकल्पोज्ज्वलाङ्गं परशुमृगवराभीतिहस्तं प्रसन्नम्। पद्मासीनं समन्तात् स्तुत-ममरगणैर्व्याघ्रकृत्तिं वसानं विश्वाद्यं विश्वबीजं निखिलभयहरं पञ्चवक्त्रं त्रिनेत्रम् ॥ पुष्पं शिरसि सन्धार्य्य मानसैः पूजनञ्चरेत्। पुनर्ध्यात्वा महेशानि शिवे पुष्पं निधाय च ॥ पिनाकधृगिति चोच्चार्य्य इहागच्छद्वयं वदेत्। इह तिष्ठ ततो द्वन्द्वं सन्निधेहिद्वयम् इह ॥ इह सन्नि ततो रुद्धत्रस्वशब्दञ्च ततो वदेत्। यावत् पूजां समुच्चार्य्य ततश्चैवं करोम्यहम् ॥ स्नानीयञ्च पशुपति ङेयुक्तञ्च नमश्चरेत्। वेदाद्यं योजयेद् देवि ब्राह्मणः साधकोत्तमः ॥ एतत् पाद्यं महेशानि षडक्षरमनुं ततः। विचार्य्य सर्वं देवेशि षोडशैरुपचारकैः ॥ पूजयित्वा

---

1. 'श्रीशिव' क-घ-ङ। 2. 'पाषाणलि-' ख-ग-ङ-प्रा। 3. '-ऽथवा' प्रा। 4. 'देवे' ख। 5. 'वैश्ये' घ। 6. 'मरकते' क-ङ। 7. '-लिङ्ग' ख-ग। 8. 'सर्वत्रैव' क।

[1]संस्कारेण विना देवि पाषाणादौ न पूजयेत् ।
संस्कारञ्च प्रवक्ष्यामि विशेष इह यद् भवेत् ॥ ६१ ॥
रौप्यञ्च [2]स्वर्णलिङ्गञ्च स्वर्णपात्रे निधाय च ।
तस्मादुत्तोल्य तं[3] लिङ्गं दुग्धमध्ये दिनत्रयम् ॥ ६२ ॥
[4]त्र्यम्बकेण [5]स्थापयित्वा कालरुद्रं प्रपूजयेत् ।
षोडशेनोपचारेण वेद्यान्तु पार्व्वतीं यजेत् ॥ ६३ ॥
तस्मादुत्तोल्य तं लिङ्गं [6]गङ्गातोये दिनत्रयम् ।
ततो वेदोक्तविधिना [7]संस्कारमाचरेत् सुधीः ॥ ६४ ॥

[8]श्रीचण्डिकोवाच—

लिङ्गप्रमाणं देवेश कथयस्व मयि प्रभो ।
पार्थिवे च शिलादौ[9] च विशेषो यदि[10] वा भवेत् ॥ ६५ ॥

महेशानि चाष्टमूर्त्तिं प्रपूजयेत् । शर्वो भवस्तथा रुद्र उग्रो भीमः पशुपतिः ॥ महादेवश्च ईशान ङेयुतं कुरु यत्नतः । क्षितिं जलं तथा चाग्निं वायुञ्चाकाशमेव च ॥ यजमानं तथा सोमं सूर्य्यञ्च मूर्त्तिना सह । सर्वत्र ङेयुतं कृत्वा पूजयेत् साधकोत्तमः ॥ प्रणवादिनमोऽन्तेन वामावर्त्तेन पूजयेत् । मूर्त्तयोऽष्टौ शिवस्यैताः पूर्वादिक्रमयोगतः ॥ आग्नेय्यान्ताः प्रपूज्याथ वेद्यां लिङ्गे शिवं यजेत् । अष्टोत्तरसहस्रं वा शतं वा प्रजपेत् ततः ॥ गुह्यातिगुह्यगोप्ता त्वं गृहाणास्मत्कृतं जपम् । सिद्धिर्भवतु मे देव त्वत्प्रसादान्महेश्वर ॥ ततस्तोयं समादाय जपञ्चैव समर्पयेत् । मुखवाद्यं ततः कृत्वा चाष्टाङ्गं प्रणमेत् सुधीः ॥ संहारेण महादेव क्षमस्वेति विसर्जयेत् ।

६३ । त्र्यम्बकेणेति । मन्त्रस्तु—"ॐ त्र्यम्बकं यजामहे सुगन्धिं पुष्टिवर्द्धनम् । उर्व्वारुकमिव बन्धनान्मृत्योर्मुक्षीय माऽमृतात् ॥" इति । शुक्लयजुः—३।६० ।

---

1. 'संस्कारञ्च' ख-ग । 2. 'ताम्रपात्रे वा' घ । 3. 'तद् द्रव्यं' ख-ग । 4. 'त्र्यम्बकेणे'त्यादि 'दिनत्रय'मित्यन्तोंऽशः' ख-ग-पुस्तकयोर्नास्ति । 5. 'स्नापयित्वा' ङ-श-प्रा० । 6. 'गाङ्गतोये' प्रा० । 7. 'संस्कारञ्च समाचरेत्' ख-ग । 8. 'श्रीदेव्युवाच'ख-ग-घ-ङ । 9. 'शिला चादौ' क । 10. 'यत्र भावयेत्' ख-ग, 'यदि भावयेत्' ङ, 'यत्र यो भवेत्' प्रा० ।

श्रीशिव उवाच—

मृत्तिकातोलकं ग्राह्यमथवा तोलकद्वयम् ।
एतदन्यं[1] न कर्त्तव्यं कदाचिदपि पार्व्वति[2] ॥ ६६ ॥
शिलादौ [3]परमेशानि स्थूलञ्च फलदायकम् ।
अङ्गुष्ठमानं देवेशि यद्वा [4]हेमाद्रिमानकम् ॥ ६७ ॥

६६ । मृत्तिकेत्यादि । अत्र संवादि प्रमाणन्तु—मृत्तिकातोलकं ग्राह्यमथवा तोलकद्वयम् । त्रिसूत्रस्य प्रमाणेन घटनं कारयेद् बुधः ॥ अङ्गुष्ठपर्वमानन्तु कृत्वा लिङ्गं प्रपूजयेत् । मृदादिलिङ्गगठने प्रमाणं परिकीर्त्तितम् ॥ फलमुक्तमवाप्नोति अन्यथा चेत् तदन्यथा । (इति षट्कर्मदीपिकाधृतविश्वसारतन्त्रम्) । मृत्तिकाभेदेन ब्राह्मणादीनां पूजाफलस्य प्राशस्त्यमुक्तं तत्रैव—शुक्लं हि पार्थिवं लिङ्गं निर्माय यस्तु पूजयेत् । स एव परमेशानि त्रिवर्गफलभाग् भवेत् ॥ क्षत्रियस्तु वरारोहे रक्तं निर्माय पार्थिवम् । पूजयेत् सततं यस्तु त्रिवर्गफलभाग्भवेत् ॥ हरितं पार्थिवं देवि निर्माय यस्तु पूजयेत् । स च वैश्यो महेशानि त्रिवर्गफलभाग्भवेत् ॥ कृष्णं हि पार्थिवं लिङ्गं निर्माय यस्तु पूजयेत् । स शूद्रः परमेशानि त्रिवर्गफलभाग् भवेत् ॥ इति । लिङ्गार्च्चनतन्त्रे द्वितीयपटले—मृत्स्ना तु परमेशानि वर्णभेदेन सुन्दरि । वर्णभेदस्तु तत्रैव तृतीयपटले—चतुर्द्धा पार्थिवं लिङ्गं मृत्स्नाभेदेन पार्व्वति । शुक्लं रक्तं तथा पीतं कृष्णञ्च परमेश्वरि ॥ शुक्लन्तु ब्राह्मणे शस्तं क्षत्रिये रक्तमिष्यते । पीतन्तु वैश्यजातौ स्यात् कृष्णं शूद्रे प्रकीर्त्तितम् ॥ इति । पार्थिवे त्रिसूत्रीकरणञ्चोक्तं कालोत्तरे—लिङ्गे वेद्यां तथा पीठे समसूत्रनिपातनात् । समञ्चैव विजानीयात् त्रिसूत्रीकरणन्त्विदम् ॥ इति । मृत्तिकाग्रहणस्थानान्याह प्राणतोषणीधृतमत्स्यसूक्ते पञ्चदशपटले—तीर्थमृत्स्नां समाहृत्य निर्माय लिङ्गमद्भुतम् । तीर्थाभावे महेशानि नदीमृत्स्नां शुचिस्मिते ॥ नद्यभावे महेशानि क्षुद्रस्य मृत्तिकां प्रिये । नदीक्षुद्रयोर्लक्षणमपि तत्रैव—पर्वतप्रभवा देवि नदी नाम्नेत्युदाहृता । एतद्भिन्ना महेशानि नदी क्षुद्रा इति प्रिये ॥ निर्झरस्य च देवेशि मृत्स्ना सम्पत्प्रदायिनी । तथा चैव सरोत्पन्ना नानासुखप्रदायिनी ॥ सर्वाभावे महेशानि गोष्पदस्थाञ्च मृत्तिकाम् । अथवा परमेशानि यत्र चित्तं प्रसीदति ॥ इति ।

६७ । शिलादौ चेति । अत्र संवदति—रुद्राक्षं शिवलिङ्गञ्च स्थूलात् स्थूलं प्रशस्यते ।

1. 'एतन्न्यूनं' क', 'एतदन्यं न कुर्वीत' श०-प्रा० । 2. 'सुन्दरि' ख-ग । 3. 'च महेशानि' प्रा० । 4. 'हेमाद्रि-' क ।

[1]एवंक्रमेण देवेशि फलं बहुविधं [2]लभेत् ।
[3]स्थूलात् स्थूलतरं लिङ्गं रुद्राक्षं परमेश्वरि ॥ ६८ ॥
पूजनाद् धारणाद्देवि फलं बहुविधं स्मृतम् ॥ ६९ ॥

इति श्रीमातृकाभेदतन्त्रे[4] हरपार्वतीसंवादे सप्तमः पटलः ॥ ७ ॥

शालग्रामो नार्मदश्च सूक्ष्मात् सूक्ष्मो विशिष्यते ॥ इति मेरुतन्त्रवचनम् । हेमाद्रिप्रमाणश्चोक्तं मत्स्यपुराणे षडशीतितमेऽध्याये—उत्तमः पलसाहस्रो मध्यमः पञ्चभिः शतैः । तदर्द्धेनाधम इति ।

६८ । स्थूलादिति । स्थूलात् स्थूलतरमिति पार्थिवलिङ्गेतरपरम्, 'मृत्तिकातोलकं ग्राह्य'मित्यादिवचनादिति ।

---

1. 'क्रमेण देवदेवेशि' क-ख-ग । 2. 'भवेत्' ङ । 3. 'स्थूला'दित्यादि 'स्मृत'मित्यन्तोंऽशः ख-ग-पुस्तकयोर्नास्ति । 4. घ-पुस्तके 'सर्वतन्त्रोत्तमोत्तमे' इत्यधिकः पाठः ।

७

अष्टमः पटलः

[1]श्रीदेव्युवाच—

श्रृणु नाथ परानन्द परापरकुलात्मक ।
त्वां विना [2]त्राणकर्त्ता च मम ज्ञाने न वर्त्तते ॥ १ ॥
[3]पूर्णलिङ्गं महेशान शिवबीजं न चान्यथा ।
[4]शिलामध्ये तथा चक्रं लक्ष्मीनारायणं परम् ॥ २ ॥
पारदस्य शतांशैकं मम ज्ञाने न वर्त्तते ।
शिवबीजं महादेव शिवरूपं न चान्यथा ।
[5]लिङ्गरूपं [6]कथं देव तद् वदस्व [7]मयि प्रभो ॥ ३ ॥

[8]श्रीशिव उवाच—

[9]यथा ज्योतिर्मयं लिङ्गं कैलासशिखरे[10] मम ।
तस्यैव षोडशांशैकः काश्यां [11]विश्वेश्वरः स्थितः[12] ॥ ४ ॥
[13]पूर्णलिङ्गं महेशानि [14]शिवबीजं न चान्यथा ।
शिलामध्ये [15]तथा चक्रं लक्ष्मीनारायणं[16] [17]परम् ॥ ५॥
पारदस्य शतांशैकं[18] लक्ष्मीनारायणं न हि ।
[19]पकारं विष्णुरूपञ्च आकारं[20] कालिका तथा[21] ॥ ६ ॥

---

1. 'पार्वत्युवाच' ख-ग । 2. 'नात्र कर्त्ता' घ । 3. 'पूर्णलिङ्ग'मित्यादि 'न वर्त्तते' इत्यन्तोंऽशः ख-ग-पुस्तकयोर्नास्ति । 4. 'शिलामध्य' इत्यादि 'न वर्त्तते' इत्यन्तोंऽशो घ-पुस्तके नास्ति । 5. 'लिङ्गं रूपं' घ । 6. 'महादेव' ङ । 7. 'दयानिधे' ग । 8. 'शङ्कर' ख-ग । 9. 'ज्योतिर्मयं महालिङ्गं' श० । 10. '-नगरे प्रिये' क-घ-ङ । 11. 'विश्वेश्वर-स्थितं' ङ-ख-ग । 12. 'अतः परं ख-ग-पुस्तकयोः 'पारदः षोडशांशैकं काश्यां विश्वेश्वरस्थितम्' इत्यधिकः । 13. 'पूर्वबीजं' ख-ग, 'पूर्णबीजं' ङ । 14. 'शिवरूपं' ख-ग । 15. 'च यच्चक्रं' ख-ग, 'यथा' घ । 16. '-यणः' श । 17. 'स्मृतम्' ख-ग । 18. '-शैकः लक्ष्मीनारायणो' श । 19. 'प्रकारं' ख-ग । 20. 'चाकालं' घ । 21. 'स्वयं' ख-ग-ङ-श ।

रेफं शिवं दकारश्च ब्रह्मरूपं न चान्यथा ।
पारदं परमेशानि ब्रह्मविष्णुशिवात्मकम् ॥ ७ ॥
यो यजेत्[1] पारदं लिङ्गं स एव शम्भुरव्ययः[2] ।
स एव धन्यो देवेशि स ज्ञानी स तु तत्त्ववित् ॥ ८ ॥
स ब्रह्मवेत्ता स धनी स राजा भुवि पूजितः[3] ।
अणिमादिविभूतीनामीश्वरः साधकोत्तमः ॥ ९ ॥
स्त्रियः स्वभावचपला[4] गोपितुं न हि शक्यते ।
अत एव हि देवेशि विरता भव पार्व्वति ॥ १० ॥

श्रीदेव्युवाच—

कथयस्व कृपानाथ करुणा यदि वर्त्तते ।
तव वाक्यं विना [5]देव क्व[6] मुक्तिः क्व च साधुता ॥ ११ ॥

श्रीशिव उवाच—

पारदं [7]शिवबीजं हि ताडनं [8]न हि कारयेत् ।
ताडनाद्वित्तनाशः स्यात् ताडनात् [9]सुतहीनता ।
ताडनाद्रोगयुक्तः स्यात् ताडनान्मरणं भवेत् ॥ १२ ॥

[10]श्रीदेव्युवाच—

एतद्विघ्नादिकं नाथ सत्यमेव न संशयः ।
विघ्नादिरहितं नाथ कथयस्व दयानिधे ॥ १३ ॥

---

1. 'जपेत्' ख-ग, '-ऽर्च्चयेत्' ङ । 2. अतः परं क-ख-ग-ङ-पुस्तकेषु 'आजन्ममध्ये यो देवि एकदा यदि पूजयेत्' इत्यधिकः । 3. 'भूरि पूज्य सः' क, 'भुवि पूज्य सः' घ-ङ । 4. '-चपलाद्-' क-ङ । 5. 'नाथ' ख-ग । 6. 'क उक्तः कश्च शब्दितः' ख-ग, 'का मुक्तिः क्व च साधुता' घ-ङ । 7. 'मम' ख-ग । 8. 'नैव', ख-ग । 9. 'वित्त-' श: । 10. 'पार्व्वत्युवाच' ख-ग ।

श्रीशिव उवाच—

पारदे शिवनिर्माणे नानाविघ्नं यतः शिवे[1] ।
अत एव हि तत्रादौ शान्ति-स्वस्त्ययनञ्चरेत् ॥ १४ ॥
द्वादशं पार्थिवं लिङ्गमुपचारैश्च षोडशैः ।
पट्टादिसूत्रनिर्माणं[2] रचितं शुक्लमेव वा[3] ॥ १५ ॥
पुरुषस्य यथायोग्यं [4]युग्मवस्त्रं निवेदयेत् ।
भोगयोग्यं प्रदातव्यं मधुपर्कं [5]सुरेश्वरि ॥ १६ ॥
अलङ्कारं यथाशक्ति दद्यात् कल्याणहेतवे ।
पूजयेद् बहुयत्नेन विल्वपत्रेण पार्वति ॥ १७ ॥
तोडलोक्तेन विधिना [6]प्रत्येकेनायुतं जपेत् ।
आदौ पञ्चाक्षरं मन्त्रमष्टोत्तरशतं जपेत् ॥ १८ ॥
पूजान्ते प्रजपेत् पश्चात् प्रासादाख्यं महामनुम् ।
दक्षिणान्तं समाचर्य्य[7] हविष्याशी जितेन्द्रियः ॥ १९ ॥
ताम्बूलञ्च तथा मत्स्यं वर्जयेन्न कदाचन ।
[8]अस्मिंस्तन्त्रे हविष्यान्नं ताम्बूलं मीनमुत्तमम् ॥२०॥

---

१५ । द्वादशमित्यादि । लिङ्गपूजाधारनियमश्च महिषमर्दिनीतन्त्रे त्रयोदशपटले—स्वर्णपात्रे तथा रौप्ये ताम्रे च प्रस्तरे तथा । पद्मपत्रे पलाशे च तथा वा कदलीदले ॥ पूजनं मृन्मयं लिङ्गं काशीक्षेत्रसमं प्रिये । तैजसे दारवे पात्रे सामान्यफलदं सदा ॥ अन्यत् पात्रञ्च चार्वङ्गि वर्जयेच्छिवपूजने । इति ।

१८ । तोडलोक्तेनेत्यादि । तदुक्तं तोडलतन्त्रे पञ्चमपटले—नमस्कारं समुद्धृत्य वान्तं नेत्रविभूषितम् । वारुणं मुखवृत्तञ्च वायुं ललाटसंयुतम् ॥ अयं पञ्चाक्षरो मन्त्रः पञ्चाम्नायफलप्रदः । एतेन "नमः शिवाय" इति मन्त्रो भवति । प्रणवादिर्यदा देवि तदा मन्त्रः षडक्षरः । एतेन च "ॐ नमः शिवाय" इति षडक्षरो मन्त्रः ।

---

1. अतः परं घ-पुस्तके 'नानाविघ्नं भवेद्देवि तत्र भक्तियुतः शिवे' इत्यधिकः पाठः । 2. 'निर्म्माणरचितं' श । 3. 'च' ख-ग । 4. 'वस्त्रयुग्मं' ख-ग, 'युग्मं वस्त्रं' ङ । 5. 'महेश्वरि' ङ, कुलेश्वरि' श । 6. 'प्रत्येकमयुतं' ख-ग । 7. 'समुच्चार्य्य' ख-ग, समाचार्य्यं' ङ । 8. 'तस्मि-' ख-ग-घ ।

होमयेत् परमेशानि दशांशं वा शतांशकम् ।
होमस्य दक्षिणा कार्य्या तदा विघ्नैर्न लिप्यते ॥ २१ ॥
ततः परस्मिन् दिवसे पारदमानयेद् बुधः[1] ।
तस्योपरि जपेन्मन्त्रं [2]सर्व्वबन्धनवात्मकम् ॥ २२ ॥
व्योमबीजं [3]शिवान्तञ्च [4]वर्गाद्यं बिन्दुमस्तकम् ।
वायुबीजं च त्रितयं[5] त्रितयं [6]त्र्यम्बकं प्रिये ॥ २३ ॥
[7]इमं मन्त्रं महेशानि प्रजपेदौषधोपरि ।
पारदे प्रजपेन्मन्त्रमष्टोत्तरशतं [8]यदि ॥ २४ ॥
[9]तदेवौषधयोगेन [10]बद्धो भवति नान्यथा ॥ २५ ॥
ततः [11]परस्मिन् दिवसे शृणु मत्प्राणवल्लभे ।
वरयेत् [12]कर्म्मकर्त्तारं यथोक्तविभवावधि ॥ २६ ॥
[13]सुवर्णं चम्पकाकारं कर्णयुग्मे [14]निवेदयेत् ।
[15]चतुष्कोणयुतं स्वर्णं ग्रीवायां सुमनोहरम् ॥ २७ ॥
हस्तद्वये महेशानि दद्याद् वलययुग्मकम् ।
वलयं शुक्लवर्णञ्च अङ्गुरीयं तथैव च ॥ २८ ॥
[16]ऊर्म्मि दद्यात् पीतवस्त्रं क्षौमवस्त्रयुगं शिवे ।
[17]एवं कृत्वा महेशानि शिवरूपं विचिन्तयेत् ॥ २९ ॥

२३। व्योमबीजमित्यादि। तेन "हँ क्षँ कँ यँ यँ यँ हँ हँ हँ" इति नवाक्षरो मन्त्रो भवति।

---

1. 'सुधीः' ख-ग-घ-श० 2 'सर्व्वबन्ध-' क-ख-ग, '-सर्व्वबद्ध-' ङ। 3. 'शिवार्णञ्च' श। 4. 'वर्णाद्यं' ख-ग-घ-ङ-श। 5. 'चेन्दुयुतं' क-घ-ङ। 6 'त्र्यम्बक-' क। 7. 'इदं' ख-ग-घ। 8. 'प्रिये' क। 9. 'तदेवौषधि-' ख-ग। 10. 'बन्धो' ख-ग। 11 'परस्य' ङ। 12. 'सर्व्व-' श। 13. 'सुवर्णचम्पका-' ख-ग। 14 'निवेशयेत' श। 15. 'चतुष्कोणेषु तं' ख-ग। 16 'वस्त्रं' ख-ग। 17. 'एवं कृतं' ख-ग।

अथातः संप्रवक्ष्यामि विधानं शृणु पार्व्वति ।
प्रस्तरे [1]चैव संस्थाप्य [2]झिण्टीपल्लरसेन च ।
[3]प्रस्तरेण समालोड्य कुर्य्यात् कर्दमवत् प्रिये ॥ ३० ॥
निर्म्माणयोग्यं[4] [5]तत्रैव यदि स्यात् सुरसुन्दरि ।
तदा निर्म्माय [6]तं लिङ्गं पुनर्दृढतरं चरेत् ॥ ३१ ॥
[7]स्वपुष्पसंयुते वस्त्रे अङ्गारे च करीषके ।
किञ्चिदुष्णं प्रकर्त्तव्यं [8]यतो दृढतरो[9] भवेत् ॥ ३२ ॥
ततो निर्म्माय तं लिङ्गं [10]पुनर्दृढतरं चरेत् ।
[11]स्वपुष्पसंयुते वस्त्रे [12]स्थापयेत् पार्थिवे पुनः ॥ ३३ ॥
किञ्चिदुष्णं प्रकर्त्तव्यं यावद् दृढतरो भवेत् ।
विना [13]ह्यौषधयोगेन भस्मो भवति नान्यथा ॥ ३४ ॥

इति श्रीमातृकाभेदतन्त्रे[14] हरगौरीसंवादेऽष्टमः पटलः ॥ ८ ॥

---

३५ । भस्मो भवतीति । अत्रावधूतैरुच्यते—मुडरीलीजे सूत पर उसको दीजे मण्डलभरके खल करीजे ॥ तव होजाय कादो प्राय उससे शिवजी निर्माय । उसमें दीजेजड़के पानी वज्रसमान करके जानी ॥ इति ।

---

1. 'हि' ख-ग । 2. 'चिञ्ची-' घ । 3. 'प्रस्तरे च' ख-ग, 'प्रणवेन' श० । 4. '-योग्यः' ख-ग, 'युग्मं' घ । 5 'तद् द्रव्यं' श । 6. 'तल्लिङ्ग'' घ-ङ । 7. 'श्व-पुष्प-' ङ-श । 8. 'अतो' ख-ग । 9. '-तरं' ङ । 10. '-दृढतरो भवेत्' ख-ग, 'स्वपुष्पं संयुतञ्चरेत्' घ । 11. ख-ग-ङ-पुस्तकेषु 'स्वपुष्पे'त्यादि 'भवे'दित्यन्तोंऽशो नास्ति' । 12. 'अङ्गारे च करीषके' घ । 13. चौषधियोगेन भस्म भवति ततक्षणात्' ख-ग । 14 ग-पुस्तके 'सर्व्व-तन्त्रोत्तमोत्तमे' इत्यधिकः ।

नवमः पटलः

[1]श्रीशिव उवाच—

भस्मप्रकारं देवेशि शृणु मत्प्राणवल्लभे ।
कर्त्तारं वरयेदादौ यथोक्तविभवावधि ॥ १ ॥
[2]सुवर्णं मौक्तिकयुतं कर्णयुग्मे निवेदयेत् ।
हस्तयुग्मे च वलयं अङ्गुरीयं तथैव च ॥ २ ॥
ताडद्वयं बाहुयुग्मे शुद्धकाञ्चननिर्म्मितम् ।
ग्रीवायां दापयेत् स्वर्णं चतुष्कोणं मनोरमम् ॥ ३ ॥
वस्त्रयुग्मं [3]पट्टसूत्रनिर्म्मितञ्च सुशोभनम् ।
[4]उष्णीषं शुक्लवर्णञ्च [5]उष्णीषं पीतवाससम् ॥ ४ ॥
एवं हि वरयेद् देवि कर्म्मयोग्यं [6]विचिन्तयेत् ।
चिन्तयेच्छिवरूपञ्च चिन्तयेत् त्रिगुणात्मकम् ॥ ५ ॥
ततः परस्मिन् दिवसे शान्तिस्वस्त्ययनञ्चरेत् ।
निर्म्मितं [7]शुद्धस्वर्णेन विल्वपत्रेण सुन्दरि ॥ ६ ॥
सहस्रसङ्ख्यया [8]देवि पार्थिवं द्वादशं यजेत् ।
षोडशेनोपचारेण पट्टवस्त्रयुगेन च ॥ ७ ॥
[9]अलङ्कारविचित्रैश्च पूजयेत् [10]परमेश्वरम् ।
भोगयोग्यं [11]प्रदातव्यं मधुपर्कं [12]निवेदयेत् ॥ ८ ॥

---

1. 'श्री' नास्ति क-घ-पुस्तकयोः । 2. 'सौवर्णं मौक्तिकं युक्तं' ख-ग । 3. 'पट्टसूत्रं निर्मि-' क-घ-ङ । 4. 'उष्णीषं पीतवस्त्रञ्च परीधानञ्च वाससम्' ख-ग । 5 'ऊर्म्मिञ्च सितवाससम्' घ, 'ऊर्म्मी च सीतवाससम्' ङ । 6. 'निवेदयेत्' ख-ग । 7. 'शुद्धवर्णेन' ख-ग-ङ । 8. 'जप्यं' ख-ग । 9. 'अलङ्कारं विचि-' ङ । 10. 'परमेश्वरि' ख-ग, 'परमेश्वरीम्' क । 11. 'महेशानि' घ-ङ । 12. 'शुचिस्मिते' ख-ग ।

स्वर्णासनेन[1] संस्थाप्य प्रत्येकं पूजनञ्चरेत् ।
पूजान्ते प्रजपेन्मन्त्रमष्टोत्तरशतं सुधीः ॥ ९ ॥
[2]षडक्षरं महामन्त्रं [3]प्रासादाख्यं मनुं ततः ।
दिक्सहस्रं जपेन्मन्त्रं तद्दशांशं हुनेत् प्रिये ॥ १० ॥
[4]होमस्य द्रव्यं देवेशि शृणु मत्प्राणवल्लभे ।
वालुकानिर्म्मिते वापि कुण्डे वा परमेश्वरि ॥ ११ ॥
द्वात्रिंशदङ्गुलिमानं विस्तृतं तत्समं प्रिये ।
षोडशाङ्गुलिमानं हि [5]कुण्डं कुर्यात् सुलक्षणम् ॥ १२ ॥
तदूर्द्ध्वे परमेशानि [6]वेदनेत्राङ्गुलिं शिवे ।
एवं हि स्वर्णकुम्भञ्च [7]ताम्रकुम्भासमर्थिना ॥ १३ ॥
एतदन्यतरं कुम्भं स्थापयेद् वेदिकोपरि ।
पट्टवस्त्रेण युग्मेन संवेष्ट्य बहुयत्नतः ॥ १४ ॥
होमयेद् विल्वपत्रेण [8]यथोक्तेन सुरेश्वरि ।
[9]त्रिमध्वक्तेन विधिना ततः सिद्धो भवेद् ध्रुवम् ॥ १५ ॥
ततस्तु दक्षिणा कार्य्या यथोक्तविभवावधि ।
सर्व्वद्रव्यमयं[10] मूल्यं द्विगुणं वा प्रदापयेत् ॥ १६ ॥
[11]दक्षिणाविहीना[12] यज्ञाः सिद्धिदा न च मोक्षदाः ।
अत एव महेशानि दक्षिणा विभवावधि ॥ १७ ॥

---

१० । षडक्षरमित्यादि । तेन 'ॐ नमः शिवाय हौँ' इति मन्त्रस्य दशसहस्र-जपतद्दशांशहोमादिकं कर्त्तव्यमिति ।

१५ । त्रिमध्वक्तेनेति । मधुत्रयमुक्तं वराहपुराणे—क्षौद्रमिक्षुरसं क्षीरं तथा त्रिमधुरं स्मृतम् । इति वैदिकसर्व्वस्वे ।

---

1. 'च'-घ । 2. '-क्षरमहा-' घ । 3. 'ततः प्रासादसंज्ञकम्' क-ख-ग-ङ । 4. 'होमद्रव्यं हि' घ । 5. 'कण्ठं' ङ । 6. 'वेदनत्राङ्गुलिं' ग । 7. 'ताम्रकुण्डासमर्थिना' ख-ग, 'ताम्रकुम्भं सम-' ङ । 8. 'यथोक्तविधिना शिवे' ख-ग । 9. 'त्रिमध्वोक्तेन' क । 10. '-समं पुण्यं' ख-ग । 11. 'दक्षिणाविहीनो यज्ञः सिद्धिदो न च मोक्षदः' ख-ग । 12. 'विहिना' घ-ङ ।

वराहवत्समानीय जन्ममात्रेऽपि सुन्दरि ।
पारदं तोलकं मानं भक्षयेद् बहुयत्नतः ॥ १८ ॥
पुनस्तोलकमानं हि मातृदुग्धं ततः परम् ।
पुनश्च भक्षयेद् धीमांस्ततो दुग्धन्तु भक्षयेत् ॥ १९ ॥
[1]ततश्च वत्समानीय [2]नवद्वारं प्रयत्नतः ।
[3]सूत्रयोगेण देवेशि [4]बद्धं कुर्य्यात् प्रयत्नतः ॥ २० ॥
ततश्च [5]हेलकीमन्त्रमष्टोत्तरशतं जपेत् ।
गजप्रमाणं देवेशि [6]दीर्घप्रस्थन्तु खातकम् ॥ २१ ॥
करीषकेण देवेशि [7]पूर्णं [8]कुर्य्याद्विचक्षणः ।
तन्मध्ये स्थापयेद् वत्सं [9]सन्दहेद् बहुयत्नतः ॥ २२ ॥
वह्निस्थिते महेशानि न स्पृशेत् कुण्डमुत्तमम् ।
[10]कुण्डे सुशीतले जाते उत्थाप्य बहुयत्नतः ॥ २३ ॥
सर्व्वप्रकाशकं मन्त्रमष्टोत्तरशतं जपेत् ।
विश्वेश्वरं प्रवक्ष्यामि शृणु पार्व्वति सादरम् ॥ २४ ॥
पारदं तोलकं मानं ताम्रपात्रे तु लेपयेत् ।
चूर्णं कुर्यान्महेशानि गन्धकं सार्द्धतोलकम् ॥ २५ ॥
समाच्छाद्य प्रयत्नेन चूर्णेन परमेश्वरि ।
सन्दहेद् बहुयत्नेन मन्दमन्देन वह्निना ॥ २६ ॥

1. 'ततस्तद्वत्समानीय' ख-ग । 2. 'सर्व्वद्वारं' घ । 3 घ-पुस्तके पद्यार्द्धमिदं नास्ति । 4. 'बन्धं' क-ख-ग । 5. 'ततश्चाहलकीमन्त्र-' ख-ग । 6. 'दीर्घपुत्रन्तु' क । 7. 'चूर्णं' ङ । 8. 'कुर्य्यात्तु खातकम्' ख-ग । 9. 'सन्दह्य च प्रयत्नतः' ख-ग । 10. 'कुम्भे सुशीतले देवि' क, कुण्डेषु शीतले' ख-ग, 'कुण्डेषु शीते जाते तु' ङ ।

कृष्णवर्णं [1]रेणुयुतं दृष्ट्वा उत्थाप्य सुन्दरि ।
[2]रक्तिप्रमाणं तद् द्रव्यं भक्षयेद् यदि सुन्दरि ॥ २७ ॥
सत्यं सत्यं [3]सर्व्वकुष्ठं भक्षणान्नाशमाप्नुयात् ।
[4]अनुपानमुष्णतोयं मत्स्यादीन् परिवर्जयेत् ॥ २८ ॥
एवं प्रयोगं देवेशि न कुर्यात् [5]पुत्रवान् गृही ।
प्रथमे दिवसे पुत्रान् [6]द्वितीये दिवसे धनम् ॥ २९ ॥
[7]तृतीये दिवसे शक्तिं [8]चतुर्थे दिवसे गृहम् ।
[9]पञ्चमे दिवसे रोगं [10]नाशं तु जायते ध्रुवम् ॥ ३० ॥
अत एव महेशानि [11]आत्मस्वस्त्ययनञ्चरेत् ।
पूर्वोक्तविधिना मन्त्री [12]चतुर्गुणं समाचरेत् ॥ ३१ ॥

इति श्रीमातृकाभेदतन्त्रे [13]हरगौरीसंवादे नवमः पटलः ॥ ९ ॥

---

1. 'रेणुयुक्तं' ख-ग। 2. 'रतिप्रमाणं' ख-ग, 'गुञ्जाप्रमाणं' घ। 3. 'सर्वारिष्टं' ख-ग। 4. 'अम्नुपात्र-' घ। 5. 'साधको' घ-ङ। 6. 'द्वितीयदिवसे' ख-ग-घ। 7. 'तृतीयदिवसे' ग-घ-ङ। 8. 'नाशयामि न संशयः' ख-ग, 'चतुर्थदिवसे' घ। 9. 'चतुर्थे दिवसे रोगं पञ्चमे शोकमाप्नुयात्' ख-ग। 10. 'नाशञ्च' घ। 11. 'शान्तिस्वस्त्ययनञ्च-' ख-ग। 12, '-र्गुणमथाचरेत' ख-ग। 13. अयमंशो नास्ति घ।

दशमः पटलः

[1]श्रीदेव्युवाच—

[2]नराकृतिं गुरुं नाथ [3]मन्त्रं वर्णात्मकं तथा ।
[4]ध्यानानुरूपिणं [5]देवमेकत्वं वा कथं वद ॥ १ ॥

[6]श्रीशिव उवाच—

गुरुवक्त्रान्महामन्त्रो[7] [8]लभ्यते [9]साधकोत्तमैः ।
[10]यद्येको जायते वीर्य्यस्तस्य [11]मूर्त्तिर्भवेद् ध्रुवम् ॥ २ ॥
देवतायाः शरीरञ्च[12] बीजादुत्पद्यते प्रिये ।
गुरोराज्ञानुसारेण चान्यमूर्त्तिस्तु जायते ॥ ३ ॥
गुर्वादिभावनाद् देवि भावसिद्धिः प्रजायते ।
अत एव महेशानि चैकत्वं परिकथ्यते ॥ ४ ॥

---

४ । गुर्वादीति । अत्र संवादि प्रमाणमुक्तं यामले—गुरुरेकः शिवः प्रोक्तः सोऽहं देवि न संशयः । गुरुस्त्वमपि देवेशि मन्त्रोऽपि गुरुरुच्यते ॥ अतो मन्त्रे गुरौ देवे न हि भेदः प्रजायते । कदाचित् स सहस्रारे पद्मे ध्येयो गुरुः सदा ॥ कदाचिद्धृदयाम्भोजे कदाचिद्दृष्टिगोचरे ॥ इति । मुण्डमालातन्त्रे च—देवतागुरुमन्त्राणामैक्यं सम्भावयन् धिया । तदा सिद्धो भवेन्मन्त्रः प्रकटे हानिरेव च ॥ मन्त्रे वा गुरुदेवे वा न भेदं यस्तु कल्पते । तस्य तुष्टा जगद्धात्री किं न दद्याद् दिने दिने ॥ इति ।

---

1. ङ-पुस्तके 'श्री' नास्ति । 2. 'नरश्चेति गुरुर्नाथ' ख-ग । 3. 'मन्त्रवर्णा-' ङ । 4. 'ध्यानानुरूपिणीं देव एकं वापि कथं वद' घ । 5. 'देव एकत्वं वा कथं भवेत्' ख-ग । 6. 'शङ्कर' ख-ग । 7. '-मन्त्री' क, '-मन्त्रं' ख-ग । 8. 'लभते' ख-ग । 9. '-त्तमः' ख-ग । 10. 'यद्देयो जायते बीज-' ख-ग, 'यज्ञे वा जायते वीर्य-' घ, 'यद्देवाज्जायते बीजन्तस्य' प्रा । 11. 'मुक्ति-' प्रा । 12. '-न्तु' ख-ग, ...'-रं हि' घ-ङ-प्रा ।

[1]श्रीदेव्युवाच—

[2]यच्चाक्षुषं महादेव तदाकारं विचिन्तयत् ।
[3]अचाक्षुषे महादेव ध्यानं[4] वा कीदृशं भवेत् ॥ ५ ॥

श्रीशिव उवाच—

[5]शब्दब्रह्ममयं देवि मम [6]वक्त्राद्विनिर्गतम् ।
आकाररहिते देवि यथा ध्यानादिकं भवेत् ॥ ६ ॥
तथैवोच्चारणेनैव भक्तियुक्तेन चेतसा ।
सत्यं सत्यं महेशानि प्रत्यक्षं नात्र संशयः ॥ ७ ॥

श्रीदेव्युवाच—

पशुप्रदाने वाक्यं तु कीदृशं वद शङ्कर ।
येन वाक्येन [7]देवेश [8]देवी तुष्टा भवत्यपि ॥ ८ ॥

[9]श्रीशिव उवाच—

मृगे महिषे चोष्ट्रे च पशुशब्दं न योजयेत् ।
छागले च तथा सिंहे व्याघ्रे च परमेश्वरि ॥ ९ ॥
पशुशब्दं योजयित्वा महादेव्यै निवेदयेत् ।
[10]पशुभावस्थितो मन्त्री महिषो दीयते यदि ॥ १० ॥

९। छागले चेति। तथाच छागादिबलिदानफलमुक्तं मुण्डमालातन्त्रे—छागे दत्ते भवेद्वाग्मी मेषे दत्ते कविर्भवेत्। महिषे धनवृद्धिः स्यान्मृगे मोक्षफलं लभेत् ॥ पक्षिदाने समृद्धिः स्याद् गोधिकायां महाफलम्। नरे दत्ते महर्द्धिः स्यादष्टसिद्धिरनुत्तमा॥ इति। एवं तत्रैव—राजा नरबलिं दद्यान्नान्यो हि परमेश्वरि। सिंहव्याघ्रनरान् दत्त्वा ब्राह्मणो रौरवं व्रजेत् ॥ इति वचनाद् ब्राह्मणानां नरादिबलिदाने नाधिकार इति। एवमपि निबन्धे तृतीयपटले—सिंहं व्याघ्रं नरञ्चापि स्वगात्ररुधिरं तथा। मद्यञ्चापि ददद् विप्रो ब्राह्मण्यादेव हीयते ॥ इति।

1. ङ-पुस्तके 'श्री' नास्ति। 2. 'यच्चाक्षरं' ख-ग। 3. 'अचक्षुषो महादेव' ख-ग। 4. 'ध्यानञ्च' ङ। 5. '-मये' ङ। 6. 'वक्त्रादि-' क। 7. 'प्राणेश' घ-ङ। 8. 'काली' ख-ग। 9. ख-ग-पुस्तकयोः 'श्री' नास्ति क। 10. 'भावस्थो यो' क-घ-ङ।

बलिदानं [1]प्रकर्त्तव्यं न मांसं भक्षयेन्नरः ।
सम्यक् फलं न लभते दशांशं [2]लभते प्रिये ॥ ११ ॥
महिषादि प्रदातव्यं दिव्यवीरमते स्थितः ।
स एव सिद्धिमाप्नोति फलं सम्यक् प्रियंवदे ॥ १२ ॥
पशुदानं विना [3]देवि पूजयेन्न कदाचन ।
तथा च नित्यपूजायां यदि शक्तो भवेन्नरः ॥ १३ ॥
केवलं बलिदानेन सिद्धो भवति नान्यथा ।
[4]निर्धनः परमेशानि यदि पूजादिकञ्चरेत् ॥ १४ ॥
वत्सरान्ते प्रदातव्यं बलिमेकं सुरेश्वरि ।
अन्यथा नैव सिद्धिः स्यादाजन्म पूजनादपि[5] ॥ १५ ॥
बलिदानं महायज्ञं कलिकाले [6]च चण्डिके ।
अश्वमेधादिकं यज्ञं कलौ नास्ति [7]सुरेश्वरि ॥ १६ ॥

---

१३ । पशुदानमित्यादि । अत्र संवादि प्रमाणमुक्तं कालीतन्त्रे एकादशपटले—न ददाति बलिं यस्तु शिवायै शिवतास्तये । स पापिष्ठो नाधिकारी कुलदेव्याः समर्च्चने ॥ इति । तथा च निबन्धे तृतीयपटले—बलिदानं विना यस्तु पूजयेत् तारिणीं नरः । न ज्ञानं न च मोक्षः स्यात् तेषां पशुधियां प्रिये ॥ इति । अत्र तारिणीत्युपलक्षणम्, यथा काली तथा च्छिन्ना यथा च्छिन्ना तथोन्मुखी । यथा दुर्गा तथा धूमा तथा महिषमर्द्दिनी ॥ यथा काली तथा तारा सर्वास्ताराविभेदकाः । इति तस्यैव वचनात् । महानील-तन्त्रीयषष्ठपटलस्य "सुन्दरी च तथा च्छिन्ना कालीतारादिकाश्च याः । महाविद्याश्च याश्चान्याः सर्वास्तारावदाचरेत् ॥ इति वचनाच्च ।

१६ । बलिदानमित्यादि । तत्र च स्त्रीपशुदाननिषेध उक्तो महानिर्वाणतन्त्रीयषष्ठोल्लासे—बलिदानविधौ देवि विहितः पुरुषः पशुः । स्त्रीपशुर्न च हन्तव्यस्तत्र शाम्भवशासनात् ॥ इति । अन्यत्रापि---शक्तिमांसं न गृह्णीयाद्ण्डजं जलजं विनेति हरतत्त्वदीधितिः ।

---

1. 'प्रवक्तव्यं' ख-ग । 2. 'लभ्यते' क-घ-ङ । 3 'देवीं' ह । 4. 'विधिना' ह । 5. 'दाजन्मावधि पूजनात्' ख-ग । 6. 'तु' ख-ग । 7. 'महेश्वरि' ख-ग ।

केवलं बलिदानेन [1]चाश्वमेधफलं भवेत् ।
यज्ञावशेषं यद् द्रव्यं भोजनीयं न चान्यथा ॥ १७ ॥
यज्ञावशेषभोगेन स [2]यज्ञी नात्र संशयः ।
[3]न भक्षेद् यदि मोहेन न यज्ञफलभाग् भवेत् ॥ १८ ॥
[4]त्याज्यं द्रव्यं कथं देवि [5]महादेव्यै निवेदयेत् ।
ब्रह्मरूपं [6]महातन्त्रं मम वक्त्राद्विनिर्गतम् ॥ १९ ॥
स पूतः सर्व्वपापेभ्यो यदि चैकाक्षरं श्रुतम् ।
महाभक्तियुतो भूत्वा शृणोति [7]पटलं यदि ॥ २० ॥
किं तस्य ध्यानपूजायां तीर्थस्नानेन तस्य किम् ।
शब्दब्रह्ममयं ज्ञात्वा समस्तं यदि चण्डिके ॥ २१ ॥
केवलं श्रवणेनैव [8]स सिद्धो नात्र संशयः ।
[9]अष्टादशपुराणानां[10] श्रवणेनैव यत् फलम् ॥ २२ ॥
चतुर्व्वेदेन [11]साङ्गेन [12]श्रवणेनैव यत् फलम् ।
[13]अस्य तन्त्रस्य देवेशि कलां नार्हन्ति षोडशीम् ॥ २३ ॥
ब्रह्मरूपमिदं तन्त्रं सारात् सारं परात् परम् ॥ २४ ॥

इति श्रीमातृकाभेदतन्त्रे[14] हरगौरीसंवादे दशमः पटलः ॥ १० ॥

१७। केवलमित्यादि। एवमपि निबन्धे पञ्चमपटले—सर्वत्रिकोटितीर्थेषु स्नात्वा यत् फलमश्नुते। तत् फलं लभते भक्त्या बलिभिः पूजनान्मम ॥ इति। वृहन्नीलतन्त्रे षष्ठपटलेऽपि—भूतहिंसा न कर्त्तव्या पशुहिंसा विशेषतः। बलिदानं विना देव्या हिंसां सर्वत्र वर्जयेत् ॥ इति ॥

---

1. 'अश्वमेध-' ख-ग। 2. 'यज्ञो' ख-ग। 3 'भक्षयेद्' घ। 4 'त्यज्यं' ख-ग। 5. 'यतो देव्यै' ख-ग। 6. 'महामन्त्रं' क। 7. 'पठनं' ख-ग। 8. 'यत् फलं लभते नरः' घ। 9. 'घ-पुस्तके पद्यार्द्धमिदं नास्ति'। 10. 'पुराणानि' क-ङ। 11. 'चाङ्गेन' ख-ग। 12. 'श्रवणे यत् फलं लभेत्' ख-ग। 13. 'तस्य तन्त्रस्य' क, 'अस्य मन्त्रस्य' ख-ग। 14. 'नास्ति' घ।

एकादशः पटलः

श्रीचण्डिकोवाच—

[1]प्रासादं मण्डपं वापि यदि देव्यै निवेदयेत् ।
विधानं [2]तस्य माहात्म्यं [3]वद मे परमेश्वर ॥ १ ॥
[4]कूपादिकं महादेव यदि देव्यै निवेदयेत् ।
विधानं तस्य माहात्म्यं वद मे परमेश्वर ॥ २ ॥

श्रीशङ्कर उवाच—

शृणु देवि प्रवक्ष्यामि येन प्रासादमुत्सृजेत् ।
तस्यैव पश्चिमे भागे [5]वेदिकां चतुरस्रकाम् ॥ ३ ॥
प्रकुर्य्याद् बहुयत्नेन वस्त्रेण वेष्टनञ्चरेत् ।
[6]तदभावे महेशानि [7]तृणेनैव च वेष्टयेत् ॥ ४ ॥
[8]कुम्भयुग्मं स्थापयित्वा क्षौमवस्त्रेण वेष्टयेत् ।
[9]युग्मं युग्मं क्षौमवस्त्रं कुम्भयुग्मे [10]नियोजयेत् ॥ ५ ॥
[11]ईशकुम्भे यजेद्देवीमाग्नेय्यामग्निदैवतम् ।
चतुःषष्ट्युपचारेण पूजयेदिष्टदेवताम् ॥ ६ ॥

---

६ । शक्तिविषये चतुःषष्टिरुपचारा यथा तन्त्रसारधृतयामले—आसनारोपणम् (१) सुगन्धितैलाभ्यङ्गः (२) मज्जनशालाप्रवेशनम् (३) मज्जनमणिपीठोपवेशनम् (४)

---

1 'प्रसादं' क, 'प्रासादमण्डलं' ख-ग । 2. 'चैव' क । 3 'श्रोतुमिच्छामि तत्त्वतः' क । 4 ख-ग-घ-ङ-पुस्तकेषु श्लोकोऽयं नास्ति । 5. 'वैदिकीं चतुरस्रिकां' ख-ग, 'वेदिकाचतुरस्रकम्' घ । 6. ख-ग-पुस्तकयोः पद्यार्द्धमिदं नास्ति । 7 'तृणेन वेष्टयेत् सुधीः' घ-ङ । 8. 'कुम्भयुग्मे क्षौमवस्त्रं रक्तपुष्पं निवेदयेत्' ख-ग । 9. ख-ग-पुस्तकयोः श्लोकार्द्धमिदं नास्ति । 10 'निवेदयेत्' घ । 11. 'ईशानकुम्भे' ख-ग ।

अभावे पूजयेद् देवीं तदर्द्धेन प्रयत्नतः ।
अथवा परमेशानि यथाशक्त्युपचारतः ॥ ७ ॥
पूजयेद् बहुयत्नेन ततो होमादिकञ्चरेत् ।
[1]आगमोक्तेन विधिना कुर्य्यात् तत्र कुशण्डिकाम् ॥ ८ ॥
त्रिमध्वक्तेन[2] देवेशि विल्वपत्रेण होमयेत् ।
सहस्रं होमयेन्मन्त्री [3]शतन्यूनं न कारयेत् ॥ ९ ॥

दिव्यस्नानीयम् (५) उद्वर्त्तनम् (६) उष्णोदकस्नानम् (७) कनककलसस्थित-सकलतीर्थाभिषेकः (८) धौतवस्त्रपरिमार्जनम् (९) अरुणदुकूलपरिधानम् (१०) अरुणदुकूलोत्तरीयम् (११) आलेपमण्डपप्रवेशनम् (१२) आलेपमणिपीठोपवेशनम् (१३) चन्दनागुरुकुङ्कुमकर्पूरकस्तूरीरोचनादिव्यगन्धसर्वाङ्गानुलेपनम् (१४) केशभारस्य कालागुरुधूप-मल्लिकामालतीजातीचम्पकाशोकशतपत्रपूगकुहरीपुन्नागकह्लार-यूथीसर्वर्तुकुसुम-मालाभूषणम् (१५) भूषणमण्डपप्रवेशनम् । (१६) भूषणमणिपीठोपवेशनम् (१७) नवमणिमुकुटम् (१८) चन्द्रशकलम् (१९) सीमन्तसिन्दूरम् (२०) तिलकरत्नम् (२१) कालाञ्जनम् (२२) कर्णपालीयुगलम् (२३) नासाभरणम् (२४) अधरयावकः (२५) ग्रथनभूषणम् (२६) कनकचित्रपदकम् (२७) महापदकम् (२८) मुक्तावलिः (२९) एकावलिः (३०) देवच्छन्दकः (३१) केयूरयुगलचतुष्कम् (३२) वलयावलिः (३३) ऊर्म्मिकावलिः (३४) काञ्चीदाम (३५) कटिसूत्रम् (३६) शोभाख्याभरणम् (३७) पादकटकम् (३८) रत्ननूपुरम् (३९) पादाङ्गुरीयकम् (४०) एककरे पाशः (४१) अन्यकरेऽङ्कुशम् (४२) इतरकरे पुण्ड्रेक्षुचापः (४३) अपरकरे पुष्पवासाः (४४) श्रीमन्माणिक्यपादुका (४५) स्वसमानवेशाभ्यावरणदेवताभिः सह सिंहासनारोहणम् (४६) कामेश्वरपर्य्यङ्कोपवेशनम् (४७) अमृताशनचषकम् (४८) आचमनीयम् (४९) कर्पूरवटिका (५०) आनन्दोल्लासविलासहासम (५१) मङ्गलारात्रिकम् (५२) श्वेतच्छत्रम (५३) चामरयुगलम् (५४) दर्पणम् (५५) तालवृन्तम् (५६) गन्धः (५७) पुष्पम् (५८) धूपः (५९) दीपः (६०) नैवेद्यम् (६१) पुनराचमनीयम् (६२) ताम्बूलम् (६३) वन्दनम् (६४) इति ।

---

1. 'आगमोक्तविधानेन' ख-ग । 2. 'त्रिमध्वोक्तेन' क । 3. 'शतान्यूनं' क ।

[1]पूर्णाहुतिं ततो दत्त्वा ततो वाक्यं समाचरेत् ।
अद्येत्यादि समुच्चार्य्य सौरमासं समुच्चरेत् ॥ १० ॥
तिथिगोत्रं चामुकोऽहं धर्म्मार्थकाममेव वा[2] ।
प्राप्तये परमेशानि ततो मूलं समुच्चरेत् ॥ ११ ॥
देवतायै नमः पश्चाद् दक्षिणां दापयेद् गुरौ ।
कुम्भतोयेन देवेशि स्नापयेद् यजमानकम् ॥ १२ ॥
[3]सुरास्त्वादीन् समुच्चार्य्य शान्तिं कुर्य्यात् ततो गुरुः ।
सर्व्वादौ गुरुदेवस्य वरणं कारयेत् [4]सुधीः ॥ १३ ॥
[5]सुवर्णं चम्पकाकारं कर्णयुग्मे निवेदयेत् ।
चतुष्कोणयुतं स्वर्णं ग्रीवायां [6]परियोजयेत् ॥ १४ ॥
उष्णीषञ्च ततो दद्यात् [7]कण्ठे मालां [8]नियोजयेत् ।
ताडयुग्मं ततो बाहौ वलयं मणिबन्धके ॥ १५ ॥
अङ्गुल्यामङ्गुरी[9] देया दिव्यवस्त्रं [10]नियोजयेत् ।
एवं हि वरणं कृत्वा कर्म्मयोग्यं विचिन्तयेत् ॥ १६ ॥
गुरुं वा गुरुपुत्रं वा वरयेद् यत्नतः सुधीः ।
सदस्यं [11]न हि कर्त्तव्यं तन्त्रधारं [12]न तत्र वै ॥ १७ ॥
[13]ब्रह्माणं न हि कर्त्तव्यं केवलं वरयेद् गुरुम् ।
[14]गुरोर्भृत्यो महेशानि भैरवो नात्र संशयः ॥ १८ ॥

1. पद्यार्द्धमिदं ख-ग-पुस्तकयोर्नास्ति । 2. 'च' ख-ग-घ-ङ । 3. 'शान्त्यादीन् स' ख-ग । 4 'बुधः' ख-ग । 5. 'सुवर्णचम्पकाकारं' ख-ग । 6. 'परिधापयेत्' ख-ग । 7. 'कण्ठमालां' ङ । 8. 'निधापयेत्' ख-ग । 9. 'मङ्गुलीं देयं' ङ । 10. 'निवेदयेत्' ख-ग । 11. 'च प्रकर्त्तव्यं' ख-ग-ङ । 12. 'च तत्र वै' ख-ग-ङ । 13. ङ-पुस्तके पद्यार्द्धमिदं नास्ति । 14. 'गुरुभृत्यो' ख-ग-ङ ।

९

स्वीयेन[1] परिधानेन वाससा तोषयेत् [2]स्वयम् ।
स्वयं होता भवेद् विप्रो गुरोराज्ञानुसारतः ॥ १६ ॥
मायाबीजं समुच्चार्य्य आधारशक्तये नमः ।
अनेन मनुना देवि [3]वेदिसंस्कारमाचरेत् ॥ २० ॥
[4]भूरसीत्यादिमन्त्रेण घट[5]-युग्माभिमन्त्रितम् ।
अस्त्रान्तेनैव मूलेन उष्णीषं परियोजयेत्[6] ॥ २१ ॥
[7]वेदोक्तञ्चैव स्मृत्युक्तं [8]मन्त्रं न योजयेत् सुधीः ।
एवं [9]कूपादिदानेषु कर्त्तव्यं परमेश्वरि ॥ २२ ॥
अन्यत् सर्वं समानं हि प्रासादादिस्थले पुनः ।
कूपादियोजनं कुर्य्यात् [10]यष्टिप्रोतनमाचरेत् ॥ २३ ॥
[11]चतुर्हस्तप्रमाणञ्च मध्यभागे[12] तु प्रोतनम् ।
मूलमन्त्रं समुच्चार्य्य ततो वह्निवधूं न्यसेत् ॥ २४ ॥
ततो यष्टिं समुच्चार्य्य [13]पोतयामि वदेत् सुधीः ।
तत्र सन्तरणं धेनुं नैव कुर्य्याद्विचक्षणः ॥ २५ ॥
धेनुसन्तरणेनैव फलहानिः प्रजायते ।
[14]स्वर्णं रूप्यं प्रवालञ्च दक्षिणां परियोजयेत् ॥ २६ ॥
स्नापयित्वा कुम्भतोयैः शान्तिं कुर्य्यात् ततो गुरुः ॥२७॥

---

२१ । भूरसीत्यादि । मन्त्रस्तु—ओँ भूरसि भूमिरस्यदितिरसि विश्वधाया विश्वस्य भुवनस्य धर्त्री । पृथिवीं यच्छ पृथिवीं दृꣳह, पृथिवीं मा हिꣳसीः । शुक्लयजुर्व्वेद, १३।१८

---

1. 'स्वांयेन' क । 2. 'गुरुम्' ख-ग । 3 'देव्याः सं-' ख-ग । 4. 'भूरस्येत्यादि-' क-घ, 'भुवस्त्वेत्यादि-' ख-ग । 5 'युग्मेऽभिऽ-' ख-ग । 6. '-योजनं' क । 7. 'वेदोक्तं नैव' ख-ग । 8. 'न मन्त्रं' ख-ग, 'मन्त्रं नानायजेत्' घ । 9. 'धूपादि' घ । 10. 'यष्टिकाष्ठविनिर्म्मितम्' ख-ग । 11. 'एवं यष्टि प्रकर्त्तव्यं' क, 'एकयष्टिप्रकर्त्तव्यं' घ-ङ । 12. 'भागेन पोतनम्' ख-ग, '-भागे तु पोतनम्' ङ । 13. 'प्रोत-' क-ख-ग-घ । 14. 'स्वर्णरौप्यं' ख-ग-ङ ।

[1]अनेनैव विधानेन कूपाद्युत्सर्गमाचरेत् ।
[2]वापीकूपतडागादि ह्यनेनोत्सर्गमाचरेत् ॥ २८ ॥
दीर्घिकाञ्च पुष्करिणीं [3]ह्यनेनैव जलाशयम् ।
[4]उत्सृज्य परया भक्त्या महादेव्यै [5]प्रयत्नतः ॥ २९ ॥
पुरुषं सप्तमं कान्ते पितृवंशे च मातरि ।
सप्तमं पुरुषं [6]कान्ते मातृवंशे समं प्रिये ॥ ३० ॥
कैलासे निवसेन्नित्यं देव्या वरप्रसादतः ।
स्वयं देवस्वरूपश्च[7] जीवन्मुक्तो न संशयः ॥ ३१ ॥
अश्वमेधसहस्रेण[8] वाजपेयशतेन[9] च ।
यत् फलं लभते देवि तस्माल्लक्षगुणं भवेत् ॥ ३२ ॥
मेरुतुल्यं[10]सुवर्णन्तु[11] ब्राह्मणे वेदपारगे ।
[12]दत्त्वा यत् फलमाप्नोति [13]तस्माल्लक्षगुणं भवेत् ॥३३॥
[14]पूर्णशस्येन देवेशि सप्तद्वीपां वसुन्धराम् ।
प्रदद्याद् बहुयत्नेन ब्राह्मणे वेदपारगे ॥
[15]तस्माल्लक्षगुणं पुण्यमनेन परमेश्वरि ॥ ३४ ॥
[16]सदक्षिणं व्रतं सर्व्वं दानं यद्वेदसम्मतम् ।
तस्माल्लक्षगुणं पुण्यमनेन परमेश्वरि ॥ ३५ ॥

[17]श्रीचण्डिकोवाच—

यज्ञसूत्रधारणेन[18] भूपूज्यो नात्र संशयः ।
इदानीं यज्ञसूत्रस्य विधानं मयि कथ्यताम् ॥ ३६ ॥

---

1. 'अनेन विधिना देवि' घ । 2. ङ-पुस्तके श्लोकार्द्धमिदं नास्ति । 3 'मूलेनैव' घ । 4. 'उदकं' ख-ग । 5. 'निवेदयेत्' ख-ग । 6. 'काण्डे' ख-ग, 'कान्तारं सेतुसमं प्रिये' घ । 7. '-श्च' क । 8. '-सहस्राणि' ङ । 9. '-शतानि' ङ । 10. '-तुल्य-' क-घ-ङ । 11. 'सुवर्णञ्च' घ-ङ । 12. 'दाने' घ । 13. 'तस्य कोटि-' ख-ग । 14. 'पूर्णमासेन' ङ । 15. 'तस्य कोटि-' ख-ग । 16. पद्यमिदं क-ख-ग-पुस्तकेषु नास्ति । 17. 'पार्वत्युवाच' ख-ग । 18. 'धारणे तु' ख-ग ।

[1]श्रीशङ्कर उवाच—

यज्ञसूत्रस्य यन्मानं तच्छृणुष्व वरानने ।
ऋग्वेदी धारयेत्[2] सूत्रं नाभेरूर्द्ध्वं स्तनादधः ॥ ३७ ॥
यजुषां सूत्रमानं [3]हि आश्चर्य्यं शैलजे परम् ।
[4]बाहुमूलप्रमाणेन यज्ञसूत्रं द्विजातिभिः ।
धारणीयं प्रयत्नेन [5]नान्यद् दैर्घ्यं कदाचन ॥ ३८ ॥
सामगस्य [6]यज्ञसूत्रं त्रिविधं [7]वरवर्णिनि ।
ब्रह्मरन्ध्रान्नाभिदेशपर्य्यन्तं यज्ञसूत्रकम् ॥ ३९ ॥
[8]अथवापि च ग्रीवायामारोप्य नाभिं संस्पृशेत् ।
तस्मात् [9]पृष्ठान्मेरुदण्डपर्य्यन्तं यज्ञसूत्रकम् ॥ ४० ॥
[10]अथवा परमेशानि प्रकारान्तरकं शृणु ।
ग्रीवाया दक्षिणाङ्गुष्ठपर्य्यन्तं [11]यज्ञसूत्रकम् ॥ ४१ ॥
[12]अथवा धारयेत् सूत्रं यत्नेन यजुषां मतम् ।
अथवा[13] धारयेत् सूत्रं सामगस्य प्रमाणतः ॥ ४२ ॥

---

३७ । यज्ञसूत्रस्येति । यज्ञसूत्रं कस्य किंनिर्म्मितं स्यादित्यपेक्षायामुक्तं महानीलतन्त्रे एकत्रिंशपटले,—कार्पासन्तु द्विजातीनां क्षौमञ्च भूभुजां तथा । वैश्यानां शणसूत्रञ्च शङ्करस्य मतेन च ॥ इति ।

---

1. 'शिव' क-घ । 2. '-न्नित्यं' ङ । 3. 'परमाश्चर्य्यं हि शैलजे' ग ; 'हि परमाश्चर्य्यंशैलजे' घ; 'तु परमाश्चर्य्यं शैलजे' ख-ङ । 4. 'बाहुमूलं' क । 5. 'नान्यद्रूपं' ख-ग, 'नान्यद्रूप' घ ; 'नान्यरूपं' ङ । 6. 'दीर्घसूत्रं' घ-ह ०त० । 7. 'परमेश्वरि' ख-ग-ङ । 8. 'श्लोकोऽयं नास्ति' ह०त० । 9. 'पृष्ठे मेरुदण्ड-' ख-ग-घ-ङ । 10 'अथवे'त्यादि 'यजुषां मत'मित्यन्तो भागः ख-ग-घ-पुस्तकेषु नास्ति । 11. 'परमेश्वरि' ङ । 12. पद्यार्द्धमिदं ङ-पुस्तके नास्ति । 13. 'अथर्वी' ख-ग-ङ ।

[1]अथर्वा धारयेद् यज्ञसूत्रं परममोहनम्।
आज्ञाचक्रान्नाभिदेशपर्य्यन्तं यज्ञसूत्रकम्॥ ४३ ॥
एतत् सङ्केतमज्ञात्वा यः कुर्य्यात् सूत्रधारणम्।
स चण्डालसमो देवि यदि व्याससमो भवेत्॥ ४४ ॥

इति श्रीमातृकाभेदतन्त्रे हरगौरीसंवादे एकादशः पटलः ॥ ११ ॥

---

1. 'अथवा' ख-ग-घ-ङ।

द्वादशः पटलः

श्रीशङ्कर उवाच—

अथातः संप्रवक्ष्यामि पूजाधारं सुदुर्लभम् ।
शालग्रामे मणौ यन्त्रे प्रतिमायां [1]घटे जले ॥ १ ॥
पुस्तिकायाञ्च गङ्गायां शिवलिङ्गे प्रसूनके ।
शालग्रामे शतगुणं मणौ तद्वत् फलं लभेत्[2] ॥ २ ॥
यन्त्रे लक्षगुणं [3]पुण्यं मूर्त्तौ लक्षं सुलोचने ।
[4]घटे चैकगुणं [5]पुण्यं जले चैकगुणं प्रिये ॥ ३ ॥
पुस्तिकायां सहस्रन्तु गङ्गायां ततसमं फलम् ।
शिवलिङ्गे ह्यनन्तं हि विना पार्थिवलिङ्गके[6] ॥ ४ ॥

१। अथात इत्यादि। अत्र संवादि गुप्तसाधनतन्त्राष्टमपटलवचनमुल्लिख्यते—अथातः संप्रवक्ष्यामि पूजाधारन्तु सिद्धिदम् । यं विना परमेशानि न हि सिद्धिः प्रजायते ॥ शालग्रामे मणौ यन्त्रे प्रतिमायां सुरेश्वरि । पुस्तिकायाञ्च गङ्गायां सामान्येन जले तथा ॥ अथवा पुष्पयन्त्रेण पूजयेच्छिवलिङ्गके । यन्त्रभेदेन देवेशि फलं सम्यक् प्रजायते ॥ शालग्रामे शतगुणं मणौ तद्वत् फलं लभेत् । यन्त्रे लक्षगुणं प्रोक्तं प्रतिमायां तथैव च ॥ पुस्तिकायाञ्च गङ्गायां समानफलमीरितम् ॥ इति ।

४। शिवलिङ्ग इत्यादि। अत्रापि गुप्तसाधनप्रमाणम्—शिवलिङ्गे महेशानि अनन्तफलमीरितम् । न कुर्य्यात् पार्थिवे लिङ्गे देवीपूजादिकाः क्रियाः ॥ पार्थिवे पूजनाद् देवि सिद्धिहानिः प्रजायते । यदि दैवान्महेशानि मृत्तिकास्खलनं भवेत् ॥ तावद् वर्ष-सहस्राणि नरके पूयशोणिते । कुम्भीपाके महाघोरे पच्यते पितृभिः सह ॥ अत एव महेशानि पार्थिवे न हि पूजयेत् । स्फटिकादीन् समानीय लिङ्गं निर्म्माय यत्नतः ॥ तल्लिङ्गे पूजनाद् देवि सर्व्वसिद्धियुतो भवेत् ॥ इति । एवमपि पार्थिवे देवताविशेष-

---

1. 'जले घटे' ख-ग। 2. 'भवेत्' ङ। 3. 'प्रोक्तं' ख-ग-ङ। 4. 'जले चैकगुणं पुण्यं घटे' ङ। 5. 'प्रोक्तं' ख-ग। 6. '-लिङ्गकम्' प्रा०ह०स०।

पुष्पयन्त्रे महेशानि पूजनात् सर्व्वसिद्धिभाक् ।
शालग्रामे च पूजायां न लिखेद् यन्त्रमुत्तमम् ॥ ५ ॥
[1]मणौ स्थिते महेशानि न लिखेद् यन्त्रमुत्तमम् ।
प्रतिमायाश्च पूजायां न लिखेद् यन्त्रमुत्तमम् ॥ ६ ॥
प्रतिमायाश्च[2] पुरतो घटं [3]संस्थाप्य यत्नतः ।
परिवारान् यजेत् तत्र घटे तु परमेश्वरि ॥ ७ ॥
[4]यन्त्राधिष्ठातृदेवांश्च [5]घटे यन्त्रे प्रपूजयेत् ।
समस्तदेवतारूपं [6]घटन्तु परिचिन्तयेत् ।
[7]सुरद्रुमस्वरूपोऽयं[8] घटो[9] हि परमेश्वरि ॥ ८ ॥
[10]जन्मस्थानं महायन्त्रं यदि [11]कुर्य्यात् तु साधकः ।
[12]तत्र मूर्त्तिं न [13]कुर्य्यात् तु [14]कदाचिदपि मोहतः ॥९॥
[15]यदि मूर्त्तिं प्रकुर्य्यात् तु तत्र यन्त्रं न कारयेत् ।
यदि कुर्य्यात् तु मोहेन यजेद् वारद्वयं प्रिये ॥ १० ॥
द्विगुणं पूजनं तत्र द्विगुणं बलिदानकम् ।
द्विगुणं प्रजपेन्मन्त्रं द्विगुणं [16]होमयेत् सुधीः ॥ ११ ॥

पूजने फलविशेषमुक्तं तन्त्रान्तरतन्त्रे—कालिकां तारिणीञ्चैव त्रिपुरां भुवनेश्वरीम् । योऽर्च्चयेत् पार्थिवे लिङ्गे स याति परमां गतिम् ॥ तारिण्याः कालिकायाश्च सुन्दर्याः परमेश्वरि । पार्थिवे पूजनाद् देवि चतुर्वर्गफलं लभेत् ॥ इति । अत्र च सामान्यविशेषन्यायेन विधिनिषेधयोरविरोधं प्रमाणयन्तोऽनूचाना वंशपरम्परया तथैव व्यवहरन्तीति ।

---

1. पद्यार्द्धमिदं ख-ग-ङ-पुस्तकेषु नास्ति । 2. '-ञ्च' क । 3. 'स्थाप्य प्रयत्नतः' ख-ग । 4. 'मन्त्राधिष्ठितदेवांश्च घटवक्त्रे च' ख-ग ; 'यन्त्राधिष्ठितदेवानां' ङ । 5. 'घटवक्त्रे' ख-ग-घ-प्रा०, इ०त० 'घटे वक्त्रे' ङ । 6. 'घटञ्च' ख-ग-घ-ङ-प्रा० । 7. 'मूलद्रुम-' ङ । 8. '-स्वरूपो हि' प्रा० । 9. 'घटोऽयं' क-घ-ङ-प्रा० । 10. 'महायन्त्रन्तु देवेशि' ख-ग । 11. 'कुर्य्याच्च' ख-ग । 12. पद्यार्द्धमिदं घ-पुस्तके नास्ति । 13. 'कुर्य्याच्च' ख-ग । 14. 'यदि यन्त्रञ्च कारयेत्' प्रा० । 15. 'यत्र मूर्त्तिः कृता देवि' घ, इदमर्द्धं नास्ति प्रा० । 16. 'होममाचरेत्' घ-प्रा० ।

अन्यथा विफला पूजा विफलं बलिदानकम् ।
सर्व्वं हि विफलं यस्मात् तस्माद् यन्त्रं न कारयेत् ॥१२॥
इति ते कथितं कान्ते पूजाधारं सुदुर्लभम्[1] ॥ १३ ॥
अथातः संप्रवक्ष्यामि शिवलिङ्गस्य लक्षणम् ।
पार्थिवे शिवपूजायां सर्व्वसिद्धियुतो भवेत् ॥ १४ ॥

---

१२ । अन्यथेत्यादि । यस्तु संस्थाप्य पूजयेत् तञ्च यन्त्रराजं घटोपरि । देव्यग्रे च घटं दिव्यं सुदृढं लक्षणान्वितम् ॥ तत्र यन्त्रं समारोप्य पूजयेद् विभवावधि ॥ इति शाम्भवीतन्त्रीयचतुर्दशपटलवचनं, तदन्नपूर्णापूजापरं प्रकरणबलात् द्विगुणपूजाभिप्रायेण वेत्यविरोधः ।

१४ । अथात इत्यादि । आधारभेदेन शिवपूजायाः फलभेदे अन्यत्रोक्तप्रमाणानि । कालोत्तरे—महाभुक्तिप्रदं हैमं राजतं भूतिवर्धनम् । आरकूटं तथा कांस्यं शृणु सामान्यमुक्तिदम् ॥ त्रपुसीसायसं लिङ्गं शत्रूणां नाशने हितम् । कीर्त्तिदं कांस्यजं लिङ्गं राजतं पुष्टिवर्धनम् ॥ पैत्तलं भुक्तिमुक्त्यर्थं मिश्रजं सर्वसिद्धिदम् ॥ इति । शिवनारदसंवादे—पितॄणां मुक्तये लिङ्गं पूज्यं रजतसम्भवम् । हैमजं सत्यलोकस्य प्राप्तये पूजयेत् पुमान् ॥ पूजयेत् ताम्रजं लिङ्गं पुष्टिकामो हि मानवः । (ताम्रादिलिङ्गन्तु कलीतरपरम्) । तथाच मत्स्यसूक्ते—ताम्रलिङ्गं कलौ नार्च्चेद् रैत्यस्य सीसकस्य च । रक्तचन्दनलिङ्गञ्च शङ्खकांस्यायसं तथा ॥ तुष्टिकामस्तु सततं लिङ्गं पित्तलसम्भवम् । कीर्त्तिकामो यजेन्नित्यं लिङ्गं कांस्यसमुद्भवम् ॥ शत्रुमारणकामस्तु लिङ्गं लौहमयं सदा । सदा सीसमयं लिङ्गमायुष्कामोऽर्च्चयेन्नरः ॥ लक्षणसमुच्चयेऽपि—स्थिरलक्ष्मीप्रदं हैमं राजतं चैव राज्यदम् । प्रजावृद्धिकरं राङ्गं ताम्रमायुःप्रवर्द्धनम् ॥ विद्वेषकारकं कांस्यं रीतिजं शत्रुनाशनम् । रोगघ्नं सैसकं लिङ्गमायसं शत्रुनाशनम् ॥ अष्टलौहमयं लिङ्गं कुष्ठरोगक्षयावहम् । त्रिलौहसम्भवं लिङ्गं विज्ञानं प्रति सिद्धिदम् ॥ लिङ्गपुराणे—श्रीप्रदं वज्रजं लिङ्गं शिलाजं सर्वसिद्धिदम् । धातुजं धनदं साक्षाद् दारुजं भोगसिद्धिदम् ॥ कालोत्तरे—गन्धपुष्पमयं लिङ्गं तथान्यादिविनिर्म्मितम् । कस्तूरीसम्भवं लिङ्गं धनाकाङ्क्षी प्रपूजयेत् ॥ लिङ्गं गोरोचनोत्थञ्च रूपकामस्तु पूजयेत् । कान्तिकामस्तु सततं लिङ्गं कुङ्कुमसम्भवम् ॥ श्वेतागुरुसमुद्भूतं महाबुद्धिविवर्द्धनम् । धारणाशक्तिदं लिङ्गं कृष्णागुरुसमुद्भवम् ॥ इति । गरुडपुराणे च—कस्तूरिकाया द्वौ भागौ चत्वार-

---

1. अतःपरं ख-ग-पुस्तकयोः 'इति श्रीमातृकाभेदतन्त्रे श्रीदुर्गाशिवसंवादे द्वादशः पटल' इत्यधिकः । पाठः' ।

पाषाणे शिवपूजायां द्विगुणं फलमीरितम् ।
स्वर्णलिङ्गे च पूजायां शत्रूणां नाशनं मतम् ॥ १५ ॥
सर्व्वसिद्धीश्वरो रौप्ये फलं [1]तस्माच्चतुर्गुणम् ।
ताम्रे पुष्टिं विजानीयात् कांस्ये च धन[2]सञ्चयम् ॥ १६ ॥
पारदस्य च माहात्म्यं पुरैव कथितं मया ।
गङ्गायाश्च लक्षगुणं लाक्षायां रोगवान् भवेत् ॥ १७ ॥
स्फाटिके सर्व्वसिद्धिः स्यात् तथा [3]मारकते प्रिये ।
लौहलिङ्गे [4]रिपोर्नाशं कामदं भस्मलिङ्गके[5] ॥ १८ ॥
वालुकायां काम्यसिद्धिर्गोमये रिपुहिंसनम् ।
[6]सर्व्वलिङ्गस्य माहात्म्यं [7]धर्म्मार्थकाममोक्षदम् ॥ १९ ॥
आधारभेदे यत् पुण्यं चाधिकं कथितं तु ते ।
अतिरिक्तफलान्येतदाधारस्य सुलोचने ॥ २० ॥
शिवस्य पूजनाद् देवि चतुर्वर्गाधिपो भवेत् ।
[8]अष्टैश्वर्य्ययुतो मर्त्त्यः शम्भुनाथस्य पूजनात् ॥ २१ ॥

श्चन्दनस्य च । कुङ्कुमस्य त्रयश्चैव शशिनश्च चतुःसमम् ॥ एतद् वै गन्धलिङ्गन्तु कृत्वा संपूज्य भक्तितः । शिवसायुज्यमाप्नोति बन्धुभिः सहितो नरः ॥ इति । पद्मपुराणे च—पारदञ्च महाभूत्यै सौभाग्याय च मौक्तिकम् । चान्द्रकान्तं मृत्युजित् स्याद्धाटकं सर्व-कामदम् ॥ इति । मत्स्यसूक्ते च—विशेषाच्छैलजं मुक्त्यै भुक्तये चानुसङ्गतः । पार्थिवं भुक्तये शस्तं मुक्तये चानुसङ्गतः ॥ एवं वै दारुजं ज्ञेयं विहलिङ्गं तथा पुनः । स्थिरलक्ष्मी-प्रदं ज्ञेयं हैमं राज्यप्रदञ्च तत् ॥ पुत्रवृद्धिकरं ताम्रं राङ्गमायुःप्रवर्द्धनम् ॥ इति ।

---

1. 'तस्याश्चतुर्गुणम्' क-ङ । 2. '-संक्षयः' श०, '-सञ्चयः' प्रा० । 3. 'मरकते' क-ङ-श० । 4. 'रिपुनाशं' ख-ग, 'रिपोर्नाशः' प्रा० । 5. '-लिङ्गकम्' श०-प्रा० । 6. 'स्वर्ण-' ख-ग-प्रा० । 7. 'सर्वार्थ-' ख-ग, 'धर्मकामार्थ-' प्रा० । 8. 'सर्व्वैश्वर्य्य-' ङ ।

१०

स्त्रयं नारायणः प्रोक्तो [1]यदि शम्भुं प्रपूजयेत् ।
[2]स्वर्गे मर्त्ये च पाताले ये देवाः संस्थिताः सदा ।
तेषां पूजा भवेद् देवि शम्भुनाथस्य पूजनात् ॥ २२ ॥
स्वर्णपुष्पसहस्रेण यत् फलं लभते नरः ।
तस्माल्लक्षगुणं [3]पुण्यं भग्नैकविल्वपत्रके ॥ २३ ॥
भग्नैकविल्वपत्रस्य सहस्रैकेन भागतः ।
मेरुतुल्यसुवर्णेन तत् फलं न हि लभ्यते ॥ २४ ॥
शुद्धाशुद्ध विचारोऽपि नास्ति तच्छिवपूजने ।
येन तेन प्रकारेण विल्वपत्रैः [4]प्रपूजनात् ।
सर्व्वसिद्धियुतो भूत्वा स नरः [5]सिद्ध एव हि ॥ २५ ॥
ब्रह्माण्डमध्ये ये देवास्तद् बाह्ये [6]याश्च देवताः ।
ते सर्व्वे तृप्तिमायान्ति केवलं शिवपूजनात् ॥ २६ ॥

२४। भग्नैकेत्यादि। अत्र संवादि प्रमाणमुक्तं योगिनीतन्त्रे—विल्वपत्रञ्च माघ्यञ्च तमालामलकीदलम्। कह्लारं तुलसीञ्चैव पद्मपुन्नागपुष्पकम्॥ एतत् पर्युषितं न स्याद् यच्चान्यत् कलिकात्मकम्। नीरजस्य च विल्वस्य तुलस्या दलमेव च॥ न दूष्येच्छिन्न-भिन्नञ्च जातिपुष्पञ्च सुन्दरि॥ इति।

२५। येनेत्यादि। अत्र विशेषमाह वरदातन्त्रे चतुर्थपटले—फलशून्यैर्वृन्त-जातैर्विल्वपत्रैर्न चार्च्चयेत्॥ इति। त्रिविक्रमसंहितायामपि—अच्छिन्नमूलं तत् पत्रं यो दद्याच्छङ्करार्च्चने। तस्य पूजा वृथा देवि मृतो नरकमाप्नुयात्॥ इति। लिङ्गार्च्चनतन्त्रे द्वादशपटलेऽपि—विल्वपत्रं महादेवि कीटादिदोषवर्ज्जितम्। कोमलं मधुरं पत्रं पत्त्रत्रययुतं शिवे॥ विल्वपत्रं विना देवि न हि पूजां समाचरेत्॥ इति। एवञ्च मूलग्रन्थेन सह पर्य्यालोचनया विशेषवचनानि फलभूयस्त्वशंसीनीति विज्ञायते।

---

1. 'शम्भुनाथस्य पूजनात्' ङ। 2. ङ-पुस्तके 'स्वर्गे' इत्यादि 'पूजना'दित्यन्ता पादचतुष्टयी नास्ति'। 3. 'प्रोक्तं' ङ। 4. 'प्रपूजयेत्' ख-ग-घ। 5. 'शिव' ख-ग-घ-ङ। 6. 'ये च' क-घ।

पुष्पं गन्धं जलं द्रव्यं लिङ्गोपरि नियोजयेत् ।
लिङ्गमध्ये महावह्निः सैव रुद्रः प्रकीर्त्तितः ॥ २७ ॥
रुद्रोपरि क्षिपेद् [1]यत्तु तदेव भस्मतां गतः ॥ २८ ॥
[2]साक्षाद्धोमो महेशानि शिवस्य पूजनाद् भवेत् ।
महायज्ञेश्वरो मर्त्त्यः शिवस्य पूजनाद् भवेत् ॥ २९ ॥
[3]कुशाग्रमानं यत् तोयं तत्तोयेन यजेद् यदि ।
सत्यं सत्यं हि गिरिजे तज्जलं सागरोपमम् ॥ ३० ॥
पुष्पञ्च मेरुसदृशं लिङ्गोपरि [4]नियोजनात् ।
लिङ्गस्य मस्तके देवि यदन्नं परितिष्ठति ॥ ३१ ॥
तदन्नस्य च दानेन क्षितिदानफलं लभेत् ॥ ३२ ॥
एकेन तण्डुलेनैव यदि लिङ्गं प्रपूजयेत् ।
ब्रह्माण्डपात्रसंपूर्ण-[5]मन्नदानफलं लभेत् ॥ ३३ ॥
[6]एकया दूर्व्वया वापि योऽर्चयेच्छिवलिङ्गकम् ।
सर्व्वदेवस्य शीर्षे तु [7]चार्घदानफलं लभेत् ॥ ३४ ॥
सामान्यतोयमानीय यदि स्नायान्महेश्वरम् ।
सार्द्धत्रिकोटितीर्थस्य स्नानस्य फलभाग् भवेत् ॥ ३५ ॥

श्रीचण्डिकोवाच—

तारिणी ब्रह्मणः शक्तिस्त्रिपुरा वैष्णवी [8]परा ।
कथं शाकम्भरी तारा त्रिपुरा शाम्भवी कथम् ॥ ३६ ॥

---

1. 'यद्‌यत् तदेव भस्मतां गतम्' ख-ग-ङ । 2. श्लोकार्द्धमिदं ख-ग-पुस्तकयोर्नास्ति । 3. 'कुशाप्रमाणं' क-ङ । 4. 'नियोजयेत्' ङ । 5. 'अन्नदान-' क । 6. 'एकेन' क । 7. 'अन्नदान-' घ । 8. 'तथा' ख-ग-घ ।

[1]श्रीशङ्कर उवाच—

कालीदेहाद् यदा जाता सावित्री वेदमातृका ।
त्रिवर्गदात्री[3] सा देवी ब्रह्मणः शक्तिरेव च ॥ ३७ ॥
[4]गुप्तरूपा महाविद्या शैवी सैकजटा परा ।
तस्माल्लक्ष्मीर्वैष्णवी या [5]त्रिवर्गदायिनी शिवा ॥ ३८ ॥
गुप्तरूपा महाविद्या श्रीमत्त्रिपुरसुन्दरी ।
[6]शाम्भवी परमा [7]माया त्रिपुरा मोक्षदायिनी ॥ ३९ ॥
एकैव हि महाविद्या नाममात्रं पृथक् पृथक् ।
तथैव [8]पुरुषश्चैको[9] नाममात्रविभेदकः ॥ ४० ॥

श्रीचण्डिकोवाच—

मन्त्रधारणमात्रेण तदात्मा तन्मयो भवेत् ।
कथं वा वातुलः सोऽपि कथं वा रोगवान् भवेत् ॥ ४१ ॥

[10]श्रीशङ्कर उवाच—

मन्त्रच्छन्नाद् वातुलत्वं रोगो देहे न जायते ।
[11]मन्त्रच्छन्नं प्रवक्ष्यामि शृणु देवि [12]समाहिता ॥ ४२ ॥
[13]अभक्तिश्चाक्षरे भ्रान्तिर्लुप्तश्छिन्नस्तथैव च ।
[14]ह्रस्वो दीर्घश्च [15]कथनं स्वप्ने तु चाष्टधा स्मृतः ॥ ४३ ॥

---

४३ । अभक्तिरित्यादि । अस्यार्थः—अभक्तिः मन्त्रेष्वक्षरबुद्ध्यादिरूपा । तदुक्तं कुलार्णवे द्वादशोल्लासे—गुरौ मनुष्यबुद्धिन्तु मन्त्रे चाक्षरभावनाम् । प्रतिमासु शिला-

---

1. 'शिव' ख-ग-घ । 2. '-देहस्वेदजाता' ख-ग । 3. '-दाता' घ । 4. 'गुरुरूपा' ङ । 5. 'त्रिवर्गफलदायिनी' ख-ग । 6. 'शाकम्भरी परा' ङ । 7. 'या सा' ख-ग । 8. 'पुरुषाश्चैकनाम-' घ । 9. '-श्चैव' ख-ग । 10. 'शिव' ख-ग । 11. 'मन्त्रच्छन्नं महेशानि आत्मा देवि' ख-ग, 'मन्त्रच्छन्नं महेशानि' घ । 12. 'समाहितः' क-ख-ग-घ । 13. 'अभक्तिं चाक्षरे भ्रान्तिं लुप्तस्थिरं तथैव च' ख-ग । 14. 'ह्रस्वदीर्घश्च कथनं' ख-ग । 15. 'कथनः' क-घ ।

अभक्त्या नैव सिद्धिः स्यात् कल्पकोटिशतैरपि ।
एवंमन्त्रश्चान्यथा वा चेति भ्रान्त्या च वातुलः ॥ ४४ ॥
लुप्तवर्णे बुद्धिनाशश्छिन्ने नाशो भवेत् किल ।
ह्रस्वोच्चारे व्याधियुक्तो [1]दीर्घजापे वसुक्षयः[2] ॥ ४५ ॥
कथने मृत्युमाप्नोति स्वप्नेऽपि [3]शृणु शैलजे ।
कालिकायाश्च ताराया मन्त्रोऽपि ज्वलदग्निवत् ॥ ४६ ॥
विप्ररूपेण[4] [5]देवेन प्रेमभावेन चेतसा ।
यदि [6]मन्त्रं हरेद् देवि शृणु साधकलक्षणम् ॥ ४७ ॥
सर्व्वाङ्गे वै भवेज्ज्वाला देहमध्ये विशेषतः ।
तोये [7]शैत्यं न जायेत तथैवौषधसेवने ॥ ४८ ॥
सदा वातुलवत् सर्व्वं प्रत्यक्षे [8]स्वप्नवद्भवेत् ।
वर्षमध्ये त्रिवर्षे वा मृत्युस्तस्य न संशयः ॥ ४९ ॥

श्रीचण्डिकोवाच—

मन्त्रच्छन्नं[9] चाष्टविधं तव वक्त्राच्छ्रुतं मया ।
यदि दैवाद् भवेद् देव तस्योपायं वदस्व मे ॥ ५० ॥

वुद्धिं कुर्व्वाणो नरकं व्रजेत् ॥ इति । देवतान्तरमन्त्रप्रशंसया स्वमन्त्रस्याफलत्वबुद्ध्यादि-रूपा च ॥ १ ॥ अक्षरे भ्रान्तिः—गुरोः शिष्यस्य वा भ्रान्त्या मन्त्रेषु वर्णवैपरीत्यं वर्णाधिक्यञ्च ॥ २ ॥ लुप्तः—मन्त्रेषु वर्णन्यूनत्वम् ॥ ३ ॥ छिन्नः—मन्त्रान्तर्गत-युक्तवर्णैक-देशन्यूनत्वम् ॥४॥ ह्रस्वः—दीर्घस्थाने ह्रस्वप्रयोगः ॥५॥ दीर्घः—ह्रस्वस्थाने दीर्घप्रयोगः ॥ ६ ॥ यद्यप्येतद्द्दोषयोरक्षरभ्रान्त्यन्तर्भूतत्वेन पौनरुक्त्यं स्यात्, तथापि पृथक्-प्रायश्चित्तस्य वक्ष्यमाणत्वाद् अक्षरभ्रान्तिस्तदितरविषया ॥ ६ ॥ कथनम्—अन्येषु स्वीयमन्त्रप्रकाशः ॥७॥ स्वप्ने त्विति—स्वप्ने ब्राह्मणरूपिदेवेन स्वीयमन्त्रस्य प्रहरणं प्रकर्षेण हरणं तस्मिन् स्वीयमन्त्रप्रकाश इति यावत् । इति ।

---

1. 'दीर्घोच्चारे' ङ । 2. 'तथा भवेत्' घ, 'वपुःक्षयः' ह०त० । 3. 'चैव' ख-ग । 4. '-जपेन' ख-ग । 5. 'देवोऽपि' ह०त० । 6. 'मन्त्रो' क-घ-ङ । 7. 'सत्यं' ख-ग । 8. '-धर-' ङ । 9. '-च्छिन्ना' घ ।

श्रीशङ्कर उवाच—

बहुजापात् तथा होमात् कायक्लेशादिविस्तरात् ।
यदि भक्तिर्भवेद् देवि तस्य सिद्धिरदूरतः ॥ ५१ ॥

गुरुणा तत्सुतेनैव साधकेन वरानने ।
अक्षरे दूषणं [1]हित्वा पुनर्मन्त्रं प्रकाशयेत् ॥ ५२ ॥

[2]गुरुणा तत्सुतेनैव साधकेन समाहितः ।
लुप्तवर्णं समुत्थाप्य पुनर्मन्त्रं प्रकाशयेत् ॥ ५३ ॥

चक्रभेदेन [3]षट्कोणं तथैव योनिमुद्रया ।
एकोच्चारे जपेन्मन्त्रं लक्षमेकं वरानने ।
गुर्वादिना महेशानि [4]छिन्नदोषनिकृन्तनम् ॥ ५४ ॥

गुरुणा लक्षजापेन तन्मन्त्रं श्रावयेत् त्रिधा ।
[5]दूषणं ह्रस्वदीर्घस्य [6]शान्तिश्चात्र न संशयः ॥ ५५ ॥

गुरुणा तत्सुतेनैव साधकेनैव शैलजे ।
उक्तमार्गेण देवेशि [7]जपेल्लक्षचतुष्टयम् ॥ ५६ ॥

तद्दशांशं हुनेत् पश्चात् तर्पणादि समाचरेत् ५७ ॥

---

५१ । अभक्तिजन्यदोषशान्तिमाह—बहुजापादित्यादि (१)
५२ । अक्षरभ्रान्तिजन्यदोषशान्तिमाह—गुरुणेत्यादि (२)
५३ । लुप्तदोषशान्तिमाह—गुरुणा तदिति (३)
५४ । छिन्नदोषशान्तिमाह—चक्रभेदेनेति (४)
५५ । ह्रस्वदीर्घदोषशान्तिमाह—गुरुणेति (५-६)
५६ । कथनदोषशान्तिमाह—गुरुणा तदिति (७)

---

1. 'छित्त्वा' घ । 2. ङ-पुस्तके 'गुरुणेत्यादि 'प्रकाशये'दित्यन्तः श्लोको नास्ति । 3. 'षट्केन' ख-ग-ङ०त० । 4. 'छिन्नदोषं' क । 5. 'दूषणे' ङ०त० । 6. 'शान्तिर्यातो' क, 'शान्तिर्जायते' घ । 7. 'जपेल्लक्षं' क-ङ ।

[1]ततोऽपि यदि नैवाभूत् साधकः स्थिरमानसः ।
चतुर्गुणं हि कर्त्तव्यं शिष्यस्य मुक्तिहेतवे ॥ ५८ ॥
यदि मृत्युर्भवेत् तस्य तथापि मुक्तिभाग् भवेत् ।
कथनस्य दोषशान्तिर्भवत्येव न संशयः ॥ ५६ ॥
स्वप्नेऽपि मन्त्रकथने [2]श्मशाने चैव शैलजे ।
[3]उक्तमार्गेण देवेशि जपेल्लक्षं चतुष्टयम् ॥ ६० ॥
तद्दशांशं हुनेत् पश्चात् तर्पणादि समाचरेत् ।
ततोऽपि यदि नैवाभूत् साधकः स्थिरमानसः ॥ ६१ ॥
चतुर्गुणं हि कर्त्तव्यं पूर्व्वोक्तं पूजनञ्चरेत् ।
[4]कुजे वा शनिवारे वा प्रथमे गमनञ्चरेत् ।
सप्ताहं वा [5]यजेद् देवीं तुरीयं वादिनं यजेत् ॥ ६२ ॥
श्मशानसाधनं वक्ष्ये [6]श्रृणु चैकाग्रचेतसा ।
स्वर्णं रौप्यं तथा वस्त्रं दत्त्वा वरणमाचरेत् ॥ ६३ ॥
स्वर्णपीठं प्रदातव्यं [7]चतुरङ्गुलिविस्तृतम् ।
भोगयोग्यं प्रदातव्यं मधुपर्कं [8]यथोदितम् ॥ ६४ ॥
राजपत्नी येन तुष्टा तोषयेत् तेन वाससा ।
अलङ्कारं यथायोग्यं तत्र तत्र[9] [10]नियोजयेत् ॥ ६५ ॥

---

६० । स्वप्ने स्वीयमन्त्रप्रकाशजनितदोषशान्तिमाह—स्वप्नेऽपीति (८)

---

1. 'ततो यदि च नैवाभूत्' ख-ग । 2. 'श्मशानसाधनञ्चरेत्' ख-ग-घ । 3. ख-ग-पुस्तकयोः 'उक्तमार्गेणे'त्यादि 'पूजनञ्चरे'दित्यन्तो भागो नास्ति । 4. 'कुजवारे शनौ वारे' ख-ग, घ-ङ-पुस्तकयोः 'कुजे वे'त्यादि पद्यार्द्धभागो नास्ति । 5. 'जपेत्' ह०त० । 6. 'श्रृणुष्वैकाग्र-' घ । 7. ख-ग-पुस्तकयोः 'चतुरङ्गुलिविस्तृतं' 'भोगयोग्यं प्रदातव्यं' इति भागो नास्ति । 8. 'यथोचितम्' ह०त० । 9. 'तस्य' ख-ग । 10. 'निवेदयेत्' ङ ।

नैवेद्यं विविधं रम्यं नानाद्रव्यसमन्वितम् ।
सामिषान्नं गुडं छागं सुरापिष्टकपायसम् ॥ ६६ ॥
[1]भोग्यद्रव्यं जले दद्याद्[2] यदि भोक्ता न तिष्ठति ।
एवं पूजां [3]समाप्यादौ शिवपूजां समाचरेत् ॥ ६७ ॥
षोडशैरुपचारैश्च [4]लिङ्गानाञ्चैकविंशतिम् ।
अष्टोत्तरशतेनैव विल्वपत्रैः सचन्दनैः ॥ ६८ ॥
प्रत्येकं [5]पूजयेन्मन्त्रं [6]गजान्तकसहस्रकम् ।
सहस्रं होमयेत् पश्चाद् विल्वपत्रैर्वरानने ॥ ६९ ॥
एवं [7]कृते लभेच्छान्तिं दीर्घायुर्नात्र संशयः ॥ ७० ॥

इति श्रीमातृकाभेदतन्त्रे [8]हरगौरीसंवादे [9]द्वादशः पटलः ॥ १२ ॥

---

६९ । प्रत्येकमित्यादि । एकविंशतिशिवलिङ्गानि सचन्दनाष्टोत्तरशतविल्वपत्रैः प्रत्येकं पूजयित्वा शिवषडक्षर-मन्त्रमष्टोत्तरसहस्रं जपेत् । ततश्च साज्यविल्वपत्रैः सहस्रं जुहुयात् । विशेषेण कथनाद् दशांशबाधः । इति ।

७० । एवं कृत इति । अत्रापि स्वस्यासामर्थ्ये गुर्वादिनैतत् कारयितव्यमिति बोध्यम् ।

1.[1] 'भोग्द्रिव्यं' ह०त० । 2. 'सर्व्वं' क-घ-ङ । 3. 'समप्यादौ' ख-ग । 4. 'लिङ्गन्तु चैक-' क-ख-ग, 'लिङ्गञ्च एक-' घ । 5. 'प्रजपेन्मन्त्रं' ह०त० । 6. 'गजान्तर-' क । 7. 'एवं कृत्वा' घ । 8. 'चण्डिकाशङ्कर-' घ । 9. 'त्रयोदशः' ख-ग ।

त्रयोदशः पटलः

श्रीचण्डिकोवाच—

श्रृणु नाथ परानन्द परापरजगत्पते ।
इदानीं श्रोतुमिच्छामि मालायाः[1] कीदृशो जपः ।
[2]का माला कस्य देवस्य तद् वदस्व समाहितः ॥ १ ॥

श्रीशङ्कर उवाच—

वैष्णवे तुलसीमाला गजदन्तैर्गणेश्वरे ।
कालिकाया [3]महामन्त्रं जपेद् रुद्राक्षमालया ॥ २ ॥
तारायाश्च जपेन्मन्त्री महाशङ्खाख्यमालया ।
महाशङ्खाख्यमालायां सर्व्वां विद्यां जपेत् सुधीः ॥ ३ ॥

---

२ । वैष्णव इत्यादि । अत्र प्रमाणम्—सुवर्णमणिभिर्मालां स्फाटिकीं शङ्खनिर्मिताम् । प्रवालैरेव वा कुर्य्यात् पुत्रजीवं विवर्ज्जयेत् ॥ पद्माक्षञ्चैव रुद्राक्षं भद्राक्षञ्च विशेषतः । रक्तचन्दनमाला तु भोगदा मोक्षदा भवेत् ॥ वैष्णवे तुलसीमाला गजदन्तैर्गणेश्वरे । त्रिपुराया जपे शस्ता रुद्राक्षै रक्तचन्दनैः ॥ इति मुण्डमालातन्त्रोक्तं संवदत्यत्र । तत्रापि मणिसंख्यामाह योगिनीतन्त्रे—मणिसंख्यां महादेवि मालायाः कथयामि ते । पञ्चविंशतिभिर्मोक्षं पुष्ट्यै तु सप्तविंशतिः ॥ त्रिंशद्भिर्धनसिद्धिः स्यात् पञ्चाशन्मन्त्रसिद्धये । अष्टोत्तरशतैः सर्वसिद्धिरेव महेश्वरि ॥······दन्तमाला जपे कार्य्या गले धार्य्या नृणां शुभा । दशनैर्यदि कर्त्तव्या संख्या दन्तस्य ते प्रिये ॥ इति ।

३ । ताराया इत्यादि । अत्र संवादि प्रमाणं मुण्डमालायाम्—महाशङ्खमयी माला नीलसारस्वते विधौ । इति । ताराकल्पेऽपि—अचिराद् विहिता सिद्धिर्महाशङ्खाख्यमालया । महाशङ्खमयी माला ज्ञेया तारामनौ प्रिये ॥ इति च ।

उक्तञ्च नित्यातन्त्रे प्रथमपटले—समाश्रित्य महाशङ्खमालां वीरपदं व्रजेत् । इति ।

---

1. '-यां' ङ । 2. 'किं मानं' क-घ-ङ । 3. 'महामन्त्रो जपेदन्ताख्य-' क ।

११

अकस्माद् वै महासिद्धिर्महाशङ्खाख्यमालया ।
तथैव [1]सकला विद्या महाशङ्खे वसेत् [2]सदा ॥ ४ ॥
[3]स्फाटिकी सर्व्वदेवस्य [4]प्रवालैः सकलां जपेत् ।
स्वर्णरौप्यसमुद्भूतां[5] सर्व्वदेवेषु योजिताम्[6] ॥ ५ ॥
कालिकायाश्च सुन्दर्य्या [7]रुद्राक्षैः प्रजपेत् सदा ।
भैरव्याः प्रजपेन्मन्त्री[8] शङ्खपद्माख्यया[9] प्रिये ॥ ६ ॥
[10]श्मशाने धुस्तुरैर्मालां जपेद् धूमावतीविधौ ।
इति ते कथितं कान्ते महामालाविनिर्णयम्[11] ॥ ७ ॥
अथ ग्रन्थिं प्रवक्ष्यामि शृणु कान्ते समाहिता[12] ।
येन माला सुसिद्धा च [13]नृणां सर्व्वफलप्रदा ॥ ८ ॥

अत एव महेशानि अस्थिमाला गले मम । इति च । योगिनीतन्त्रे द्वितीयपटलेऽपि—वर्णमाला शुभा प्रोक्ता सर्वमन्त्रप्रदीपनी । तस्याः प्रतिनिधिर्देवि महाशङ्खमयी शुभा ॥ महाशङ्खः करे यस्य तस्य सिद्धिरदूरतः । तदभावे वीरवन्द्ये स्फाटिकी सर्व्वसिद्धिदा ॥ इति ।

४ । अकस्मादित्यादि । अत्र च संवादि प्रमाणमुक्तं गुप्तसाधनतन्त्रे एकादश-पटले—महाशङ्खाख्यमालायां यो जपेत् साधकोत्तमः । अणिमादिविभूतीनामीश्वरो नात्र संशयः ॥……यदि भाग्यवशाद् देवि महाशङ्खश्च लभ्यते । स सिद्धः स गणः सोऽपि स च विष्णुर्न संशयः ॥ तदैव सहसा सिद्धिर्नात्र कार्य्या विचारणा ॥ इति ।

७ । श्मशान इत्यादि । अत्र संवादि प्रमाणमुक्तं मुण्डमालातन्त्रे—श्मशानधुस्तुरै-र्माला ज्ञेया धूमावतीविधौ । इति ।

८ । अथ ग्रन्थिमित्यादि । ग्रन्थौ सूत्रादिनियममप्याह सनत्कुमारतन्त्रे—कार्पास-सम्भवं सूत्रं धर्म्मकामार्थमोक्षदम् । तच्च विप्रेन्द्रकन्याभिर्निर्म्मितञ्च सुशोभनम् ॥ श्वेतं रक्तं तथा कृष्णं पट्टसूत्रमथापि वा । शान्तिवश्याभिचारेषु मोक्षैश्वर्य्यजयेषु च ॥ शुक्लं रक्तं तथा पीतं कृष्णं वर्णेषु च क्रमात् । सर्व्वेषामेव वर्णानां रक्तं सर्व्वेप्सितिप्रदम् ॥

---

1. 'सकलां विद्यां' क-घ-ङ । 2. 'प्रिये' ङ । 3. 'स्फाटिकीं' क-घ-ङ । 4. 'पुराणैः' घ । 5. '-भूतं' क-घ-ङ । 6. '-तम्' व-ङ । 7. 'रुद्राक्षे' ख-ग । 8. '-न्मन्त्रं' ङ । 9. '-ख्ययोः' ख-ग । 10. 'श्मशानधुस्तुरै-' ख-ग, 'श्मशानधुस्तुरभवां' ङ । 11. '-र्णयः' ख-ग । 12. '-हितः' क । 13. 'सर्वेप्सितफलप्रदा' ङ ।

मालायाश्चाधिका[1] कान्ते [2]ग्रन्थिश्चैका फलप्रदा ।
एकपञ्चाशिकायाञ्च मालायां परमेश्वरि ॥ ९ ॥
[3]ब्रह्मग्रन्थियुतां मालां सार्द्धद्वितयवेष्टिताम्[4] ।
सपादवेष्टनं देवि नागपाशं मनोहरम् ॥ १० ॥
सर्व्वदेवस्य मालायां सर्व्वत्र परमेश्वरि ।
ब्रह्मग्रन्थिं विधायेत्थं नागपाशमथापि वा ॥ ११ ॥
[5]मालायां त्वधिकां देवि चैकां ग्रन्थिं प्रदापयेत् ।
मूलेन [6]ग्रथितं कुर्यात् प्रणवेनाथवा प्रिये ॥ १२ ॥

त्रिगुणं त्रिगुणीकृत्य ग्रथयेच्छिल्पशास्त्रतः । एकैकं मातृकावर्णं सतारं प्रजपन् सुधीः ॥ मालामादाय सूत्रेण ग्रथयेन्मध्यमध्यतः । ब्रह्मग्रन्थिं विधायेत्थं मेरुञ्च ग्रन्थिसंयुतम् ॥ ग्रथयित्वा पुरो मालां ततः संस्कारमारभेत् ॥ एकवीराकल्पे च—मातृकावर्णतो ग्रन्थिं विद्यया वाथ कारयेत् । सुवर्णादिगुणैर्वापि ग्रथयेत् साधकोत्तमः ॥ इति ।

ग्रन्थिनियमश्च एकवीराकल्पे—ब्रह्मग्रन्थिं ततो दद्यान्नागपाशमथापि वा । इति । छन्दःसारेऽपि—त्रिरावृत्तिग्रन्थिकेन तथार्धेन विधीयते । सार्द्धद्वयावर्त्तनेन ग्रन्थिं कुर्य्याद् यथा दृढम् ॥ कालिकापुराणे च—ब्रह्मग्रन्थियुतं कुर्य्यात् प्रतिबीजं यथास्थितम् । अथवा ग्रन्थिरहितं दृढरज्जुसमन्वितम् ॥ एवं निर्माय मालां वै शोधयेन्मुनिसत्तम ॥ इति ।

९ । मालाया इत्यादि । माला कीदृशी कर्त्तव्या इत्यपेक्षायामुक्तं गुप्तसाधनतन्त्रे एकादशपटले—गोपुच्छसदृशीं कुर्य्यादथवा सर्परूपिणीम् । स्थूला सूक्ष्मा च पर्य्यन्तं क्रमेण ग्रथनञ्चरेत् ॥ मूलेन ग्रथनं कार्य्यं प्रणवेनाथवा प्रिये । ब्रह्मग्रन्थिं प्रयत्नेन दद्यात् साधकसत्तमः ॥ सूत्रद्वयं परेशानि मिलितं कारयेत् ततः । मेरुञ्च ग्रथनं कार्य्यं तदूर्द्ध्वं ग्रन्थिसंयुतम् ॥ समीपे गुरुदेवस्य संस्कारमाचरेत् सुधीः । स्थूलावधि जपेन्मन्त्रं सूक्ष्मभागे समापयेत् ॥ पुच्छावधि जपाद् देवि सिद्धिहानिः प्रजायते ॥ इति ।

---

1. '-श्चाधिकां' क । 2. 'ग्रन्थिचैकां' क । 3. '-ग्रन्थियुतां मातां सा-' ग, 'ग्रन्थिं युग्मवाणसार्द्धत्रि-' क-घ-ङ । 4. '-वेष्टिती' ङ । 5. 'मालायामधिकां' ख-ग, 'मालायाश्चाधिकां' ङ । 6. 'ग्रथनं' ख-ग ।

[1]ग्रन्थिमध्ये [2]च गुटिकां [3]कुर्य्यादतिमनोहराम्[4]।
सूत्रद्वयं महेशानि [5]मिलनं कारयेत् ततः ॥ १३ ॥
मेरुञ्च ग्रथनं कुर्यात् तदूर्द्ध्वे ग्रन्थिसंयुतम्।
एवं मालां विनिर्माय गोपयेद् बहुयत्नतः ॥ १४ ॥
कम्पनं धूननं शब्दं [6]नैव तत्र प्रकाशयेत्।
करभ्रष्टं तथा छिन्नं महाविघ्नस्य कारणम् ॥ १५ ॥
कम्पने सिद्धिहानिः स्याद् धूननं बहुदुःखदम्।
शब्दे जाते [7]भवेद्रोगः [8]करभ्रष्टाद्विनाशकृत् ॥ १६ ॥
[9]छिन्नसूत्रे भवेन्मृत्युस्तस्माद् यत्नपरो भवेत्।
एवं ज्ञात्वा महेशानि शान्तिस्वस्त्ययनं चरेत् ॥ १७ ॥

१४। मेरुञ्चेत्यादि। अत्र संवादि प्रमाणम् एकवीराकल्पे—कवचेनाथ बध्नीयान्मालां ध्यानपरायणः। सर्व्वशेषं ततो मेरुं सूत्रद्वयसमन्वितम् ॥ ग्रथयेत् तारयोगेण बध्नीयात् साधकोत्तमः। इति। गौतमीये च—मुखे मुखञ्च संयोज्य पुच्छे पुच्छञ्च योजयेत्। गोपुच्छसदृशी माला यद्वा सर्पाकृतिर्भवेत् ॥ मुखपुच्छनियमश्च छन्दःसारे—रुद्राक्षस्योन्नतं प्रोक्तं मुखं पुच्छन्तु निम्नगम्। कमलाक्षस्य सूक्ष्मांशं सबिन्दुद्वितयं मुखम् ॥ सबिन्दुकस्य स्थूलांशं पुच्छं श्लक्ष्णमिति स्थितम्। एवं ज्ञात्वा मुखं पुच्छं रुद्राक्षाम्भोरुहाक्षयोः ॥ तत्सजातीयमेकाक्षं मेरुत्वेनाग्रतो न्यसेत्। एकैकं मणिमादाय ब्रह्मग्रन्थिं प्रकल्पयेत् ॥ एकैकं मातृकावर्णं ग्रथनादौ तु संजपेत् ॥ इति।

१५। कम्पनमित्यादि। अत्र संवादि प्रमाणन्तु मालाशोधनमधिकृत्योक्तं योगिनीहृदये—होमकर्म ततः कुर्य्याद् देवताभावसिद्धये। अष्टोत्तरशतं हुत्वा सम्पाताज्यं विनिक्षिपेत् ॥ होमकर्मण्यशक्तश्चेद् द्विगुणं जपमाचरेत्। नान्यमन्त्रं जपेन्मन्त्री कम्पयेन्न विधूनयेत् ॥ कम्पनात् सिद्धिहानिः स्याद् धूननं बहुदुःखदम्। शब्दे जाते भवेद्रोगः करभ्रष्टा विनाशकृत् ॥ छिन्ने सूत्रे भवेन्मृत्युस्तस्माद् यत्नपरो भवेत्। जपान्ते कर्णदेशे वा उच्चदेशेऽथवा न्यसेत् ॥ इति। कम्पनं जपकर्त्तुः शरीरस्य, धूननं मालाया इति केचिद् व्याचक्षते।

---

1. 'ग्रन्थिं मध्ये' क-घ-ङ। 2. 'तु' ङ। 3. 'कुर्यादन्ति-' ङ। 4. '-मनोरमम्' क-घ-। 5. 'मीलनं' ख-ग। 6. 'नैवं' ख-ग। 7. 'भवेद्रोगं' ख-ग। 8. 'करभ्रष्टादि-' क। 9. 'छिन्ने सूत्रे' ख-ग।

कम्पने यो जपेन्मन्त्रं यदि सिद्धिं प्रयच्छति ।
यत्नेन गुरुमानीय [1]द्वाविंशदुपचारतः ॥ १८ ॥
कुम्भस्थापनकं कृत्वा पूजयेदिष्टदेवताम् ।
ततो हुनेद् विल्वपत्रैरष्टोत्तरशताहुतिम् ॥ १९ ॥
[2]त्रिमध्वक्तेन विधिना धूननेऽपि च सुन्दरि ।
सशब्दे [3]जपने चण्डि ह्येवं कुर्याद् विचक्षणः ॥ २० ॥
करभ्रष्टे तथा छिन्ने पुरश्चरणमाचरेत् ।
जपाद्यन्ते यजेद् देवीं षोडशैरुपचारकैः ॥ २१ ॥

२१। करभ्रष्ट इत्यादि । अत्र---जीर्णे सूत्रे पुनः सूत्रं ग्रथयित्वा शतं जपेत् । प्रमादात् पतिता हस्ताच्छतमष्टोत्तरं जपेत् ॥ जपेन्निषिद्धसंसर्गे क्षालयित्वा यथोदितम् । इति वैशम्पायनसंहितोक्तप्रमाणम् । छिन्ने सूत्रे पुनः सूत्रं ग्रथयित्वा शतं जपेत् । इति कुब्जिकातन्त्रोक्तप्रमाणञ्चोपजीव्य यदुक्तं तन्त्रसारकृता 'छिन्नेऽपि अष्टोत्तरशतजपः कार्य्यः, करभ्रष्टच्छिन्नयोस्तुल्यत्वादिति', तत्तु ग्रन्थमेतमनालोच्यैवेति सुधीभिश्चिन्तनीयम् । पुरश्चरणमिति ।—पुरश्चरणविधिश्चोक्तस्तन्त्रसारे—"कुलार्णवे···एवं जपं पुरा कृत्वा गन्धाक्षतकुशोदकैः । जपं समर्पयेद् देव्या वामहस्ते विचक्षणः ॥ जपान्ते प्रत्यहं मन्त्री होमयेत् तद्दशांशतः । तर्पणञ्चाभिषेकञ्च तत्तद्दशांशतो मुने ॥ प्रत्यहं भोजयेद् विप्रान् न्यूनाधिकप्रशान्तये ॥ तथा होमाद्यशक्तौ च योगिनीहृदये—होमकर्म्मण्यशक्तानां विप्राणां द्विगुणो जपः"। इत्यादिना । गन्धर्व्वतन्त्रेऽष्टाविंशतिपटले च—···जपसंख्यादशांशतः । यथोक्तविहिते कुण्डे जुहुयात् संस्कृतेऽनले ॥ अथवा प्रत्यहं जप्त्वा जुहुयात् तद्दशांशतः । तथा होमदशांशन्तु जले सम्पूज्य देवताम् ॥ तर्पयामीति मन्त्रान्ते प्रोक्ताभिर्मूर्द्धि तर्पयेत् । जपो होमस्तर्पणञ्च पूजा ब्राह्मणभोजनम् ॥ पूर्व्वपूर्व्वदशांशेन कुर्य्यात् पञ्चाङ्गसंयुतम् । स्वाभिषेकाघमर्षौ च सूर्य्यार्घ्यं जलपानकम् ॥ प्राणायामं ततः कुर्य्यात् पूर्व्वपूर्व्वदशांशतः । दशाङ्गोपासनं भक्त्या पुरश्चरणमुच्यते ॥ तत् पुरश्चरणं नाम मन्त्रसिद्ध्यर्थमात्मनः । यथोक्तं नियमं कृत्वा स्वकल्पोक्तजपस्य च ॥ करणं विजयान्तं तत् प्रोक्तं देशिकसत्तमैः । तदन्ते महतीं

---

1. 'द्वात्रिंशदुप-' ख-ग-ङ । 2. 'त्रिमध्वोक्तेन' क । 3. 'जल्पमाने च' ख-ग ।

प्रत्यहं प्रजपेन्मन्त्रं प्रत्यहं बलिदानकम् ।
पञ्चाङ्गस्य प्रमाणेन सर्वकर्म्म समापयेत् ॥ २२ ॥
दरिद्रः परमेशानि यदि विघ्नपरायणः ।
आद्यन्ते महतीं पूजां [1]दिक्सहस्रं जपेन्मनुम् ॥ २३ ॥
सहस्रैकं हुनेत् पश्चात् [2]सर्वविघ्नस्य शान्तये ।
कुम्भतोयैः स्नापयित्वा पुनर्मालां प्रदापयेत् ॥ २४ ॥
[3]अनेनैव विधानेन विघ्नजालैर्न लिप्यते ॥ २५ ॥

इति श्रीमातृकाभेदतन्त्रे हरगौरीसंवादे [4]त्रयोदशः पटलः ॥ १३ ॥

पूजां कुर्य्याद् ब्राह्मणभोजनम् ॥ गुरुं सन्तोषयेदेवं मन्त्राः सिद्ध्यन्ति मन्त्रिणः । होम-कर्म्मण्यशक्तानां विप्राणां द्विगुणो जपः ॥ इति ।

२३ । दिक्सहस्रमिति—दशसहस्रमित्यर्थः ।

२४ । सहस्रैकमिति । अत्रापि होमाद्यशक्तौ होमसंख्याद्विगुणजपादिकं कर्त्तव्य-मिति बोध्यम् ।

---

1. 'कुर्य्यात् साधकसत्तमः' ङ । 2. 'सर्वविघ्नोपशान्तये' ख-ग । 3. 'ध्याने-' क-घ । 4. 'चतुर्दशः' ख-ग ।

चतुर्द्दशः पटलः

श्रीचण्डिकोवाच—

मन्त्रधारणमात्रेण तत्क्षणे[1] तन्मयो भवेत् ।
जीवात्मा कुण्डलीमध्ये प्रदीपकलिका यथा ॥ १ ॥
निजेष्टदेवतारूपा देहसंस्था च कुण्डली ।
भुज्यते सैव देहस्था का चिन्ता साधकस्य च ।
तन्मे ब्रूहि महादेव यद्यहं तव वल्लभा ॥ २ ॥

[2]श्रीशङ्कर उवाच—

[3]भोगस्तु त्रिविधो देवि दिव्यवीरपशुक्रमात् ।
निर्लिप्तो दिव्यभावस्थः कुण्डली भुज्यते [4]यदि ॥ ३ ॥
आजिह्वान्ता कुण्डलिनी वीरस्य वीरवन्दिते[5] ।
महादेव्याः प्रीतये च प्रसादं भुज्यते पशुः ॥ ४ ॥
द्विजातेर्दिव्यभावश्च[6] सदा निर्वाणदायकः ।
विप्रो वीरश्च निर्वाणी भवत्येव न संशयः ॥ ५ ॥
सायुज्यादि महामोक्षं नियुक्तं क्षत्रियादिषु ।
पशुना भक्तियुक्तेन प्रसादं भुज्यते यदि ॥ ६ ॥
स्वर्गभोगी[7] भवत्येव मरणे नाधिकारिता ।
जन्मान्तरमवाप्नोति महादेव्याः प्रसादतः ॥ ७ ॥

---

३ । भोगस्त्वित्यादि । रुद्रयामले षष्ठपटले भावत्रयमुक्तमनुलोमक्रमेण, यथा— आदौ भावं पशोः कृत्वा पश्चात् कुर्य्यादवश्यकम् । वीरभावं महाभावं सर्व्व-भावोत्तमोत्तमम् ॥ तत्पश्चादतिसौन्दर्य्यं दिव्यभावं महाफलम् । कुर्य्याद्व भावत्रयं दिव्यं भावसाधनमुत्तमम् ॥ इति । अत्र च भावस्य प्रातिलोम्येन कथनेऽपि क्रम-शब्दोपादानं भोगस्य क्रमापकर्षज्ञापनार्थम् । तथाच दिव्यभावे सर्व्वोत्कर्षेण भोगः, ततः क्रमेण तस्य ह्रास इति सुधीभिर्व्विवेच्यम् ॥

---

1. '-क्षणमत्' ख-ग । 2. क-पुस्तके 'श्री' नास्ति । 3. 'भोगन्तु त्रिविधं' क । 4. 'यदा' ङ । 5. '-वल्लभे' ङ । 6. '-भावेश' क । 7. '-भागी' ङ ।

दिव्यवीरमते दृष्टिर्जायते नात्र संशयः ।
दिव्यवीरप्रसादेन निर्वाणी नात्र संशयः ॥ ८ ॥
प्रसादभोगी यो देवि स पशुर्नात्र संशयः ।
मरणे नाधिकारोऽस्ति पशुभावस्थितस्य च ॥ ९ ॥
नैव मुक्तिर्भवेत् तस्य जन्म [1]चाप्नोति निश्चितम् ॥१०॥

श्रीचण्डिकोवाच—

वद मे परमेशान दिव्यवीरस्य [2]लक्षणम् ।
यत् कृते दिव्यवीरस्य महामुक्तिर्भविष्यति ॥ ११ ॥

श्रीशङ्कर उवाच—

साक्षाद् ब्रह्ममयी देवी चाभिशप्ता च वारुणी ।
शापमोचनमात्रेण [3]ब्रह्मरूपा सुधा परा ॥ १२ ॥
निवेदनान्महादेव्यै तत्तद् देवी भवेत् किल ।
मूलाधारात् कुण्डलिनीमाजिह्वान्तां [4]विभावयेत् ॥१३॥

८। दिव्यवीरेत्यादि। दिव्यस्य वीरस्य च लक्षणमुक्तं कामाख्यातन्त्रे चतुर्थपटले—दिव्यः सर्व्वमनोहारी मितवादी स्थिरासनः। गभीरः श्लिष्टवक्ता च शतावधानकः सुखी॥ गुरुपादाम्बुजे भीरुः सर्व्वत्र भयवर्जितः। सर्व्वदर्शी सर्व्ववक्ता सर्व्वदुष्टनिवारकः॥ सर्व्वगुणान्वितो दिव्यः सोऽहं किं बहुवाक्यतः॥ इति। निर्भयो भयदो वीरो गुरुभक्तिपरायणः। वाचालो बलवान्क्षुब्धः पञ्चतत्त्वे सदा रतिः॥ महोत्साहो महाबुद्धिर्महासाहसिकोऽपि च। महाशयः सदा देवि साधूनां पालने रतः॥ तमोमयः सदा वीरो विनयेन महोत्सुकः। एवं बहुगुणैर्युक्तो वीरो रुद्रः स्वयं प्रिये॥ इति च।

९। प्रसादेत्यादि। अत्र संवादि प्रमाणमुक्तं कामाख्यातन्त्रे चतुर्थपटले—य उक्तः पशुभावो हि कलौ कस्तस्य पालकः। पञ्चतत्त्वं न गृह्णाति तत्र निन्दां करोति न॥ शिवेन गदितं यत्तु तत् सत्यमिति भावयन्।······यदि चंक्रमणे शक्तः खडगधारे सदा नरः। पश्वाचारं सदा कुर्य्यात् किन्तु सिद्धिर्न जायते॥ इत्यादि।

---

1. 'नाप्नोति' क। 2. 'सम्मतम्' ख-ग। 3. 'ब्रह्मरूपधरा' ख-ग। 4. 'हि भावयेत्' ख-ग

तन्मुखे दानमात्रेण [1]ज्ञानवान् साधको भवेत् ।
यथैव कुण्डली देवी देहमध्ये व्यवस्थिता ॥ १४ ॥
तथैव [2]वारुणीं ध्यायेत् [3]कलाङ्गे स्वेष्टदेवताम् ।
कुण्डल्या [4]समभावेन शक्तिवक्त्रे प्रदापयेत् ॥ १५ ॥
[5]आत्मोच्छिष्टं महापूतं तन्मुखात् परमामृतम् ।
अवश्यमेव गृह्णीयात् [6]तादात्म्येन वरानने ॥ १६ ॥
उत्सृष्टादिविचारोऽपि कदाचिन्नास्ति ब्रह्मणि ।
गङ्गातोयं परं ब्रह्म प्रसादं [7]कस्य तद् वद ॥ १७ ॥
गङ्गासागरतोयं वा प्रसादं कस्य वा भवेत् ।
शृणु [8]देवि प्रवक्ष्यामि तज्जले स्नानमात्रतः ॥ १८ ॥
मुक्तिभागी भवेन्मर्त्यः[9] स्नानावगाहनात् किल ।
[10]पादादिमस्तकान्तं वै स्नानकाले प्रमज्जति ॥ १९ ॥
पादस्पर्शो[11] न दोषाय परंब्रह्मणि शैलजे ।
परमात्मनि लीने च तथैव परमेश्वरि ॥ २० ॥

१५। शक्तिवक्त्रे इति। अत्र विशेषस्तु निरुत्तरतन्त्रे पञ्चमपटले—निजशक्तिं विना देवि शक्त्युच्छिष्टं पिबेद् यदि। रौरवे नरके घोरे यावदिन्द्राश्चतुर्दश ॥ एकासने वसेद् यस्तु भुञ्जीत चैकभाजने। परस्परमुखस्पर्शी स याति नरकं ध्रुवम् ॥ एकासनस्थो यो वीरो दिव्यो वा कुलसुन्दरि ॥ सुधां पीत्वा वीरचक्रे रौरवं नरकं व्रजेत् ॥ महासिद्धीश्वरो वापि भुङ्क्ते पीत्वा परस्परम्। सिद्धिहानिं पुरस्कृत्य स याति नरकं ध्रुवम् ॥ विना शक्तिं पिबेद् द्रव्यं वीरो गुरुपरायणः। तथापि नरके घोरे पतत्येव न संशयः। शक्त्यभावे कुलेशानि तद् द्रव्यं जलतः क्षिपेत्। गुर्वभावे च तद् द्रव्यं जलतो विनिवेदयेत्। इति ॥

---

1. 'साधको ज्ञानवान्' ङ। 2. 'चाबलां' ख-ग। 3. 'कलाङ्के' ख-ग, 'संकलाङ्के' क। 4. 'मध्यभागे तु' ङ। 5. 'आत्मोत्सृष्टं' ख-ग। 6. 'तदात्मानं' ख-ग, तद्वक्त्रे न' ङ। 7. 'कस्यचिद् वद' ङ। 8. 'जाये महामाये' ख-ग। 9. '-र्त्यस्तज्जले चावगाहनात्' ख-ग, '-र्त्योजले स्नानावगाहनात्' ङ। 10. 'पदादि-' ख-ग। 11 '-स्पर्शो न दोषाय' ख-ग।

१२

इति ते कथितं [1]देवि दिव्यवीरस्य लक्षणम् ।
[2]वीरतन्त्रे च कथितं माहात्म्यं प्राणवल्लभे ॥ २१ ॥

शृणु देवि प्रवक्ष्यामि [3]साधिकायाश्च लक्षणम् ।
दिव्यशक्तिर्वीरशक्तिर्गुरुशक्तिस्तथा परा ॥ २२ ॥

कुलशक्तिः कामिनी च नवशक्तिः कुमारिका ।
श्रीगुरुं पूजयेद् भक्त्या स्वदेहदानपूर्व्वकम् ॥ २३ ॥

अन्यथा [4]तु स्वदेहस्य निग्रहो जायते ध्रुवम् ॥
सप्तजन्मनि सा देवी [5]पुक्कसी पतिवर्ज्जिता ॥ २४* ॥

शिवं [6]मत्वा स्वकान्तञ्च पूजासाधनमाचरेत् ।
कदाचिन्न यजेच्चान्यं पुरुषं परमेश्वरि ॥ २५ ॥

अन्यस्य यजनाच्चण्डि सर्वनाशो भवेद् ध्रुवम् ।
[7]कान्तस्यायुर्विहीनत्वं [8]विपत्तिश्च पदे पदे ॥ २६ ॥

धननाशो भवेन्नित्यं देव्याः [9]क्रोधश्च जायते ।
अवश्यं पूजयेन्नित्यं गुरुदेवं सनातनम् ॥ २७ ॥

भद्राभद्रविचारञ्च[10] या करोति गुरुस्थले ।
तस्या मन्त्रं क्रोधयुक्तं [11]विपत्तिश्च पदे पदे ॥ २८ ॥

वरं जनमुखान्निन्दा वरं प्राणान् परित्यजेत् ।
तथापि [12]पूजयेद् देवं साक्षान्निर्वाणदायकम् ॥ २९ ॥

---

* अत्रैव 'ङ'-पुस्तके चतुर्दशः पटलः समाप्तो जात इति ॥

---

1. 'कान्ते' ख-ग । 2. 'योनि-' ख-ग, 'वीरतन्त्रेऽपि' ङ । 3. 'वीरिकायाश्च' ख-ग 4. 'स्वस्य देहस्य' ख-ग । 5. 'पुंश्चली जायते ध्रुवम्' ङ । 6. 'नत्वा' ख-ग । 7. 'कान्तस्या-युक्तहीनत्वं' क । 8. 'पुत्राणां नाशमाप्नुयात्' ख-ग—कटीप्पनी । 9. 'क्रोधेश' क । 10. 'विचारोऽपि' क । 11. '-त्तिश्च' क । 12. 'पूजयेच्चैवं' ख-ग ।

सदा भयञ्च[1] कापट्यं वर्जयेद् गुरुपूजने ॥ ३० ॥
श्रीगुरोस्तेजसं भक्त्या यदि धारणमाचरेत् ।
सत्यं सत्यं [2]पुनः सत्यं काशी सा नात्र संशयः ॥ ३१ ॥
अभक्त्या परमेशानि यदि धारणमाचरेत् ।
जपपूजादिकं [3]तस्याः सन्दहेत् तेन तेजसा ॥ ३२ ॥

श्रीचण्डिकोवाच—

सपत्नीकं यजेद् देवं गुरुं निर्वाणदायकम् ।
[4]तस्य सङ्गं परित्यज्य कथमात्मनियोजनम् ॥ ३३ ॥

श्रीशङ्कर उवाच—

शृणु देवि प्रवक्ष्यामि गुरोराज्ञानुसारतः ।
धारयेत् तेजसं भक्त्या स्वयं लिप्साविवर्ज्जिता ॥ ३४ ॥
गुरुपत्न्याश्चात्मजश्च श्रीगुरो[5]रात्मजो यतः ।
गुरुपत्नी गुरुः साक्षाद् गुरुपुत्रो न संशयः ॥ ३५ ॥
एकस्य पूजनात् कान्त उभयोः पूजनं भवेत् ।
गुरुपुत्रो गणेशश्च गुरुपुत्रः षडाननः ॥ ३६ ॥
एकं गुरुसुतं कान्ते पूजने या सदा रता ।
अन्यं गुरुसुतं कान्ते पूजयेन्न कदाचन ॥ ३७ ॥
वीरं वा दिव्यमूर्त्तिं वा कदाचिन्न हि [6]पूजयेत् ।
एकस्य पूजनाद् देवि महासिद्धीश्वरो भवेत् ॥ ३८ ॥
उभयोस्त्रीणि चत्वारि या नारी पूजनञ्चरेत् ।
तस्याः समस्तं विफलं ध्यानादि-जप-पूजनम् ॥ ३९ ॥

---

1. 'भक्तिञ्च' ख-ग । 2. 'महेशानि' क । 3. 'तस्य वर्द्धते तेजसाधिकम्' ख-ग ।
4. 'तस्याः' ख-ग । 5. '-रात्मयोषितः' ख-ग । 6. 'पूजनात्' ख-ग ।

यदि भाग्यवशाद् देवि एकं गुरुसुतं लभेत् ।
मनोज्ञं शास्त्रवेत्तारं निग्रहानुग्रहे रतम्[1] ॥ ४० ॥
सुन्दरं यौवनोन्मत्तं गुरुतुल्यं [2]जितेन्द्रियम् ।
प्राणान्तेऽपि च कर्त्तव्यं पूजनं मोक्षदायकम् ॥ ४१ ॥
नो यजेद् यदि मोहेन सैव [3]पापमयी भवेत् ॥ ४२ ॥

इति श्रीमातृकाभेदतन्त्रे हरगौरीसंवादे [4]चतुर्दशः पटलः ॥ १४ ॥

---

1. 'तरम्' क । 2. 'न संशयः' ख-ग । 3. 'पापालया' ख-ग । 4. 'पञ्चदशः ख-ग ।

अथ श्रीमद्गुरुपादुकास्तोत्रम्

ब्रह्मरन्ध्रसरसीरुहोदरे नित्यलग्नमवदातमद्भुतम् ।
कुण्डलीविवरकाण्डमण्डितं द्वादशार्णसरसीरुहं भजे ॥ १ ॥
तस्य कन्दलितकर्णिकापुटे क्लृप्तरेखमकथादिरेखया ।
कोणलक्षितहलक्षमण्डलीभाव[1]लक्ष[2]ममलालयं भजे ॥ २ ॥
तत्पुटे[3] पटुतडित्कडारिमस्पर्द्धमानमणिपाटलप्रभम् ।
चिन्तयामि हृदि चिन्मयं वपु[4]र्बिन्दुनादमणिपीठमण्डलम् ॥३॥
ऊर्द्ध्वमस्य हुतभुक्शिखासखं[5] तद्विलासपरिबृंहणास्पदम् ।
विश्वघस्मर[6]महोत्सवोत्कटं व्यामृषामि युगमादिहंसयोः ॥४॥
तत्र नाथचरणारविन्दयोः कुङ्कुमासव[7]झरीमरन्दयोः[8] ।
द्वन्द्वमिन्दुकरकन्दशीतलं मानसं स्मरति मङ्गलास्पदम् ॥५॥

निषक्तमणिपादुकानियमिताघकोलाहलं
स्फुरत्किशलयारुणं नखसमुल्लसच्चन्द्रकम् ।
परामृतसरोवरोदितसरोजसद्रोचिषं
भजामि शिरसि स्थितं गुरुपदारविन्दद्वयम् ॥ ६ ॥
पादुकापञ्चकस्तोत्रं पञ्चवक्त्राद् विनिर्गतम् ।
षडाम्नायदलोपेतं[9] प्रपञ्चे चातिदुर्लभम् ॥ ७ ॥

इति श्रीमातृकाभेदतन्त्रे सर्वतन्त्रोत्तमोत्तमे हरगौरीसंवादे श्रीशिववक्त्राद्
विनिर्गतं श्रीमद्गुरुपादुकास्तोत्रं समाप्तम् ।

---

१ । स्तोत्रमिदं कुलमूलावतारकल्पसूत्रटीकायामिति प्राणतोषण्यामुक्तम् । तत्रान्तौ श्लोकोऽयमधिको वर्त्तते :—आदि कादि किल थादितारकं वर्णमण्डलमखण्डसिद्धिदम् । अन्तरुल्लसितहक्षलाक्षरं लक्षयन्ति पशवः कथं शिवे ।

---

1. 'लक्ष्य-' प्रा, Ta । 2. '-मबला-' प्रा, Ta । 3. 'पुट-' प्रा । 4. '-र्नादविन्दु-' Ta । 5. '-श्रयं' Ta । 6. '-महोत्सदोत्कटं' प्रा, '-महोविदोत्-' Ta । 7. '-परी-' Ta । 8. '-ममन्दयोः' 9. 'फलप्रासं' Ta 'फलं-'-प्रा ।

मातृकाभेदतन्त्रस्य मातृकानुसारिणी

श्लोकानुक्रमणी

श्लोकानुक्रमणी

श्लोकानुक्रमणी

श्लोकानुक्रमणी

१२

श्लोकानुक्रमणी

श्लोकानुक्रमणी

श्लोकानुक्रमणी

श्लोकानुक्रमणी

श्लोकानुक्रमणी

श्लोकानुक्रमणी

श्लोकानुक्रमणी

मातृकाभेदतन्त्रस्थविशेषशब्दानां सूची